John Ruskin

The Bible References of John Ruskin

John Ruskin

The Bible References of John Ruskin

ISBN/EAN: 9783337096533

Printed in Europe, USA, Canada, Australia, Japan

Cover: Foto ©Lupo / pixelio.de

More available books at **www.hansebooks.com**

The Bible References
in the Works of
John Ruskin

London: George Allen

ARRANGED BY
MARY AND ELLEN GIBBS

PREFACE

THE compilers of this little volume desire, first of all, to express their sincere thanks to the great author from whose works and by whose permission the quotations have been made.

They trust that the work will be found as exhaustive of its subject and as accurate in detail as the immense option of selection could allow. A short list of supplementary references has been added; and, for convenience, a table giving in order the books of the Bible quoted from. These will be found at the end of the volume.

It may interest readers to know how the root and foundation of all Mr. Ruskin's Scripture knowledge was laid. He says, in *Præterita*, vol. i., p. 52: 'I have with deeper gratitude to chronicle what I owe to my mother for the resolutely consistent lessons which so exercised me in the Scriptures as to make every word of them familiar to my ear in habitual music,—yet in that familiarity reverenced, as transcending all thought, and ordaining all conduct.'

ABBREVIATIONS

The reference is always to the *small* edition of the work, where such an edition exists; and to the *paragraph*, in the case of all those works which are paragraphed continuously throughout.

CONTENTS

SUBJECTS ALPHABETICALLY ARRANGED

	PAGES
AARON, DEATH OF—BEAUTY OF HOLINESS	1—11
BEAUTY OF HOLINESS—CHARITY	11—29
CHARITY—DAVID	29—57
DAVID—EARLY CHRISTIANITY	57—67
EARLY CHRISTIANITY—FAITH	67—83
FAITH—GARDEN OF EDEN, THE	83—87
GARDEN OF EDEN, THE—HAPPINESS	87—104
HAPPINESS—IDLENESS	104—121
IDLENESS—JACOB'S LADDER	121—130
JACOB'S LADDER—KINGDOM, THE	130—136
KINGDOM, THE—LANGUAGE OF THE BIBLE	136—138
LANGUAGE OF THE BIBLE—MADONNA, THE	138—153
MADONNA, THE—'NATIONS OF THE EARTH'	153—167
'NATIONS OF THE EARTH'—OBEDIENCE	167—169
OBEDIENCE—PARABLES	169—177
PARABLES—REFORMATION	177—195
REFORMATION—SACRED CHORD OF COLOUR	195—203
SACRED CHORD OF COLOUR—TABERNACLE	203—228
TABERNACLE—UNITY	228—244
UNITY—VAINGLORY	244—245
VAINGLORY—WEALTH	245—247
WEALTH—ZEDEKIAH	247—253

CONTENTS

SAINTS

	PAGE
BARBARA	257
BARNABAS AND MARK	258
BENEDICT	258
BERNARD	260
CATHERINE	261
CECILIA	261
FIRMIN	262
GENEVIEVE	263
GEOFFROY	265
GEORGE	266
JEROME	266
MARGARET	268
MARTIN	268
MATTHEW	271
SOPHIA	273
THEODORE	274
URSULA	275
ZITA	275

APPENDICES

I. SUPPLEMENTARY REFERENCES	279
II. THE BOOKS OF THE BIBLE AS QUOTED OR REFERRED TO IN THIS VOLUME	288

THE BIBLE REFERENCES
OF JOHN RUSKIN

'There is need, bitter need to bring back into men's minds, that to live is nothing, unless to live be to know Him by whom we live.'—*Modern Painters*, vol. ii., sec. i., ch. i., § 7.

Aaron, Death of.

Although the *time* of the deaths of Aaron and Moses was hastened by God's displeasure, we have not, it seems to me, the slightest warrant for concluding that the *manner* of their deaths was intended to be grievous or dishonourable to them. Far from this: it cannot, I think, be doubted that in the denial of the permission to enter the Promised Land, the whole punishment of their sin was included; and that as far as regarded the manner of their deaths, it must have been appointed for them by their Master in all tenderness and love; and with full purpose of ennobling the close of their service upon the earth. It might have seemed to *us* more honourable that both should have been permitted to die beneath the shadow of the Tabernacle, the congregation of Israel watching by their side; and all whom they loved gathered together to receive the last message from the lips of the meek lawgiver, and the last blessing from the prayer of the anointed priest. But it was not thus they were permitted to die. Try to realize that going forth of Aaron from the midst of the congregation. He who had so often done sacrifice for their sin, going forth now to offer up his own spirit. He who had stood, among them, between the dead and the living, and had seen the eyes of all that great multitude turned to him, that by his intercession their breath might yet be drawn a moment more, going forth now to meet the Angel of Death face to face, and deliver himself into his hand. Try if you cannot walk, in thought, with those two brothers, and the son, as they passed the outmost tents of Israel, and turned, while yet the dew lay round about the camp, towards the slopes of Mount Hor; talking together for the last time, as, step by step, they felt the steeper rising of the rocks, and hour after hour, beneath the ascending sun, the horizon grew broader as they climbed, and all the folded hills of Idumea, one by one subdued, showed amidst their hollows in the haze of noon, the windings of that long desert journey, now at last to close. But who shall enter into the thoughts of the High Priest, as his eye followed those paths of ancient pilgrimage; and, through the silence of the arid and endless hills, stretching even to the dim peak of Sinai, the whole history of those forty years was unfolded before him, and the mystery of his own ministries revealed to him; and that other Holy of Holies, of which the mountain peaks were the altars, and the mountain clouds the veil, the firmament of his Father's dwelling, opened to him still more brightly and infinitely as he drew nearer his death; until at last, on the shadeless summit,—from him on whom sin was to be laid no more—from him, on whose heart the names of sinful nations were to press their graven fire no longer,—the brother and the son took breastplate and ephod, and left him to his rest?—*Modern Painters*, vol. iv., ch. xx., § 46.

<small>Num. xx. 27.</small>

<small>Num. xx. 28.</small>

Abraham.

'The word of God came to Abram.' Of course you can't imagine such a thing as that the word of God should ever come to *you*? Is that because you are worse, or better, than Abram?—because you are a more, or less, civilized person than he? I leave you to answer that question for yourself;—only as I have told you often before, but cannot repeat too often, find out first what the word *is*. . . .   Gen. xv. 1.

On the Mount of the Amorite. On the slope of it, down to the vale of Eshcol, sat Abram, as the sun ripened its grapes through the glowing day; the shadows lengthening at last under the crags of Machpelah;— the golden light warm on Ephron's field, still Ephron's, wild with wood. 'And as the sun went down, an horror of great darkness fell upon Abram.'—*Fors Clavigera*, Letter LXV.   Gen. xv. 12.

Adamite Fall.

There is not any part of our nature, nor can there be through eternity, uninfluenced or unaffected by the fall, and that not in any way of degradation, for the renewing in the divinity of Christ is a nobler condition than that of Paradise; and yet throughout eternity it must imply and refer to the disobedience, and the corrupt state of sin and death, and the suffering of Christ Himself, which can we conceive of any redeemed soul as for an instant forgetting, or as remembering without sorrow? . . . *There is a perfect ideal to be wrought out of every face around us* that has on its forehead the writing and the seal of the angel ascending from the East.—*Modern Painters*, vol. ii., sec. i., ch. xiv., §§ 11, 12.   Rev. vii. 2.

Advent, The Second.

I find it written very distinctly that God loved the world, and that Christ is the light of it. What the much-used words, therefore, mean, I cannot tell. But this, I believe, they *should* mean. That there is, indeed, one world which is full of care, and desire, and hatred: a world of war, of which Christ is not the light, which indeed is without light, and has never heard the great 'Let there be.' Which is,   John viii. 12.   Gen. i. 3.

therefore, in truth, as yet no world; but chaos, on the face of which, moving, the Spirit of God yet causes men to hope that a world will come. The better one, they call it: perhaps they might, more wisely, call it the real one. Also, I hear them speak continually of going to it, rather than of its coming to them; which, again, is strange, for in that prayer which they had straight from the lips of the Light of the world, and which He apparently thought sufficient prayer for them, there is not anything about going to another world; only something of another government coming into this; or rather, not another, but the only government,—that government which will constitute it a world indeed. New heavens and new earth. Earth, no more without form and void, but sown with fruit of righteousness. Firmament, no more of passing cloud, but of cloud risen out of the crystal sea—cloud in which, as He was once received up, so He shall again come with power, and every eye shall see Him, and all kindreds of the earth shall wail because of Him.—*Modern Painters*, vol. v., Pt. ix., ch. xii., §§ 18, 19.

<small>Rev. xxi. 1.
Gen. i. 2.
S. Matt. xxiv. 30.
Rev. i. 7.</small>

Alms-giving.

The tithe may, indeed, be set aside for some special purpose—for the maintenance of a priesthood—for distant labour, or any other purpose out of their own immediate range of action. But to the Charity or Alms of men—to Love, and to the God of Love, *all* their substance is due—and all their strength—and all their time. That is the first commandment: Thou shalt love the Lord with all thy strength and soul. Yea, says the false disciple—but not with all my money. And of these it is written, after that thirty-third verse of Luke xiv.: 'Salt is good; but if the salt have lost his savour, it is neither fit for the land nor the dunghill. He that hath ears to hear, let him hear.'—*Fors Clavigera*, Letter LIII.

<small>S. Matt. xxii. 37.
S. Luke x. 27.
S. Mark iv. 9.</small>

Ambassadors for God.

Ecclesiastical tyranny has, for the most part, founded itself on the idea of Vicarianism, one of the most pestilent of the Romanist theories, and most plainly denounced in Scripture. Of this I have a word or two to say to the modern 'Vicarian.' All powers that be are unquestionably ordained of God; so that they that resist the Power, resist the ordinance of God. Therefore, say some in these offices, We, being ordained of God, and having our credentials, and being in the English Bible called ambassadors for God, do, in a sort, represent God. We are Vicars of Christ, and stand on earth in place of Christ. I have heard this said by Protestant clergymen. [Rom. xiii. 1, 2.]

Now the word ambassador has a peculiar ambiguity about it, owing to its use in modern political affairs; and these clergymen assume that the word, as used by St. Paul, means an Ambassador Plenipotentiary; representative of his King, and capable of acting for his King. What right have they to assume that St. Paul meant this? St. Paul never uses the word ambassador at all. He says, simply, 'We are in embassage from Christ; and Christ beseeches you through us.' Most true. And let it further be granted, that every word that the clergyman speaks is literally dictated to him by Christ; that he can make no mistake in delivering his message; and that, therefore, it is indeed Christ Himself who speaks to us the word of life through the messenger's lips. Does, therefore, the messenger represent Christ? Does the channel which conveys the waters of the Fountain represent the Fountain itself? Suppose, when we went to draw water at a cistern, that all at once the Leaden Spout should become animated, and open its mouth and say to us, See, I am Vicarious for the Fountain. Whatever respect you show to the Fountain, show some part of it to me. Should we not answer the Spout, and say, Spout, you were set there for our service, and may be taken away and thrown aside¹ if anything goes wrong with you? But the Fountain will flow for ever.

Observe, I do not deny a most solemn authority vested in every Christian messenger from God to men. I am prepared to grant this to the uttermost; and all that George **Herbert** says, in the end of 'The Church-porch,' I would **enforce,** at another time than this, to the uttermost. But the Authority is **simply** that of a King's *Messenger;* not of a King's *Representative.—On the Old Road,* vol. ii., § 208.

Amiens Cathedral. Its Theology.

Who built it, shall we ask? God, and Man,—is the first and most true answer. The stars in their courses built it, and the Nations. Greek Athena labours here —and Roman Father Jove, and Guardian Mars. The Gaul labours here, and the Frank: knightly Norman,— mighty Ostrogoth,—and wasted anchorite of Idumea.

The actual Man who built it scarcely cared to tell you he did so. . . .

The northern porch is dedicated to St. Firmin, the first Christian missionary to Amiens. The southern porch, to the Virgin. But these **are both** treated as withdrawn behind the great foundation of Christ and the Prophets. What you have first to think of, and read, is the scripture of the great central porch, and the façade itself. You have then in the centre of the front, the image of Christ Himself, receiving you: 'I am the Way, the truth and the life.' . . .

<small>S. John xiv. 6.</small>

Throughout the Sermon on this Amiens Mount, Christ never appears, or is for a moment thought of, as the Crucified, nor as the Dead; but as the Incarnate Word —as the present Friend—as the Prince of Peace on Earth,—and as the Everlasting King in Heaven. What His life *is,* what His commands *are,* and what His judgment *will be,* are the things here taught: not what He once did, nor what He once

<small>Isaiah ix. 6.</small>

---

¹ 'By just judgment be deposed.'—Art. **26.**

suffered, but what He is now doing—and what He requires us to do. That is the pure, joyful, beautiful lesson of Christianity; and the fall from that faith, and all the corruptions of its abortive practice, may be summed briefly as the habitual contemplation of Christ's death instead of His Life, and the substitution of His past suffering for our present duty. Then, secondly, though Christ bears not *His* cross, the mourning prophets, —the persecuted apostles—and the martyred disciples *do* bear theirs. For just as it is well for you to remember what your undying Creator is *doing* for you —it is well for you to remember what your dying fellow-creatures *have done:* the Creator you may at your pleasure deny or defy—the Martyr you can only forget; deny, you cannot. Every stone of this building is cemented with his blood, and there is no furrow of its pillars that was not ploughed by his pain.

Keeping, then, these things in your heart, look back now to the central statue of Christ, and hear His message with understanding. He holds the Book of the Eternal Law in His left hand; with His right He blesses,—but blesses on condition. 'This do, and thou shalt live;' nay, in stricter and more piercing sense, This *be*, and thou shalt live: to show Mercy is nothing —thy soul must be full of mercy; to be pure in act is nothing—thou shalt be pure in heart also. And with this further word of the unabolished law—'This if thou do *not*, this if thou art not, thou shalt die.' Die (whatever Death means)—totally and irrevocably. There is no word in thirteenth-century Theology of the pardon (in our modern sense) of sins; and there is none of the Purgatory of them. Above that image of Christ with us, our Friend, is set the image of Christ over us, our Judge. For this present life—here is His helpful Presence. After this life—there is His coming to take account of our deeds, and of our desires in them; and the parting asunder of the Obedient from the Disobedient, of the Loving from the Unkind, with no hope

S. Luke x. 28.

given to the last of recall or reconciliation. I do not know what commenting or softening doctrines were written in frightened minuscule by the Fathers, or hinted in hesitating whispers by the prelates of the early Church. But I know that the language of every graven stone and every glowing window,—of things daily seen and universally understood by the people, was absolutely and alone, this teaching of Moses from Sinai in the beginning, and of St. John from Patmos in the end, of the Revelation of God to Israel.—*Our Fathers Have Told Us*, ch. iv., §§ 12, 28, 52.

Amorites.

We habitually **speak of the Holy Land** as the Land of 'Canaan.' The 'promised' land was indeed that of Canaan, with others. But Israel never got it. **They got** only the Mount of the Amorites; for the promise was only to be perfected on condition of their perfect obedience. . . . For *all* the Canaanites were left, to prove Israel, (Judges iii. 3,) and a good many of the Amorites and Jebusites too, (Judges iii. 5–7,) but in the main Israel subdued the last two races, and held the hill country from Lebanon to Hebron, and the capital, Jerusalem, for their own. . . . And above all, you will, or may, understand that the Amorites had a great deal of good in them: that they and the Jebusites were on the whole a generous and courteous people,—so that, when Abram dwells with the Amorite princes, Mamre and Eshcol, they are faithful allies to him; and when he buys his grave from Ephron the Hittite, and David the threshing floor from Araunah the Jebusite, both of the mountaineers behave just as the proudest and **truest** Highland chief would. 'What is that between me and thee?' 'All these things did Araunah, as a King, give unto the King—and Araunah said unto the King, The Lord thy God accept thee.' Not *our* God, you see;—but giving sadly, as the Sidonian widow begging,

Gen. xv. 18.

Gen. xiv. 13.

Gen. xxiii. 3.

2 Sam. xxiv. 23.

—with claim of no part in Israel.—*Fors Clavigera,* Letter LXV.

Anchorites.

While we mourn over the fictitious shape given to the religious visions of the anchorite, we may envy the sincerity and the depth of the emotion from which they spring: in the deep feeling, we have to acknowledge the solemn influences of the hills; but for the erring modes or forms of thought, it is human wilfulness, sin, and false teaching, that are answerable. We are not to deny the nobleness of the imagination because its direction is illegitimate, nor the pathos of the legend because its circumstances are groundless; the ardour and abstraction of the spiritual life are to be honoured in themselves, though the one may be misguided and the other deceived; and the deserts at Osma, Assisi, and Monte Viso are still to be thanked for the zeal they gave, or guarded, whether we find it in St. Francis and St. Dominic, or in those whom God's hand hid from them in the clefts of the rocks.— *Modern Painters,* vol. iv., Pt. v., ch. xx., § 12. [Exod. xxxiii. 21, 22.]

Anchorites and Saints.

The evidence respecting them has never yet been honestly collected, much less dispassionately examined: but assuredly, there is in that direction a probability, and more than a probability, of dangerous error, while there is none whatever in the practice of an active, cheerful, and benevolent life. The hope of attaining a higher religious position, which induces us to encounter, for its exalted alternative, the risk of unhealthy error, is often, as I said, founded more on pride than piety; and those who, in modest usefulness, have accepted what seemed to them here the lowliest place in the kingdom of their Father, are not, I believe, the least likely to receive hereafter the command, then unmistakable, 'Friend, go up higher.'—*Ethics of the Dust,* § 87. [S. Luke xiv. 10.]

Angel of the Sea.

Far away in the **south** the strong river Gods have all hasted, and gone down to the **sea**. Wasted and burning, white furnaces of blasting sand, **their** broad beds lie ghastly and bare; but here in the moss-lands, the soft wings of the Sea Angel droop still with dew, and the shadows of their plumes falter on the hills: strange laughings and glitterings of silver streamlets, born suddenly, and twined about the mossy heights in trickling tinsel, answering to them as they wave. Nor are those wings colourless. We habitually think of the rain-cloud only as dark and gray; not knowing that we owe to it perhaps the fairest, though not the most dazzling of the hues of heaven. Often in our English mornings, the rain-clouds **in the dawn form** soft, level fields, which melt imperceptibly into the blue; or, when of less extent, gather into apparent bars, crossing the sheets of broader cloud above; and all these bathed throughout in an unspeakable light of pure rose-colour, and purple, and amber, and blue; not shining, but misty-soft; the barred masses, when seen nearer, composed of clusters or tresses of cloud, like floss silk; looking as if each knot **were** a little swathe or sheaf of lighted rain. No clouds **form such skies, none are so** tender, various, inimitable. For these are the robes of love of the Angel of the Sea.

Job xxxvi. 29. To these that name is chiefly given, the 'spreadings of the clouds,' from their extent, their gentleness, their fulness of rain. Note how they are spoken of in Job xxxvi. 5, 29–31. 'By them judgeth

Job xxxvi. 32. He the people; He giveth meat in abundance. With clouds He covereth the light. He hath hidden the light in His hands and commanded it that it should return. He speaks of it to His friend; that it is His possession, and that He may ascend thereto.'

That, then, is the Sea Angel's message to God's friends; *that*, the meaning of those strange golden lights and purple flushes before the morning rain. The rain is sent to judge, and feed us; but the light is the possession of the friends of God, and they may ascend thereto,—where the tabernacle veil will cross and part its rays no more.—*Modern Painters*, vol. v., Pt. vii., ch. iv., §§ 5, 6, 7.

Apostles, The—Baptistery of St. Mark's.

Each of the Apostles, over the font, is seen baptizing in the country to which he is sent. Their legends, written above them, begin over the door of entrance into the church, with St. John the Evangelist, and end with St. Mark.

Most careful reference is made to the various traditions concerning the places of each Apostle's special ministry, the main tradition being always followed in cases of doubt. Thus, St. John was bishop of Ephesus; St. James the Less bishop of Jerusalem, where he received St. Paul, and introduced him to the Church; St. Philip laboured in Phrygia, and is said to have died at Hierapolis; St. Matthew chiefly in Ethiopia; St. Simeon in Egypt; and **St. Thomas** (though this may be by confusion with another Thomas) is said to have preached in India and founded the Church at Malabar, where his tomb is shown, and 'Christians of St. Thomas' is still a name for the Church. So, again, St. Andrew preached in Achaia, and was there crucified at Patræ; the connection of St. Peter with Rome needs no comment; both Jerome and Eusebius assign India to St. Bartholomew; St. Thaddæus or Jude preached in Syria and Arabia, and died at Edessa; the first fifteen years of the ministry of St. Matias were spent in Palestine; and lastly, **St. Mark** is reported to have been sent by St. Peter to Egypt, and there founded the Church at Alexandria.—*St. Mark's Rest*, pp. 95, 156.

Beauty of Holiness.

And perfect the day shall be, when it is of all men understood that the beauty of Holiness must be in labour as well as in rest. Nay! *more*, if it may be, in **labour**; in our strength, rather than

Psalm xxix. 2.

in our weakness; and in the choice of what we shall work for through the six days, and may know to be good at their evening time, than in the choice of what we pray for on the seventh, of reward or repose. Psalm xlii. 4. With the multitude that keep holiday, we may perhaps sometimes vainly have gone up to the house of the Lord, and vainly there asked for what we fancied would be mercy; but for the few who labour as their Lord would have them, the mercy needs no seeking, and their wide home no hallowing. Surely Psalm xxiii. 6. goodness and mercy shall *follow* them, *all* the days of their life; and they shall dwell in the house of the Lord—FOR EVER.—*Lectures on Art*, § 96. *On the Old Road*, vol. i., Pt. i., § 252.

Beholding this our Natural Face in a Glass.

We come at last to set ourselves face to face with ourselves; expecting that in creatures made after Gen. i. 26. the image of God, we are to find comeliness and completion more exquisite than in the fowls of the air and the things that pass through the paths of the sea.

But behold now a sudden change from all former experience. No longer among the individuals of the race is there equality or likeness, a distributed fairness and fixed type visible in each; but evil diversity, and terrible stamp of various degradation: features seamed by sickness, dimmed by sensuality, convulsed by passion, pinched by poverty, shadowed by sorrow, branded with remorse; bodies consumed with sloth, broken down by labour, tortured by disease, dishonoured in foul uses; intellects without power, hearts without hope, minds earthly and devilish; our bones full of the sin Psalm xxv. 7. **of our** youth, the heaven revealing our iniquity, **the** earth rising up against us, the roots dried up beneath, and the branch cut off above; well for us only, S. James i. 23. if, after beholding this our natural face in a glass, we desire not straightway to forget what manner of men we be.

Herein there is at last something, and too much for that short-stopping intelligence and dull perception of ours to accomplish, whether in earnest fact, or in the seeking for the outward image of beauty :—to undo the devil's work; to restore to the body the grace and the power which inherited disease has destroyed; to restore to the spirit the purity, and to the intellect the grasp, that they had in Paradise. . . . And so the only restoration of the body that we can reach is not to be coined out of our fancies, but to be collected out of such uninjured and bright vestiges of the old seal as we can find and set together: and the ideal of the good and perfect soul, as it is seen in the features, is not to be reached by imagination, but by the seeing and reaching forth of the better part of the soul to that of which it must first know the sweetness and goodness in itself, before it can much desire, or rightly find, the signs of it in others.—*Modern Painters*, vol. ii., sec. i., ch. xiv., § 1.

Benediction, The.

'The Grace of our Lord Jesus Christ, and the Love of God, and the Fellowship of the Holy Ghost, be with you.' Now I do not know precisely what sense is attached in the English public mind to those expressions. But what I have to tell you positively is that the three things do actually exist, and can be known if you care to know them, and possessed if you care to possess them; and that another thing exists, besides these, of which we already know too much. (2 Cor. xiii. 14.)

'First, by simply obeying the orders of the Founder of your religion, all grace, graciousness, or beauty and favour of gentle life, will be given to you in mind and body, in work and in rest. The Grace of Christ exists, and can be had if you will.

Secondly, as you know more and more of the created world, you will find that the true will of its Maker is that its creatures should be happy;—that He has made

everything beautiful in its time and its place, and that
it is chiefly by the fault of men, when they are allowed
<small>Rom. viii. 22.</small> the liberty of thwarting His laws, that Creation
groans or travails in pain. The Love of God
exists, and you may see it, and live in It if you will.
Lastly, a spirit does actually exist which teaches the ant
her path, the bird her building, and men, in an instinctive and marvellous way, whatever lovely arts and noble
deeds are possible to them. Without it you can do no
good thing. To the grief of it you can do many bad ones.
In the possession of it is your peace and your power.

And there is a fourth thing, of which we already know
too much. **There is** an evil spirit whose dominion is
in blindness and in cowardice, **as the** dominion of the
Spirit of wisdom is in clear sight and in courage. And
this blind and cowardly spirit is for ever telling you
that evil things are pardonable, and you shall not die
for them, and that good things are impossible, and you
need not live for them; and that gospel of his is now
the loudest that is preached in your Saxon tongue.
You will find some day, to your cost, if you believe the
first part of it, that it is not true; but you may never,
if you believe the second part of it, find, to your gain,
that also, untrue; and therefore I pray you with all
earnestness to prove, and know within your hearts, that
all things lovely and righteous are possible for those who
believe in their possibility, and who determine that, for
their part, they will make every day's work contribute to
them.—*Lectures on Art*, § 125.

Bible.

Not book, merely; but 'Bibliotheca,' Treasury of
Books: and it is, I repeat, a singular question, how far,
if Jerome, at **the very** moment when Rome, his tutress,
ceased from her **material** power, had not made her language the oracle of Hebrew prophecy, a literature of
their own, and a religion unshadowed by the terrors
of the Mosaic law, might have developed itself in the

hearts of the Goth, the Frank, and the Saxon, under Theodoric, Clovis, and Alfred. Fate had otherwise determined, and Jerome was so passive an instrument in her hands that he began the study of Hebrew as a discipline only, and without any conception of the task he was to fulfil, still less of the scope of its fulfilment. I could joyfully believe that the words of Christ, 'If they hear not Moses and the Prophets, neither will they be persuaded though one rose from the dead,' had haunted the spirit of the recluse, until he resolved that the voice of Moses and the Prophets should be made audible to the Churches of all the earth. But so far as we have evidence, no such will or hope exalted the quiet instincts of his natural industry; partly as a scholar's exercise, partly as an old man's recreation, the severity of the Latin language was softened, like Venetian crystal, by the variable fire of Hebrew thought; and the 'Book of Books' took the abiding form of which all the future art of the Western nations was to be an hourly enlarging interpretation. **And in this** matter you have to note that the gist of it lies, not in the translation of the Hebrew and Greek Scriptures into an easier and a common language, but in their *presentation to the Church as of common authority.* The earlier Gentile Christians had naturally a tendency to carry out in various oral exaggeration or corruption, the teaching of the Apostle of the Gentiles, until their freedom from the bondage of the Jewish law passed into doubt of its inspiration; and, after the fall of Jerusalem, even into horror-stricken interdiction of its observance. So that, only a few years after the remnant of exiled Jews in Pella had elected the Gentile Marcus for their Bishop, and obtained leave to return to the Ælia Capitolina built by Hadrian on Mount Zion, 'it became a matter of doubt and controversy whether a man who sincerely acknowledged Jesus as the Messiah, but who still continued to observe the law of Moses, could possibly hope for salvation!'[1] While, on

[Side note: S. Luke xvi. 31.]

---

[1] Gibbon, chap. 15 (II. 277).

the other hand, the most learned and the most wealthy of the Christian name, under the generally recognized title of 'knowing' (Gnostic), had more insidiously effaced the authority of the Evangelists by dividing themselves, during the course of the third century, 'into more than fifty numerably distinct sects, and producing a multitude of histories, in which the actions and discourses of Christ and His Apostles were adapted to their several tenets.'[1] It would be a task of great, and in no **wise** profitable difficulty to determine in what measure the **consent** of the general Church, and in what measure the **act and** authority of Jerome, contributed to fix in their **ever since** undisturbed harmony and majesty, the canons of Mosaic and Apostolic Scripture. All that the young reader need know is, that when Jerome died at Bethlehem, this great deed was virtually accomplished: and the series of historic and didactic books **which** form our present Bible, (including the Apocrypha), were established in and above the nascent thought of the noblest **races of men** living on the terrestrial globe, as a direct message to them from its Maker, containing whatever it was necessary for them to learn of His purposes towards them; and commanding, or advising, with divine authority and infallible wisdom, all that was best for them to do, and happiest to desire. And it is only for those who have obeyed the law sincerely, to say how far the hope held out to them by the law-giver, has been fulfilled. The worst 'children of disobedience' are those who accept, of the Word, what they like, and refuse what they hate: nor is this perversity in them always conscious, for the greater part of the sins of the Church have been brought on it by enthusiasm which, in passionate contemplation and advocacy of parts of Scripture easily grasped, neglected the study, and at last betrayed the balance, of the rest. What forms and methods of self-will are concerned in the wresting of the Scriptures to a man's

Ephes. ii. 2; v. 6. Col. iii. 6.

---

[1] Gibbon, chap. 15 (II. 283).

destruction, is for the keepers of consciences to examine, not for us. The history we have to learn must be wholly cleared of such debate, and the influence of the Bible watched exclusively on the persons who receive the Word with joy, and obey it in truth. There has, however, been always a farther difficulty in examining the power of the Bible, than that of distinguishing honest from dishonest readers. The hold of Christianity on the souls of men must be examined, when we come to close dealing with it, under these three several heads: there is first, **the power of the** Cross itself, **and of the** theory of salvation, upon the heart,—then, the operation of the Jewish and Greek Scriptures on the intellect,— then, the influence on morals of the teaching and example of the living hierarchy. And in the comparison **of men** as they are and as they might have been there are **these** three questions to be separately kept in mind,—first, what would have been the temper of Europe without the charity and labour meant by 'bearing the **Cross**'; then, secondly, what would the intellect **of** Europe have become without **Biblical literature;** and lastly, what would the social order of Europe have become without its hierarchy. You see I have connected the words 'charity' and 'labour' under the general term of 'bearing the cross.' 'If any man will come after me, let him deny himself, (for charity) **and** take up his cross (of pain) and follow me.' . . . [S. Matt. xvi. 24. S. Mark viii. 34; x. 21.]

Only, therefore, in days when the Cross was received with courage, the Scripture searched with honesty, and the Pastor heard in faith, can the pure word of God, and the bright **sword** of the Spirit, be recognised in the heart and **hand of** Christianity. [Ephes. vi. 17.]

The effect of Biblical poetry and legend on its intellect, must be traced farther, through decadent ages, and in unfenced fields;—producing 'Paradise Lost' for us, no less than the 'Divina Commedia';— Goethe's 'Faust,' and **Byron's** 'Cain,' no less than

B

the 'Imitatio Christi.' Much more, must the scholar, who would comprehend in any degree approaching to completeness, the influence of the Bible on mankind, be able to read the interpretations of it which rose into the great arts of Europe at their culmination. . . .

But this is demonstrably true of the entire volume of them, as we have it, and read,—each of us as it may be rendered in his native tongue; that, however mingled with mystery which we are not required to unravel, or difficulties which we should be insolent in desiring to solve, it contains plain teaching for men of every rank of soul and state in life, which so far as they honestly and implicitly obey, they will be happy and innocent to the utmost powers of their nature, and capable of victory over all adversities, whether of temptation or pain. Indeed, the Psalter alone, which practically was the service book of the Church for many ages, contains merely in the first half of it the sum of personal and social wisdom. The 1st, 8th, 12th, 14th, 15th, 19th, 23rd, and 24th psalms, well learned and believed, are enough for all personal guidance; the 48th, 72nd, and 75th, have in them the law and the prophecy of all righteous government; and every real triumph of natural science is anticipated in the 104th. For the contents of the entire volume, consider what other group of historic and didactic literature has a range comparable with it. There are—

i. The stories of the Fall and of the Flood, the grandest human traditions founded on a true horror of sin.

ii. The story of the Patriarchs, of which the effective truth is visible to this day in the polity of the Jewish and Arab races.

iii. The story of Moses, with the results of that tradition in the moral law of all the civilized world.

iv. The story of the Kings—virtually that of all Kinghood, in David, and of all Philosophy, in Solomon: culminating in the Psalms and Proverbs, with the still more close and practical wisdom of Ecclesiasticus and the Son of Sirach.

v. The story of the Prophets—virtually that of the deepest mystery, tragedy, and permanent fate, of national existence.

vi. The story of Christ.

vii. The moral law of St. John, and his closing Apocalypse of its fulfilment.

Think, if you can match that table of contents in any other—I do not say 'book' but 'literature.'

Think, so far as it is possible for any of us—either adversary or defender of the faith—to extricate his intelligence from the habit and the association of moral sentiment based upon the Bible, what literature could have taken its place, or fulfilled its function, though every library in the world had remained, unravaged, and every teacher's truest words had been written down.—*Our Fathers Have Told Us*, ch. iii., § 37.

Bible of Venice, Church of St. Mark.

The old architect was sure of readers. He knew that every one would be glad to decipher all that he wrote; that they would rejoice in possessing the vaulted leaves of his stone manuscript; and that the more he gave them, the more grateful would the people be. We must take some pains, therefore, when we enter St. Mark's, to read all that is inscribed, or we shall not penetrate into the feeling either of the builder or of his times.

A large atrium or portico is attached to two sides of the church, a space which was especially reserved for unbaptized persons and new converts. It was thought right that, before their baptism, these persons should be led to contemplate the great facts of the Old Testament history; the history of the Fall of Man, and of the lives of Patriarchs up to the period of the covenant by Moses; the order of the subjects in this series being very nearly the same as in many Northern churches, but significantly closing with the Fall of the Manna in order to mark to the catechumen the insufficiency of the Mosaic covenant for salvation,—'Our fathers did eat manna in the wilderness, and are dead,' —and to turn his thoughts to the true Bread of which that **manna was the type.** Then, when after his baptism **he was permitted to enter** the church, over its main entrance **he saw, on looking back,** a mosaic of Christ **enthroned, with the Virgin** on one side and St. Mark on the other, in attitudes of adoration. Christ is represented as holding a book open upon His knee, on which is written: 'I AM THE DOOR; BY ME IF ANY MAN ENTER IN, HE SHALL BE SAVED.' On the red marble moulding which surrounds the mosaic is written: 'I AM THE GATE OF LIFE; LET THOSE WHO ARE MINE ENTER BY ME.' Above, on the red marble fillet which forms the cornice of the west end of the church, is written, with reference to the figure of Christ below: 'WHO HE WAS, AND FROM WHOM HE CAME, AND AT WHAT PRICE HE REDEEMED THEE, AND WHY HE MADE THEE, AND GAVE THEE ALL THINGS, DO THOU CONSIDER.' Now observe, this was not to be seen and read only by the catechumen when he first entered the church; every one who at any time entered was supposed to look back **and** to read this writing; their daily entrance into the church was thus made a daily memorial of their first entrance into the spiritual church; and we shall find that the rest of **the** book which was open for them upon its walls continually led them in **the** same manner to regard the visible temple as in every part a type of the invisible Church of God. Therefore the mosaic of the first dome, which is over the head of the spectator as soon as he has entered by the great **door** (that door being the type of baptism) represents the effusion of the Holy Spirit, as the first consequence **and** seal of the entrance into the church of God. In the centre of the cupola **is** the Dove, enthroned in the Greek manner, as the Lamb is enthroned, when the Divinity of the Second and Third Persons is to be

S. John vi. 49-58.

S. John x. 9.

insisted upon, together with their peculiar offices. From the central symbol of the Holy Spirit twelve streams of fire descend upon the heads of the twelve apostles, who are represented standing around the dome; and below them, between the windows which are pierced in its walls, are represented, by groups of two figures for each separate people, the various nations who heard the apostles speak, at Pentecost, every man in his own tongue. Finally, on the vaults, at the four angles which support the cupola, are pictured four angels each bearing a tablet upon the end of a rod in his hand: on each of the tablets of the three first angels is inscribed the word 'Holy'; on that of the fourth is written 'Lord'; and the beginning of the hymn being thus put into the mouths of the four angels, the words of it are continued around the border of the dome, uniting praise to God for the gift of the Spirit, with welcome to the redeemed soul received into His Church: [Acts ii. 8.]

'HOLY, HOLY, HOLY, LORD GOD OF SABAOTH:
HEAVEN AND EARTH ARE FULL OF THY GLORY.
HOSANNA IN THE HIGHEST:
BLESSED IS HE THAT COMETH IN THE NAME
OF THE LORD.' [S. Matt. xxi. 9.]

And observe in this writing that the convert is required to regard the outpouring of the Holy Spirit especially as a work of *sanctification*. It is the *holiness* of God manifested in the giving of His Spirit to sanctify those who had become His children, which the four angels celebrate in their ceaseless praise; and it is on account of this holiness that the heaven and earth are said to be full of His glory.

After thus hearing praise rendered to God by the angels for the salvation of the newly-entered soul, it was thought fittest that the worshipper should be led to contemplate, in the more comprehensive forms possible, the past evidence and the future hopes of Christianity, as summed up in the three facts without assurance of which all faith is vain; namely, that Christ died, that He rose again, and that He ascended into heaven, there to prepare a place for His elect. On the vault between the first and second cupolas are represented the crucifixion and resurrection of Christ, with the usual series of intermediate scenes,—the treason of Judas, the judgment of Pilate, the crowning with thorns, the descent into Hades, the visit of the women to the Sepulchre, and the apparition to Mary Magdalene. The second cupola itself, which is the central and principal one of the church, is entirely occupied by the subject of the Ascension. At the highest point of it Christ is represented as rising into the blue heaven, borne up by four angels, and throned upon a rainbow, the type of reconciliation. Beneath Him, the twelve apostles are seen upon the Mount of Olives, with the Madonna, and, in the midst of them, the two men in white apparel who appeared at the moment of the Ascension, above whom, as uttered by them, are inscribed the words, 'Ye men of Galilee, why stand ye gazing up into heaven? This Christ, the Son of God, as He is taken from you, shall so come, the arbiter of the earth, trusted to do judgment and justice.'

Beneath the circle of the apostles, between the windows of the cupola, are represented the Christian virtues, as sequent upon the crucifixion of the flesh, and the spiritual ascension together with Christ. Beneath them, on the vaults which support the angles of the cupola, are placed the four Evangelists, because on their evidence our assurance of the fact of the Ascension rests: and, finally, beneath their feet, as symbols of the sweetness and fulness of the Gospel which they declared, are represented the four rivers of Paradise, Pison, Gihon, Tigris, and Euphrates.

The third cupola, that over the altar, represents the witness of the Old Testament to Christ; showing Him enthroned in its centre, and surrounded by the patriarchs and prophets. But this dome was little seen by the people; their contemplation was intended to be chiefly drawn to that of the centre of the church, and thus the mind of the worshipper was at once fixed on the main groundwork and hope of Christianity,—'Christ is risen,' and 'Christ shall come.' If he had time to explore the minor lateral chapels and cupolas, he could find in them the whole series of New Testament history, the events of the life of Christ, and the Apostolic miracles in their order, and finally the scenery of the Book of Revelation [1]; but if he only entered, as often the common people do to this hour, snatching a few moments before beginning the labour of the day to offer up an ejaculatory prayer, and advanced but from the main entrance as far as the altar screen, all the splendour of the glittering nave and variegated dome, if they smote upon his heart, as they might often, in strange contrast with his reed cabin among the shallows of the lagoon, smote upon it only that they might proclaim the two great messages,—'Christ is risen,' and 'Christ shall come.' Daily, as the white cupolas rose like wreaths of sea-foam in the dawn, while the shadowy campanile and frowning palace were still withdrawn into the night, they rose with the Easter Voice of Triumph,—'Christ is risen;' and daily, as they looked down upon the tumult of the people, deepening and eddying in the wide square that opened from their feet to the sea, they uttered above them the sentence of warning,—'Christ shall come.' And this thought may surely dispose the reader to look with some change of temper upon the gorgeous building and wild blazonry of that shrine of St. Mark's. He now perceives that it was in the hearts of the old Venetian people far more than a place of worship It was at once a type of the Redeemed Church of God, and a scroll for the written word of God. It was to be to them, both an image of the Bride,

1 Cor. xv. 20.

---

[1] The old mosaics from the Revelation have perished, and have been replaced by miserable work of the seventeenth century.

all glorious within, her clothing of wrought gold; and the actual Table of the Law and the Testimony, written within and without. And whether honoured as the Church or as the Bible, was it not fitting that neither the gold nor the crystal should be spared in the adornment of it; that, as the symbol of the Bride, the building of the wall thereof should be of jasper, and the foundations of it garnished with all manner of precious stones; and that, as the channel of the Word, that triumphant utterance of the Psalmist should be true of it,—'I have rejoiced in the way of Thy testimonies, as much as in all riches'? And shall we not look with changed temper down the long perspective of St. Mark's Place towards the sevenfold gates and glowing domes of its temple, when we know with what solemn purpose the shafts of it were lifted above the pavement of the populous square? Men met there from all countries of the earth, for traffic or for pleasure; but, above the crowd swaying for ever to and fro in the restlessness of avarice or thirst of delight, was seen perpetually the glory of the temple, attesting to them, whether they would hear or whether they would forbear, that there was one treasure which the merchantmen might buy without a price, and one delight better than all others, in the word and the statutes of God. Not in the wantonness of wealth, not in vain ministry to the desire of the eyes or the pride of life, were those marbles hewn into transparent strength, and those arches arrayed in the colours of the iris. There is a message written in the dyes of them, that once was written in blood; and a sound in the echoes of their vaults, that one day shall fill the vault of heaven,— 'He shall return to do judgment and justice.' The strength of Venice was given her, so long as she remembered this: her destruction found her when she had forgotten this; and it found her irrevocably, because she forgot it without excuse. Never had city a more glorious Bible. Among the nations of the North, a rude and shadowy sculpture filled their temples with confused and hardly legible imagery; but, for her, the skill and the treasures of the East had gilded every letter, and illumined every page, till the Book-Temple shone from afar off like the star of the Magi.—*Stones of Venice*, vol. ii., ch. iv., § LXIV.

Bishops.

As for the rank or name of the officers in whom the authorities, either of teaching or discipline, are to be vested, they are left undetermined by Scripture. I have heard it said by men who know their Bible far better than I, that careful examination may detect evidence of the existence of three orders of Clergy in the Church. This may be; but one thing is very clear, without any laborious examination, that 'bishop' and 'elder' sometimes mean the same thing; as indisputably, in Titus i. 5 and 7, and 1 Peter v. 1 and 2, and that the office of the bishop or overseer was one of considerably less importance than it is with us. This is palpably evident from 1 Timothy iii., for what divine among us, writing of episcopal proprieties, would think of saying that bishops 'must not be given to wine,' must be 'no strikers,' and must not be 'novices'? We are not in the habit of making bishops of novices in these days; and it would be much better that, like the early Church, we sometimes ran the risk of doing so; for the fact is we have not bishops enough—by some hundreds. The idea of overseership has been practically lost sight of, its fulfilment having gradually become physically impossible, for want of more bishops. The duty of a bishop is, without doubt, to be accessible to the humblest clergyman of his diocese, and to desire very earnestly that all of them should be in the habit of referring to him in all cases of difficulty; if they do not do this of their own accord, it is evidently his duty to visit them, live with them sometimes, and join in their ministrations to their flocks, so as to know exactly the capacities and habits of life of each; and if any of them complained of this or that difficulty with their congregations, the bishop should be ready to go down to help them, preach for them, write general epistles to their people, and so on: besides this, he should of course be watchful of their errors—ready to hear complaints from their congregations of inefficiency or aught else; besides having general superintendence of all the charitable institutions and schools in his diocese, and good knowledge of whatever was going on in theological matters, both all over the kingdom and on the Continent. This is the work of a right overseer; and I leave the reader to calculate how many additional bishops—and those hard-working men, too—we should need to have it done, even decently. Then our present bishops might all become archbishops with advantage, and have general authority over the rest.—*On the Old Road*, vol. ii., § 206.

Blasphemy.

The real sin of blasphemy is not in the saying, nor even in the thinking; but in the wishing which is father to thought and word: and the nature of it is simply in wishing evil to anything; for as the quality of Mercy is not strained, so neither that of Blasphemy, the one distilling from the clouds of Heaven, the other from the steam of the Pit. He that is unjust in little is unjust in much, he that is malignant to the least is to the greatest, he who hates the earth which is God's footstool, hates yet more Heaven which is God's throne, and Him that sitteth thereon.—*On the Old Road*, vol. ii., § 96.

[S. Luke xvi. 10.]

Blessed are the Pure in Heart.

The Christian Theoria seeks not, though it accepts and touches with its own purity, what the Epicurean sought; but finds its food and the objects of its love everywhere, in what is harsh and fearful as well as in what is kind: nay, even in all that seems coarse and commonplace, seizing that which is good; and sometimes delighting more at finding its table spread in strange places, and in the presence of its enemies, and its honey coming out of the rock, than if all were harmonized into a less wondrous pleasure; hating only what is self-sighted and insolent of men's work, despising all that is not of God, unless reminding it of God, yet able to find evidence of Him still where all seems forgetful of Him, and to turn that into a witness of His working which was meant to obscure it; and so with clear and unoffended sight beholding Him for ever, according to the written promise, <small>S. Matt. v. 8.</small> 'Blessed are the pure in *heart,* for they shall see God.' —*Modern Painters,* vol. ii., sec. i., ch. ii., § 10.

Blindness and Neglect of God's Warning.

Where chiefly the beauty of God's working was manifested to men, warning was also given, and that to the full, of the enduring of His indignation against sin. It seems one of the most cunning and frequent of self-deceptions to turn the heart away from this warning, and refuse to acknowledge anything in the fair scenes of the natural creation but beneficence. Men in general lean towards the light, so far as they contemplate such things at all, most of them passing 'by on the other side,' either in mere plodding pursuit of <small>S. Luke x. 31.</small> their own work, irrespective of what good or evil is around them, or else in selfish gloom, or selfish delight, resulting from their own circumstances at the moment. Of those who give themselves to any true contemplation, the plurality, being humble, gentle, and kindly hearted, look only in nature for what is lovely and kind; partly, also, God gives the disposition to every healthy human mind in some degree to pass over or even harden itself against evil things, else the suffering would be too great to be borne; and humble people, with a quiet trust that everything is for the best, do not fairly represent the facts to themselves, thinking them none of their business. So, what between hard-hearted people, thoughtless people, busy people, humble people, and cheerfully-minded people,—giddiness of youth, and preoccupations of age,—philosophies of faith, and **cruelties of** folly,—priest and Levite, masquer and merchantman, all agreeing to keep their own side of the way,—the evil that **God sends to warn** us gets to be forgotten, and the evil that He sends to be mended by us gets left unmended. And then, because people shut their eyes to the dark indisputableness of the facts in front of them, their Faith, such as it is, is shaken **or** uprooted by every darkness in what is revealed to them. In the present day it **is not** easy to find a well-meaning **man among** our more earnest thinkers, who will not take upon himself to dispute **the whole** system of redemption, because he cannot unravel the mystery of the punishment of sin. But can he unravel the mystery of the punishment of *No* sin? . . . We cannot reason of these things. But this I know—and this may by all men be known—that no good or lovely thing exists in this world without its correspondent darkness; and that the universe presents itself continually to mankind under the stern aspect of warning, or of choice, the good and the evil set on the right hand and the left.—*Modern Painters*, vol. iv., ch. xix., § 32.

<small>S. Matt. xxv. 33.</small>

Bread of Heaven.

The most helpful and **sacred work,** which can at present be done for humanity, is to teach people (chiefly by example, as all best teaching must be done) not how 'to better themselves,' but how to 'satisfy themselves.' It is the curse of every evil nation and evil creature to eat, and *not* be satisfied. The words of blessing are, that they shall 'eat and be satisfied.' And as there is only one kind of water which quenches all thirst, so there is only one kind of bread which satisfies all hunger — the bread of

<small>Deut. xiv. 29.</small>
<small>S. John iv. 14; vi. 35.</small>

justice, or righteousness; which hungering after, men shall always be filled, that being the bread of Heaven; but hungering after the bread, or wages, of unrighteousness, shall not be filled, that being the bread of Sodom.—*Modern Painters*, vol. v., Pt. ix., ch. xi., § 20.

In the parable in Luke, the bread asked for is shown to be also, and chiefly, the Holy Spirit, and the prayer, 'Give us each day our daily bread,' is, in its fulness, the disciples', 'Lord, evermore give us *this* bread,'—the clergyman's question to his whole flock, primarily literal: 'Children, have ye here any meat?' must ultimately be always the greater spiritual one: 'Children, have ye here any Holy Spirit?' or, 'Have ye not heard yet whether there *be* any? and, instead of a Holy Ghost the Lord and Giver of Life, do you only believe in an unholy mammon, Lord and Giver of Death?' {S. Luke xi. 13. S. John vi. 34. S. John xxi. 5.}

The opposition between the two Lords has been, and will be as long as the world lasts, absolute, irreconcilable, mortal; and the clergyman's first message to his people of this day is—if he be faithful—'Choose ye this day whom ye will serve.'—*On the Old Road*, vol. ii., § 239. {Joshua xxiv. 15.}

Breaking of Bread.

Whatever is good for human life is also made beautiful to human sight, not by 'association of ideas,' but by appointment of God that in the bread we rightly break for our lips, we shall best see the power and grace of the Light He gave for our eyes.—*The Laws of Fésole*, ch. vii., § 12.

Charity.

You know how often it is difficult to be wisely charitable, to do good without multiplying the sources of evil. You know that to give alms is nothing unless you give thought also; and that therefore it is written, not 'blessed is he that *feedeth* the poor,' but, 'blessed is he that *considereth* the poor.' {Psalm xli. 1.}

And you know that a little thought and a little kindness are often worth more than a great deal of money.

Now this charity of thought is not merely to be exercised towards the poor; it is to be exercised towards all men. There is assuredly no action of our social life, however unimportant, which, by kindly thought, may not be made to have a beneficial influence upon others; and it is impossible to spend the smallest sum of money, for any not absolutely necessary purpose, without a grave responsibility attaching to the manner of spending it. The object we ourselves covet may, indeed, be desirable and harmless, so far as we are concerned, but the providing us with it may, perhaps, be a very prejudicial occupation to some one else. And then it becomes instantly a moral question, whether we are to indulge ourselves or not. Whatever we wish to buy, we ought first to consider not only if the thing be fit for us, but if the manufacture of it be a wholesome and happy one; and if, on the whole, the sum we are going to spend will do as much good spent in this way as it would if spent in any other way. It may be said that we have not time to consider all this before we make a purchase. But no time could be spent in a more important duty; and God never imposes a duty without giving the time to do it. Let us, however, only acknowledge the principle;—once make up your mind to allow the consideration of the *effect* of your purchases to regulate the *kind* of your purchase, and you will soon easily find grounds enough to decide upon. The plea of ignorance will never take away our responsibilities.

Prov. xxiv. 12.   It is written, 'If thou sayest, Behold, we knew it not; doth not He that pondereth the heart consider it? and He that keepeth thy soul, doth not He know it?'—*Lectures on Architecture and Painting*, § 44.

For truly it is fine Christianity we have come to, which, professing to expect the perpetual grace or charity of its Founder, has not itself grace or charity enough to hinder it from over-reaching its friends in sixpenny bargains; and which, supplicating evening and morning the forgiveness of its own debts, goes forth at noon to take its fellow-servants by the throat, saying,—not merely 'Pay me that thou owest,' but 'Pay me that thou owest me *not.*' S. Matt. xviii. 28.

It is true that we sometimes wear Ophelia's rue with a difference, and call it 'Herb o' grace o' Sundays,' taking consolation out of the offertory with—'Look, what he layeth out, it shall be paid him again.' Comfortable words indeed, and good to set against the old royalty of Largesse—

> Whose moste joie was, I wis,
> When that she gave, and said, 'Have this.'

I am glad to end, for this time, with these lovely words of Chaucer. We have heard only too much lately of 'Indiscriminate charity,' with implied reproval, not of the Indiscrimination merely, but of the Charity also. We have partly succeeded in enforcing on the minds of the poor the idea that it is disgraceful to receive; and are likely, without much difficulty, to succeed in persuading not a few of the rich that it is disgraceful to give. But the political economy of a great state makes both giving and receiving graceful; and the political economy of true religion interprets the saying that 'it is more blessed to give than to receive,' not as the promise of reward in another life for mortified selfishness in this, but as pledge of bestowal upon us of that sweet and better nature, which does not mortify itself in giving.—*Munera Pulveris*, Appendix 6. Acts xx. 35.

Christmas.

Standing as it were astonished in the midst of this gaiety of yours, will you tell—what it is all about? Your little children would answer, doubtless, fearlessly, 'Because the Child Christ was born to-day': but you, wiser than your children, it may be,—at least, should be,— are you also sure that He was? . . .

What is, or may be, this Nativity, to you, then, I repeat? Shall we consider, a little, what, at all events, it was to the people of its time; and so make ourselves more clear as to what it might be to us? We will read slowly.

'And there were, in that country, shepherds, staying <small>S. Luke ii. 8, 9.</small> out in the field, keeping watch over their flocks by night.' . . . 'And behold, the Messenger of the Lord stood above them, and the glory of the Lord lightened round them, and they feared a great fear.'

'Messenger.' You must remember that, when this was written, the word 'angel' had only the effect of our word—'messenger'—on men's minds. Our translators say 'angel' when they like, and 'messenger' when they <small>Joshua ii. 15, 16.</small> like; but the Bible, messenger only, or angel only, as you please. For instance, 'Was not <small>S. James ii. 25.</small> Rahab the harlot justified by works, when she had received the angels, and sent them forth another way?' . . .

<small>S. Luke ii. 11.</small> The shepherds were told that their Saviour was that day born to them 'in David's village.' We are apt to think that this was told, as of special interest to them, because David was a King. Not so. It was told them because David was in youth *not* a King; <small>S. Luke ii. 11.</small> but a Shepherd like themselves. 'To you, shepherds, is born this day a Saviour in the shepherd's town'; that would be the deep sound of the message in their ears. For the great interest to them in the story of David himself must have been always, not that he had saved the monarchy, or subdued Syria, or <small>S. Luke ii. 15.</small> written Psalms, but that he had kept sheep in those very fields they were watching in; . . . and they said hastily, 'Let us go and see.'

Will you note carefully that they only think of *seeing*, not of worshipping? Even when they do see the Child, it is not said that they worshipped. They were simple people, and had not much faculty of worship; even though the heavens had opened for them, and the hosts of heaven had sung. They had been at first only frightened; then curious, and communicative to the bystanders: they do not think even of making any offering, which would have been a natural thought enough, as it was to the first of shepherds: but they brought no firstlings of their flock. . . . It is not said here that they brought anything, but they looked, and talked, and went away praising God, as simple people,—yet taking nothing to heart; only the mother did that. . . . Some days later, another kind of persons came. On that first day, the simplest people of His own land;—twelve days after, the wisest people of other lands, far away: persons who had received, what you are all so exceedingly desirous to receive, a good education. . . .

The uneducated people came only to see, but these highly trained ones to worship; and they have allowed themselves to be led, and governed, and directed into the way which they should go, (and that a long one,) by the mere authority and prestige of a superior person, whom they clearly recognize as a born king, S. Matt. though not of their people. 'Tell us, where is ii. 2. He that is born King of the Jews, for we have come to worship Him.' . . .

Therefore, the Magi bring treasures, as being discerners of treasures, knowing what is intrinsically worthy, and worthless; what is best in brightness, best in sweetness, best in bitterness—gold, and frankincense, and myrrh. Finders of treasure hid in fields, and goodliness in strange pearls, such as produce no effect whatever on the public mind, bent passionately on its own fashion of pearl-diving at Gennesaret.

And you will find that the essence of the mis-teaching, of your day, concerning wealth of any kind, is in this denial of intrinsic value. What anything is worth, or not worth, it cannot tell you: all that it can tell is the exchange value. . . . I repeat to you, now, the question I put at the beginning. What is this Christmas to you? What Light is there, for your eyes, also, pausing yet over the place where the Child lay?

C

I will tell you, briefly, what Light there should be;—
what lessons and promise are in this story, at the least.
There may be infinitely more than I know, but there
is certainly, this. The Child is born to bring you the
promise of new life. Eternal or not, is no matter; pure,
and redeemed, at least.

He is born twice on your earth; first, from the womb,
to the life of toil; then, from the grave, to that of rest.

To His first life He is born in a cattle-shed, the supposed son of a carpenter; and afterwards brought up to
a carpenter's craft.

But the circumstances of His second life are, in great
part, hidden from us: only note this much of it. The
three principal appearances to His disciples are
accompanied by giving or receiving of food.
He is known at Emmaus in breaking of bread;
at Jerusalem He Himself eats fish and honey to
show that He is not a spirit; and His charge to Peter
is 'when they had dined,' the food having been
obtained under His direction.

<small>S. Luke xxiv. 30, 31;</small>
<small>xxiv. 42.</small>
<small>S. John xxi. 13, 15.</small>

But in His first showing Himself to the person who
loved Him best, and to whom He had forgiven most,
there is a circumstance more singular and significant
still. Observe—assuming the accepted belief to be
true,—this was the first time when the Maker of men
showed Himself to human eyes, risen from the dead, to
assure them of immortality. You might have thought
He would have shown Himself in some brightly glorified
form,—in some sacred and before unimaginable beauty.

He shows Himself in so simple aspect, and dress,
that she, who, of all people on the earth,
should have known Him best, glancing quickly
back through her tears, does not know Him. Takes
Him for 'the gardener.'

<small>S. John xx. 15.</small>

Now, unless absolute orders had been given to us, such
as would have rendered error impossible, (which would
have altered the entire temper of Christian probation);
could we possibly have had more distinct indication

of the purpose of the Master—borne first by witness of shepherds, in a cattle-shed, then by witness of the person for whom He had done most, and who loved Him best, in the garden, and in gardener's guise, and not known even by His familiar friends till He gave them bread—could it be told us, I repeat, more definitely by any sign or indication whatsoever, that the noblest human life was appointed to be by the cattle-fold and in the garden; and to be known as noble in breaking of bread?

Now, but a few words more. You will constantly hear foolish and ignoble persons conceitedly proclaiming the text, that 'not many wise and not many noble are called.' Nevertheless, of those who are truly wise, and truly noble, all are called that exist. And to sight of this Nativity, you find that, together with the simple persons, near at hand, there were called precisely the wisest men that could be found on earth at that moment. [1 Cor. i. 26.]

And these men, for their own part, came—I beg you very earnestly again to note this—not to see, nor talk —but to do reverence. They are neither curious nor talkative, but submissive.

And, so far as they came to teach, they came as teachers of one virtue only: Obedience. For of this Child, at once Prince and Servant, Shepherd and Lamb, it was written: 'See, mine elect, in whom my soul delighteth. He shall not strive, nor cry, till He shall bring forth Judgment unto Victory.' [Isaiah xlii. 1, 2, 3.]

My friends, you may have wondered at my telling you so often,—I tell you nevertheless, once more, that one main purpose of the education I want you to seek is, that you may see the sky, with the stars of it again; and be enabled, in their material light—'riveder le stelle.'

But, much more, out of this blackness of the smoke of the Pit, the blindness of heart, in which the children of *Dis*obedience blaspheme God and each other, heaven grant to you the vision of that sacred light, at pause over the place where the young Child was laid; and ordain that more and more in each coming Christmas it may be said of you, 'When they saw the Star, they rejoiced with exceeding great joy.'—*Fors Clavigera*, Letter XII.

<small>S. Matt. ii. 10.</small>

Christ's Church.

Christ does not order impossibilities, and He *has* ordered us to be at peace one with another. Nay, it is answered—He came not to send peace, but a sword. Yes, verily: to send a sword upon earth, but not within His Church; for to His Church He said, 'My Peace I leave with you.'—*On the Old Road*, vol. ii., § 222.

<small>S. Matt. x. 34.</small>
<small>S. John xiv. 27.</small>

Christ, Life of.

You have had various 'lives of Christ,' German and other, lately provided among your other severely historical studies. Some, critical; and some, sentimental. But there is only one light by which you can read the life of Christ,—the light of the life you now lead in the flesh; and that not the natural, but the won life. 'Nevertheless, I live; yet not I, but Christ liveth in me.'—*St. Mark's Rest*, § 127.

<small>Gal. ii. 20.</small>

Christ your Master.

With those whom you *know* to be honest, *know* to be innocent, *know* to be striving, with main purpose, to serve mankind and honour their God, you are humbly and lovingly to associate yourselves: and with none others. 'You don't like to set yourself up for being better than other people? You dare not judge harshly of your fellow-creatures?'

I do not tell you to judge them. . . . To their own Master they stand or fall; but to *your* Master, Christ, *you* must stand, with your best might; and in this manner only, self asserting as you may think it, can you confess Him before men. Why do you suppose that thunderous word of His impends over your denial of Him, 'Whosoever shall deny me before men, him will I also deny before Angels,' but because you are sure to be constantly tempted to such denial.— *Fors Clavigera*, Letter LXIII.

<small>Matt. x. 33.</small>

Christ at the Lake of Galilee.

There is no event in the whole life of Christ to which, in hours of doubt or fear, men turn with more anxious thirst to know the close facts of it, or with more earnest and passionate dwelling upon every syllable of its recorded narrative, than Christ's showing Himself to His disciples at the Lake of Galilee. There is something pre-eminently open, natural, full fronting our disbelief, in this manifestation. The others, recorded after the resurrection, were sudden, phantom-like, occurring to men in profound sorrow and wearied agitation of heart; not, it might seem, safe judges of what they saw. But the agitation was now over. They had gone back to their daily work, thinking still their business lay net-wards, unmeshed from the literal rope and drag. 'Simon Peter saith unto them, "I go a fishing." They say unto him, "We also go with thee."' True words enough, and having far echo beyond those Galilean hills. That night they caught nothing; but when the morning came, in the clear light of it, behold, a figure stood on the shore. They were not thinking of anything but their fruitless hauls. They had no guess who it was. It asked them simply if they had caught anything. They said No; and it tells them to cast yet again. And John shades his eyes from the morning sun with his hand, to look who it is; and though the glinting of the sea, too, dazzles him, he makes out who it is, at last; and poor Simon, not to be outrun this time, tightens his fisher's coat about him, and dashes in, over the nets. One would have liked to see him swim those hundred yards, and stagger to

<small>S. John xxi. 3.</small>

his knees on the beach. Well, the others get to the beach, too, in time, in such slow way as men in general do get, in this world, to its true shore, much impeded by that wonderful 'dragging the net with fishes;' but they get there—seven of them in all;—first the Denier, and then the slowest believer, and then the quickest believer, and then the two throne-seekers, and two more, we know not who. They sit down on the shore face to face with Him, and eat their broiled fish as He bids. And then, to Peter, all dripping still, shivering and amazed, staring at Christ in the sun, on the other side of the coal fire,—thinking a little, perhaps, of what happened by another coal fire, when it was colder, and having had no word once changed with him by his Master since that look of His,—to him, so amazed, comes the question, 'Simon, lovest thou Me?' Try to feel that a little, and think of it till it is true to you.—*Modern Painters*, vol. iii., ch. iv., § 16.

<small>S. John xxi. 8.</small>

<small>S. John xxi. 15.</small>

Christ's Teachings.

Have you ever observed that all Christ's main teachings, by direct order, by earnest parable, and by His own permanent emotion, regard the use and misuse of *money?* We might have thought, if we had been asked what a divine teacher was most likely to teach, that he would have left inferior persons to give directions about money; and himself spoken only concerning faith and love, and the discipline of the passions, and the guilt of the crimes of soul against soul. But not so. He speaks in general terms of these. But He does not speak parables about them for all men's memory, nor permit Himself fierce indignation against them, in all men's sight. The Pharisees bring Him an adulteress. He writes her forgiveness on the dust of which He had formed her. Another, despised of all for known sin, He recognized as a giver of unknown love. But He acknowledges no

<small>S. John viii. 3-6.</small>

<small>S. Luke vii. 37, 47.</small>

love in buyers and sellers in His house. One should have thought there were people in that house twenty times worse than they;—Caiaphas and his like—false priests, false prayer-makers, false leaders of the people—who needed putting to silence, or to flight, with darkest wrath. But the scourge is only against the *traffickers and thieves*. The two most intense of all the parables: the two which lead the rest in love and terror (this of the Prodigal, and of Dives), relate, both of them, to management of riches. The practical order given to the only seeker of advice, of whom it is recorded that Christ 'loved him,' is briefly about his property. 'Sell that thou hast.' [S. Mark x. 21.]

And the arbitrament of the day of the Last Judgment is made to rest wholly, neither on belief in God, nor in any spiritual virtue in man, nor on freedom from stress of stormy crime, but on this only, 'I was an hungred and ye gave me drink; naked, and ye clothed me; sick, and ye came unto me.'—*Time and Tide*, § 174. [S. Matt. xxv. 35, 36.]

Christ waiting at the Gate.

You have heard it said—(and I believe there is more than fancy even in that saying, but let it pass for a fanciful one)—that flowers only flourish rightly in the garden of some one who loves them. I know you would like that to be true; you would think it a pleasant magic if you could flush your flowers into brighter bloom by a kind look upon them: nay, more, if your look had the power, not only to cheer, but to guard;—if you could bid the black blight turn away, and the knotted caterpillar spare—if you could bid the dew fall upon them in the drought, and say to the south wind, in frost—'Come, thou south, and breathe upon my garden, that the spices of it may flow out.' This you would think a great thing? And do you think it not a greater thing, that all this, (and how much more than this!) you *can* do, for fairer flowers [Cant. iv. 16.]

than these—flowers that could bless you for having
blessed them, and will love you for having loved them;
—flowers that have thoughts like yours, and lives like
yours; and which, once saved, you save **for ever?** Is
this only a little power? Far among the moorlands
and the rocks,—far in the darkness of the terrible
streets,—these feeble florets are lying, with all their
fresh leaves torn, and their stems broken—will you
never go down to them, nor set them in order in their
little fragrant beds, nor fence them, in their trembling,
from the fierce wind? Shall morning follow morning,
for you, but not for them; and the dawn rise to watch,
far away, those frantic Dances of Death; but no dawn
rise to breathe upon these living banks of wild violet,
and woodbine, and rose; nor call to you, through your
casement,—call (not giving you the name of the English
poet's lady, but the name of Dante's great Matilda, who
on the edge of happy Lethe, stood, wreathing flowers
with flowers)? . . . Will you not go down among them?
—among those sweet living things, whose new courage,
sprung from the earth with the deep colour of heaven
upon it, is starting up in strength of goodly spire; and
whose purity, washed from the dust, is opening, bud by
bud, into the flower of promise;—and still they turn
to you and for you, 'The Larkspur listens—I hear, I
hear! And the Lily whispers—I wait.' . . . Who is it,
think you, who stands at the gate of this sweeter garden,
alone, waiting for you? Did you ever hear, not of a
Maud, but a Madeleine, who went down to her garden
<small>S. John</small> in the dawn, and found One waiting at the gate,
<small>xx. 15.</small> whom she supposed to be the gardener? Have
you not sought Him often; sought Him in vain, all
through the night; sought Him in vain at the gate of
<small>Gen.</small> that old garden where the fiery sword is set?
<small>iii. 24.</small> He is never there; but at the gate of *this*
garden He is waiting always—waiting to take your hand
—ready to go down to see the fruits of the valley, to see
whether the vine has flourished, and the pomegranate

budded. There you shall see with Him the little tendrils of the vines that His hand is guiding—there you shall see the pomegranate springing where His hand cast the sanguine seed;—more: you shall see the troops of the angel keepers that, with their wings, wave away the hungry birds from the pathsides where He has sown, and call to each other between the vineyard rows, 'Take us the foxes, the little foxes, [Cant. ii. 15.] that spoil the vines, for our vines have tender grapes.' Oh—you queens—you queens; among the hills and happy greenwood of this land of yours, shall [S. Luke ix. 58.] the foxes have holes and the birds of the air have nests; and in your cities shall the stones cry out against you, that they are the only pillows where the Son of Man can lay His head?—*Sesame and Lilies*, §§ 94, 95.

Christianity.

Briefly, the entire doctrine of Christianity, painted so that a child could understand it. And what a child cannot understand of Christianity, no one need try to. . . . The total meaning was, and is, that the God who made earth and its creatures, took at a certain time upon the earth, the flesh and form of man; in that flesh sustained the pain and died the death of the creature He had made; rose again after death into glorious human life, and when the date of the human race is ended, will return in visible human form, and render to every man according to [Prov. xxiv. 12; Romans ii. 6.] his work. Christianity is the belief in, and love of, God thus manifested. Anything less than this, the mere acceptance of the sayings of Christ, or assertion of any less than divine power in His Being, may be, for aught I know, enough for virtue, peace, and safety; but they do not make people Christians, or enable them to understand the heart of the simplest believer in the old doctrine.—*Præterita*, vol. ii., pp. 207–9.

Christian Ministers.

We shall find the offices of the Clergy, whatever names we may choose to give to those who discharge them, falling mainly into two great heads :—Teaching ; including doctrine, warning, and comfort : Discipline ; including reproof and direct administration of punishment. . . .

Teaching.—It appears natural and wise that certain men should be set apart from the rest of the Church that they may make Theology the study of their lives : and that they should be thereto instructed specially in the Hebrew and Greek tongues ; and have entire leisure granted them for the study of the Scriptures, and for obtaining general knowledge of the grounds of Faith, and best modes of its defence against all heretics : and it seems evidently right, also, that with this Scholastic duty should be joined the Pastoral duty of constant visitation and exhortation to the people ; for, clearly, the Bible, and the truths of Divinity in general, can only be understood rightly in their practical application ; and clearly, also, a man spending his time constantly in spiritual ministrations, must be better able, on any given occasion, to deal powerfully with the human heart than one unpractised in such matters. The unity of Knowledge and Love, both devoted altogether to the service of Christ and His Church, marks the true Christian Minister ; who, I believe, whenever he has existed, has never failed to receive due and fitting reverence from all men,—of whatever character or opinion ; and I believe that if all those who profess to be such were such indeed, there would never be question of their authority more.

But, whatever influence they may have over the Church, their authority never supersedes that of either the intellect or the conscience of the simplest of its lay members. They can assist those members in the search for truth, or comfort their over-worn and doubtful minds; they can even assure them that they are in the way of truth, or that pardon is within their reach : but they can neither manifest the truth, nor grant the pardon. Truth is to be discovered, and Pardon to be won, for every man by himself. This is evident from innumerable texts of Scripture, but chiefly from those which exhort every man to seek after Truth, and which connect knowing with doing. We are to seek after knowledge as silver, and search for her as for hid treasures; Prov. ii. 3, 4. therefore, from every man she must be naturally hid, and the discovery of her is to be the reward only of personal search. The kingdom of God is as treasure hid in a field; and of those who profess S. Matt. xiii. 44. to help us to seek for it, we are not to put confidence in those who say,—Here is the treasure, we have found it, and have it, and will give you some of it; but in those who say,—We think that is a good place to dig, and you will dig most easily in such and such a way.

Farther, it has been promised that if such earnest search be made, Truth shall be discovered: as much truth, that is, as is necessary for the person seeking. These, therefore, I hold, for two fundamental principles of religion,—that, without seeking, truth cannot be known at all; and that, by seeking, it may be discovered by the simplest. I say, without seeking it cannot be known at all. It can neither be declared from pulpits, nor set down in Articles, nor in anywise 'prepared and sold' in packages, ready for use. Truth must be ground for every man by himself out of its husk, with such help as he can get, indeed, but not without stern labour of his own. In what science is knowledge to be had cheap? or truth to be told over a velvet cushion, in half an hour's talk every seventh day? Can you learn chemistry so?—zoology?—anatomy? and do you expect to penetrate the secret of all secrets, and to know that whose price is above rubies; and of which the depth saith,—It is not in me,—in so Job xxviii. 14. easy fashion? There are doubts in this matter which evil spirits darken with their wings, and that is true of all such doubts which we were told long ago—

they can 'be ended by action alone.'[1] As surely as we live, this truth of truths can only so be discerned: to those who act on what they know, more shall be revealed; and thus, if any man will do His will, he shall know the doctrine whether it be of God. Any man,—not the man who has most means of knowing, who has the subtlest brains, or sits under the most orthodox preacher, or has his library fullest of most orthodox books,—but the man who strives to know, who takes God at His word, and sets himself to dig up the heavenly mystery, roots and all, before sunset, and the night come, when no man can work. Beside such a man, God stands in more and more visible presence as he toils, and teaches him that which no preacher can teach—no earthly authority gainsay. By such a man, the preacher must himself be judged.—*On the Old Road*, vol. ii., §§ 198–201.

<small>S. John vii. 17.</small>

<small>S. John ix. 4.</small>

Church, The.

In the minds of all early Christians the Church itself was most frequently symbolized under the image of a ship, of which the bishop was the pilot. Consider the force which this symbol would assume in the imaginations of men to whom the spiritual Church had become an ark of refuge in the midst of a destruction hardly less terrible than that from which the eight souls were saved of old, a destruction in which the wrath of man had become as broad as the earth and as merciless as the sea, and who saw the actual and literal edifice of the Church raised up, itself like an ark in the midst of the waters. No marvel if with the surf of the Adriatic rolling between them and the shores of their birth, from which they were separated for ever, they should have looked upon each other as the disciples did when the storm came down on the Tiberias Lake, and have yielded ready and loving obedience to those who ruled them

<small>1 S. Peter iii. 20.</small>

<small>S. Mark iv. 37–39.</small>

<small>S. Luke viii. 22, 24.</small>

---

[1] Carlyle, *Past and Present*, Ch. ii.

in His name, who had there rebuked the winds and commanded stillness to the sea. And if the stranger would yet learn in what spirit it was that the dominion of Venice was begun, and in what strength she went forth conquering and to conquer, let him not seek to estimate the wealth of her arsenals or number of her armies, nor look upon the pageantry of her palaces, nor enter into the secrets of her councils; but let him ascend the highest tier of the stern ledges that sweep round the altar of Torcello, and then, looking as the pilot did of old along the marble ribs of the goodly temple-ship, let him repeople its veined deck with the shadows of its dead mariners, and strive to feel in himself the strength of heart that was kindled within them, when first, after the pillars of it had settled in the sand, and the roof of it had been closed against the angry sky that was still reddened by the fires of their homesteads,—first, within the shelter of its knitted walls, amidst the murmur of the waste of waves and the beating of the wings of the sea-birds round the rock that was strange to them,—rose that ancient hymn in the power of their gathered voices:

THE SEA IS HIS, AND HE MADE IT; Psalm
AND HIS HANDS PREPARED THE DRY LAND. xcv. 5.

—*Stones of Venice*, vol. ii., ch. ii., § XVI.

Church Decoration.

What is the purpose of your decoration? Let us take an instance—the most noble with which I am acquainted, the Cathedral of Chartres. You have there the most splendid coloured glass, and the richest sculpture, and the grandest proportions of building, united to produce a sensation of pleasure and awe. We profess that this is to honour the Deity; or, in other words, that it is pleasing to Him that we should delight our eyes with blue and golden colours, and solemnize our spirits by the sight of large stones laid one on another, and ingeniously carved.

I do not think it can be doubted that it *is* pleasing to

Him when we do this; **for He has** Himself prepared for us, nearly every morning and evening, windows painted with Divine art, in blue and gold and vermilion: windows lighted from within by the lustre **of** that heaven which we may assume, at least with more certainty than any consecrated ground, to be one of His dwelling-places. Again, in every mountain side, and cliff of rude **sea shore, He has heaped** stones one upon another of greater magnitude than those of Chartres **Cathedral, and** sculptured them with floral ornament,—surely **not less** sacred because living?

Must it not then be only because we love our own work better than His, **that we respect the lucent glass, but not the lucent clouds; that we weave** embroidered robes with ingenious fingers, **and make** bright the gilded vaults we have beautifully ordained—while **yet we have** not considered the heavens, the work **of** His fingers, nor the stars of the strange vault which He has ordained? And do we dream that by carving fonts and lifting pillars in His honour, who cuts the way of the rivers among the rocks, and at whose reproof the pillars of the earth are astonished, **we** shall obtain pardon for the **dishonour** done **to the hills and streams** by which He has appointed our dwelling-place;—**for** the infection **of their sweet air** with **poison;**—for the burning **up of** their tender grass and **flowers** with fire, and for spreading such a shame **of mixed** luxury and misery over our native land, as if **we** laboured **only that,** at least here in England, we might be able to give the lie to the song, whether of the Cherubim above, or Church beneath— 'Holy, holy, Lord God of all creatures; **Heaven**—*and Earth*—are full of Thy glory'?

<small>Psalm viii. 3.</small>

<small>Job xxvi. 11.</small>

<small>Rev. iv. 8-11.</small>

That we *may* have splendour of art again, and with that, we may truly praise and honour our Maker, and with that set forth the beauty and holiness of all that **He** has made: but only after we have striven with our whole hearts first to sanctify the temple of the body and spirit of every child that has no roof to cover its head from the cold, and no walls to guard its soul from corruption, in this our English land.—*Lectures on Art*, §§ 62–65.

I do not know, as I have repeatedly stated, how far the splendour of architecture, or other art, is compatible with the honesty and usefulness of religious service. The longer I live, the more I incline to severe judgment in this matter, and the less I can trust the sentiments excited by painted glass and coloured tiles. But if there be indeed value in such things, our plain duty is to direct our strength against the superstition which has dishonoured them; since there are thousands to whom they are now merely an offence, owing to their association with absurd or idolatrous ceremonies. I have but this exhortation for all who love them,—not to regulate their creeds by their taste in colours, but to hold calmly to the right, at whatever present cost to their imaginative enjoyment; sure that they will one day find in heavenly truth a brighter charm than in earthly imagery, and striving chiefly to gather stones for the eternal building, whose walls shall be salvation, and whose gates shall be praise.—*Stones of Venice*, vol. i. Appendix 12. [Isaiah lx. 18.]

Church and State.

In all human institutions certain evils are granted, as of necessity; and, in organizing such institutions, we must allow for the consequences of such evils, and make arrangements such as may best keep them in check. Now, in both the civil and ecclesiastical governments there will of necessity be a certain number of bad men. The wicked civilian has comparatively little interest in overthrowing ecclesiastical authority; it is often a useful help to him, and presents in itself little which seems covetable. But the wicked ecclesiastical officer has much interest in overthrowing the civilian, and getting the political power into his own hands. As far as wicked men are concerned, therefore, it is better that the State should have power over the Clergy, than the Clergy over the State.

Secondly, supposing both the Civil and Ecclesiastical officers to be Christians; there is no fear that the civil officer should underrate the dignity or shorten the serviceableness of the minister; but there is considerable danger that the religious enthusiasm of the minister might diminish the serviceableness of the civilian. (The History of Religious Enthusiasm should be written by some one who had a life to give to its investigation; it is one of the most melancholy pages in human records, and one the most necessary to be studied.) Therefore, as far as good men are concerned, it is better the State should have power over the Clergy than the Clergy over the State.

This we might, it seems to me, conclude by unassisted reason. But surely the whole question is, without any need of human reason, decided by the history of Israel. If ever a body of Clergy should have received independent authority, the Levitical Priesthood should; for they were indeed a Priesthood, and more holy than the rest of the nation. But Aaron is always subject to Moses. All solemn revelation is made to Moses, the civil magistrate, and he actually commands Aaron as to the fulfilment of his priestly office, and that in a necessity of life and death: 'Go, and make an atonement for the people.' Nor is anything more remarkable throughout the whole of the Jewish history than the perfect subjection of the Priestly to the Kingly Authority. Thus Solomon thrusts out Abiathar from being priest, 1 Kings ii. 27; and Jehoahaz administers the funds of the Lord's House, 2 Kings xii. 4, though that money was actually the Atonement Money, the Ransom for Souls (Exod. xxx. 12).

_{Num. xvi. 46, 47.}

We have, however, also the beautiful instance of Samuel uniting in himself the offices of Priest, Prophet, and Judge; nor do I insist on any special manner of subjection of Clergy to civil officers, or *vice versâ;*

but only on the necessity of their perfect unity and influence upon each other in every Christian kingdom. Those who endeavour to effect the utter separation of ecclesiastical and civil officers, are striving, on the one hand, to expose the Clergy to the most grievous and most subtle of temptations from their own spiritual enthusiasm and spiritual pride; on the other, to deprive the civil officer of all sense of religious responsibility. . . . Whereas, the ideal of all government is the perfect **unity of the two** bodies of officers, each supporting and correcting the other; **the Clergy** having due weight in all the national councils; **the civil** officers having a solemn reverence for **God in all** their acts; the Clergy hallowing all worldly policy by their influence; and the magistracy repressing all religious enthusiasm by their practical wisdom. **To separate** the two is to endeavour to separate the daily life of the nation from God.—*On the Old Road*, vol. ii., §§ 217–19.

Clouds.

What noble things these clouds are, and with what feeling it seems to be intended by their Creator that we should contemplate them.

The account given of the stages of Creation in the first chapter of Genesis, is in every respect clear and intelligible to the simplest reader, except in the statement of the work of the second day. I suppose that this statement **is passed over by** careless readers **without an endeavour to understand** it; and contemplated by simple and **faithful readers as** a sublime mystery, which was **not intended to** be understood. But **there is** no mystery in **any** other part of the chapter, and **it seems to me unjust to** conclude that any was intended here.

And the passage ought to be peculiarly interesting to us, as **being** the first in the Bible in which the *heavens* are named, and the only one in which the word 'Heaven,' all important as that word is to our understanding of the most precious promises of Scripture, receives a definite explanation. . . .

Gen. i. 8.

In the first place, the English word 'Firmament' itself is obscure and useless; because we never employ it but as a synonym of heaven; it conveys no other distinct idea to us; and the verse, though from our familiarity with it we imagine that it possesses meaning, has in reality no more point or value than if it were written, 'God said, Let there be a something in the midst of the waters, and God called the something Heaven.'

<small>Gen. i. 6.</small>

But the marginal reading, 'Expansion,' has definite value; and the statement that 'God said, Let there be an expansion in the midst of the waters, and God called the expansion Heaven,' has an apprehensible meaning. . . .

<small>Gen. i. 8.</small>

An unscientific reader knows little about the manner in which the volume of the atmosphere surrounds the earth; but I imagine that he could hardly glance at the sky when rain was falling in the distance, and see the level line of the bases of the cloud from which the shower descended, without being able to attach an instant and easy meaning to the words 'Expansion in the midst of the waters.' And if, having once seized this idea, he proceeded to examine it more accurately, he would perceive at once, if he had ever noticed *any*thing of the nature of clouds, that the level line of their bases did indeed most severely and stringently divide 'waters from waters,' that is to say, divide water in its collective and tangible state, from water in its divided and aërial state; or the waters which *fall* and *flow*, from those which *rise* and *float*. Next, if we try this interpretation in the theological sense of the word *Heaven*, and examine whether the clouds are spoken of as God's dwelling-place, we find God going before the Israelites in a pillar of cloud; revealing Himself in a cloud on Sinai; appearing in a cloud on the mercy seat; filling the Temple of Solomon with the cloud when its dedication is accepted; appearing in a great cloud to Ezekiel; ascending into a cloud before

<small>Gen. i. 6.</small>

<small>Exodus xiii. 21; xix. 9.</small>
<small>Lev. xvi. 2.</small>
<small>2 Chron. v. 13.</small>

the eyes of the disciples on Mount Olivet; and in like manner returning to Judgment. 'Behold, He cometh with clouds, and every eye shall see Him.' 'Then shall they see the Son of man coming in the clouds of heaven, with power and great glory.'¹ While farther, the 'clouds' and 'heavens' are used as interchangeable words in those Psalms which most distinctly set forth the power of God: 'He bowed the heavens also, and came down; He made darkness pavilions round about Him, dark waters, and thick clouds of the skies.' And, again: 'Thy mercy, O Lord, is in the heavens, and Thy faithfulness reacheth unto the clouds.' And, again: 'His excellency is over Israel, and His strength is in the clouds.' Again: 'The clouds poured out water, the skies sent out a sound, the voice of Thy thunder was in the heaven.' Again, 'Clouds and darkness are round about Him, righteousness and judgment are the habitation of His throne; the heavens declare His righteousness, and all the people see His glory.' *[margin: Ezekiel i. 4. Acts i. 9. Rev. i. 7. S. Matt. xxiv. 30. Psalm xviii. 9, 11. Psalm xxxvi. 5. Psalm lxviii. 34. Psalm lxxvii. 17, 18. Psalm xcvii. 2-6.]*

In all these passages the meaning is unmistakable, if they possess definite meaning at all. We are too apt to take them merely for sublime and vague imagery, and therefore gradually to lose the apprehension of their life and power.—*Modern Painters*, vol. iv., ch. vi., §§ 1-6.

Coming of the Day of God.

Whether the opportunity is to be permitted us to redeem the hours that we have lost; whether He, in whose sight a thousand years are as one day, has appointed us to be tried by the continued possession of the strange powers with which He has lately endowed us; or whether the periods of childhood *[margin: Psalm xc. 4.]*

---

[1] The reader may refer to the following texts: Exod. xiii. 24, xvi. 10, xix. 9, xxiv. 16, xxxiv. 5; Levit. xvi. 2; Numb. x. 34; Judges v. 4; 1 Kings viii. 10; Ezek. i. 4; Dan. vii. 13; Matt. xxiv. 30; 1 Thess. iv. 17; Rev. i. 7.

and of probation are to cease together, and the youth of mankind is to be one which shall prevail over death, and bloom for ever in the midst of a new heaven and a new earth, are questions with which we have no concern. It is indeed right that we should look for, and hasten, so far as in us lies, the coming of the Day of God; but not that we should check any human efforts **by anticipations of** its approach. We shall hasten it best by endeavouring **to work** out the tasks that are appointed for us here; and, therefore, reasoning as if the world were to continue under its existing dispensation, and the powers which have just been granted to us were to be continued through myriads of future ages.—*Stones of Venice*, vol. iii., ch. iv., § 11.

<small>Rev. xxi. 1.</small>

<small>2 S. Peter iii. 12.</small>

Confession.

I find in my concordance (confess and confession together) forty-two occurrences of the word. Sixteen of these, including John's confession that he was not the Christ, and the confession of the faithful fathers that they were pilgrims on the earth, do indeed move us strongly to confess Christ before men. Have you ever taught your congregations what that confession means? They are ready enough to confess Him in church, that is to say, in their own private synagogue. Will they in Parliament? Will they in a ball-room? Will they in a shop? Sixteen of the texts are to enforce their doing *that*.

The next most important one (1 Tim. vi. 13) refers to Christ's own good confession, which I suppose was not of His sins, but of His obedience. How many of your congregations can make any such kind of confession, or wish to make it?

The eighteenth, nineteenth, and twentieth (1 Kings viii. 33, 2 Chron. vi. 26, Heb. xiii. 15) speak of confessing thankfully that God is God, and the twenty-first (Job xl. 14) speaks of God's own confession, that no doubt we are the people, and that wisdom shall die with us, and on what conditions He will make it.

There remain twenty-one texts which do speak of the confession of our sins—very moving ones indeed—and Heaven grant that some day the British public may be moved by them.

(1) The first is Lev. v. 5, 'He shall confess that he hath sinned *in that thing.*' And if you can get any soul of your congregation to say he has sinned in *any*thing, he may do it in two words for one if he likes, and it will yet be good liturgy.

(2) The second is indeed general—Lev. xvi. 21: the command that the whole nation should afflict its soul on the great day of atonement once a year. The Church of England, I believe, enjoins no such unpleasant ceremony. Her festivals are passed by her people often indeed in the extinction of their souls, but by no means in their intentional affliction.

(3, 4, 5) The third, fourth, and fifth (Lev. xxvi. 40, Numb. v. 7, Nehem. i. 6) refer all to national humiliation for definite idolatry, accompanied with an entire abandonment of that idolatry, and of idolatrous persons. How soon *that* form of confession is likely to find a place in the English congregations the defences of their main idol, mammon, in the vilest and cruellest shape of it—usury—show very sufficiently.

(6) The sixth is Psalm xxxii. 5—virtually the whole of that psalm, which does, indeed, entirely refer to the greater confession, once for all opening the heart to God, which can be by no means done fifty-two times a year, and which, once done, puts men into a state in which they will never again say there is no health in them; nor that their hearts are desperately wicked; but will obey for ever the instantly following order, 'Rejoice in the Lord, ye righteous, and shout for joy, all ye that are true of heart.'

(7) The seventh (Acts xxiv. 14) is the one confession in which I can myself share:—'After the way which they call heresy, so worship I the Lord God of my fathers.'

(8) The eighth (James v. 16) tells us to confess **our** faults—not to God, but 'one to another'—a practice not favoured by English catechumens—(by the way, **what** *do* you all mean by 'auricular' confession—confession that can be heard? and **is the** Protestant pleasanter form one that can't be?).

(9) The ninth is that passage of St. John (i. 9), the favourite evangelical text, which **is** read and preached by thousands of false preachers every day, without once going on to read its great companion, 'Beloved, if our heart condemn us, God is greater than our heart, and knoweth all things; but if our heart condemn us *not*, then have we confidence toward God.' Make your people understand the second text, and they will understand the first. At present you leave them understanding **neither**.

<small>1 S. John iii. 21.</small>

And the entire body of the remaining texts is summed in Joshua vii. 19 and Ezra x. 11, in which, whether it be Achan, with his Babylonish garment, or the people of Israel, with their Babylonish lusts, the meaning of confession is simply what it is to every brave boy, girl, man, and woman, who knows the meaning of the word 'honour' before God or man — namely, to say what they have done wrong, and to take the punishment of it (not to get it blanched over by any means), and to do it no more.—*On the Old Road*, vol. ii., § 259-62.

Conscience, Divine.

One thing we know, or may know, if we will,—that the heart and conscience of man are divine; that in his perception of evil, in his recognition of good, he is himself a God manifest in the flesh; that his joy in love, his agony in anger, his indignation at injustice, his glory in self-sacrifice, are all eternal, indisputable proofs of his unity with a great Spiritual Head; that in these, and not merely in his more availing form, or manifold instinct, he is king over the lower animate world; that, so far as he denies or forfeits these, he dishonours the Name of his **Father**, and makes it unholy and unadmirable in the earth; that so far as he confesses, and rules **by**, these, **he** hallows and makes admirable the Name **of** his Father, and receives, in his sonship, **fulness** of power with Him, whose **are** the kingdom, the power, and **the** glory, **world** without end.—*Fors Clavigera*, Letter **LIII**. _{S. Matt. vi. 13.}

Covetousness.

The first and great Commandment, so called by Christ,—and the **Second** which is like unto it. . . . **You vow, then,** that you will at least strive to keep both of these commandments— as far as, what some would call the corruption, but what in honest people is the weakness, of flesh, permits. If you cannot watch an hour, because you don't love Christ enough to care about His agony, **that is your** weakness; but if you first **sell** Him, and then kiss Him, that is your corruption. . . . Be sure that you are serving Christ, till you are tired and can do no more; for that time: and then, even if you have not breath enough left to say 'Master, Master' with,—He will not mind. Begin therefore 'to-day'— . . . to do good for Him,—whether you live or die. . . . And see that every stroke of this work—be it weak or strong,— shall therefore be done in love of God and your neighbour, and in hatred of covetousness.—*Fors Clavigera*, Letter LXII. _{S. Matt. xxii. 37, 39.}

'A lover of silver,' this latter word being the common **and** proper word for covetous, in the Gospels and Epistles; as of the Pharisees in Luke xvi. 14; and associated with the other characters of men in perilous times, 2 Timothy iii. 2, and its relative noun φιλαργυρία, given in sum for the root of *all* evil in 1 Timothy vi. **10, while** even the authority of Liddell and Scot in the interpretation of πλεονεξία itself as only the desire of getting more than our share, may perhaps be bettered **by** the authority of the teacher, who, _{Eccle. v. 10.}

declining the appeal made to him as an equitable μεριστής (Luke xii. 14–46), tells his disciples to beware of covetousness, simply as the desire of getting more than we have got. 'For a man's life consisteth not in the *abundance* of the things which he possesseth.' —*On the Old Road*, vol. ii., § 162.

<small>S. Luke xii. 15.</small>

Creator, The.

Whether taught or untaught, whether of mean capacity or enlarged, it is necessary that communion with their Creator should be possible to all; and the admission to such communion must be rested, not on their having a knowledge of astronomy, but on their having a human soul. In order to render this communion possible, the Deity has stooped from His throne, and has not only, in the person of the Son, taken upon Him the veil of our human *flesh*, but, in the person of the Father, taken upon Him the veil of our human *thoughts*, and permitted *us*, by His own spoken authority, to conceive Him simply and clearly as a loving Father and Friend;—a being to be walked with and reasoned with; to be moved by our entreaties, angered by our rebellion, alienated by our coldness, pleased by our love, and glorified by our labour; and, finally, to be beheld in immediate and active presence in all the powers and changes of creation. This conception of God, which is the child's, is evidently the only one which can be universal, and therefore the only one which *for us* can be true. The moment that, in our pride of heart, we refuse to accept the condescension of the Almighty, and desire Him, instead of stooping to hold our hands, to rise up before us into His glory,—we hoping that by standing on a grain of dust or two of human knowledge higher than our fellows, we may behold the Creator as He rises,—God takes us at our word; He rises, into His own invisible and inconceivable majesty; He goes forth upon the ways which are not our ways, and retires into the thoughts which are not our

<small>Isaiah lv. 8.</small>

thoughts; and we are left alone. And presently we say in our vain hearts, 'There is no God.'—*Modern Painters*, vol. iv., ch. vi., § 7.   Psalm liii. 1.

Creed.

It is a creed with a great part of the existing English people, that they are in possession of a book which tells them, straight from the lips of God, all they ought to do, and need to know. I have read that book, with as much care as most of them, for some forty years; and am thankful that, on those who trust it, I can press its pleadings. My endeavour has been uniformly to make them trust it more deeply than they do; trust it, not in their own favourite verses only, but in the sum of all; trust it, not as a fetish or talisman, which they are to be saved by daily repetitions of; but as a Captain's order, to be heard and obeyed at their peril.—*Crown of Wild Olive*, § 12.

Cross.

It means simply that you are to go the road which you see to be the straight one: carrying whatever you find is given you to carry, as well and stoutly as you can; without making faces or calling people to come and look at you. Above all, you are neither to load, nor unload, yourself; nor cut your cross to your own liking.—*Ethics of the Dust*, p. 141.

Cross of Christ.

Remember that Christ Himself never says anything about holding by His Cross. He speaks a good deal of bearing it; but never for an instant of holding by it. It is His Hand, not His Cross, which is to save either you, or St. Peter, when the waves are rough.—*Ariadne Florentina*, § 29.

David.

And, though rightness of moral conduct is ultimately the great purifier of race, the sign of nobleness is not in this rightness of moral conduct, but in sensitiveness. When the make of the creature is fine, its temptations are strong, as well as its perceptions; it is liable to all kinds of impressions from without in their most violent form; liable therefore to be abused and hurt by all kinds of rough things which would do a coarser creature little harm, and thus to fall into frightful wrong if its fate will have it so. Thus David, coming of gentlest as well as royalist race of Ruth as well as of Judah, is sensitiveness through all flesh and spirit; not that his compassion will restrain him from murder when his terror urges him to it; nay, he is driven to the murder all the more by his sensitiveness to the shame which otherwise threatens him. But when his own story is told him under a disguise, though only a lamb is now concerned, his passion about it leaves him no time for thought. 'The man shall die'—note the reason—'because he had no pity.' He is so eager and indignant that it never occurs to him as strange that Nathan hides the name.—*Modern Painters*, vol. v., Pt. ix., ch. vii., § 6.

<small>2 Sam. xii. 5.</small>
<small>2 Sam. xii. 6.</small>

King and Prophet, type of all Divinely right doing, and right claiming, and right proclaiming, kinghood, for ever.—*Our Fathers Have Told Us*, ch. iv., § 32.

Dawn.

Let every dawn of morning be to you as the beginning of life, and every setting sun be to you as its close:—then let every one of these short lines leave its sure record of some kindly thing done for others— some goodly strength or knowledge gained for yourselves; so, from day to day, and strength to strength, you shall build up indeed, by Art, by Thought, and by Just Will, an Ecclesia of England, of which it shall not be said, 'See what manner of stones are here,' but, 'See what manner of men.'—*Lectures on Art*, § 125.

<small>S. Mark xiii. 1.</small>

'Day' of Genesis.

'And God said, Let the waters which are under the heaven be gathered together unto one place, and let the dry land appear.' _{Gen. i. 9.}

We do not, perhaps, often enough consider the deep significance of this sentence. We are too apt to receive it as the description of an event vaster only in its extent, not in its nature, than the compelling the Red Sea to draw back, that Israel might pass by. We imagine the Deity in like manner rolling the waves of the greater ocean together on an heap, and setting bars and doors to them eternally. But there is a far deeper meaning than this in the solemn words of Genesis, and in the correspondent verse of the Psalm, 'His hands prepared the dry land.' Up to that moment _{Psalm xcv. 5.} the earth had been *void*, for it had been *without form*. The command that the waters should be *gathered* was the command that the earth should be *sculptured*. The sea was not driven to his place in suddenly restrained rebellion, but withdrawn to his place in perfect and patient obedience. The dry land appeared, not in level sands, forsaken by the surges, which those surges might again claim for their own; but in range beyond range of swelling hill and iron rock, for ever to claim kindred with the firmament, and be companioned by the clouds of heaven. What space of time was in reality occupied by the 'day' of Genesis, is not, at present, of any importance for us to consider. By what furnaces of fire the adamant was melted, and by what wheels of earthquake it was torn, and by what teeth of glacier and weight of sea-waves it was engraven and finished into its perfect form, we may perhaps hereafter endeavour to conjecture; but here, as in few words the work is summed by the historian, so in few broad thoughts it should be comprehended by us; and as we read the mighty sentence, 'Let the dry land appear,' we should try to follow the finger of _{Gen. i. 9.} God, as it engraved upon the stone tables of the earth the letters and the law of its everlasting form; as, gulf by gulf, the channels of the deep were ploughed; and, cape by cape, the lines were traced, with Divine foreknowledge, of the shores that were to limit the nations; and, chain by chain, the mountain walls were lengthened forth, and their foundations fastened for ever; and the compass was set upon the face of the depth, and the fields, and the highest part of the dust of the world were made; and the right hand of Christ first strewed the snow on Lebanon, and smoothed the slopes of Calvary.—*Modern Painters*, vol. iv., ch. vii., §§ 1, 2.

Death.

The longer I live, the more clearly I see how all souls are in His hand — the mean and the great. Fallen on the earth in their baseness, or fading as the mist of morning in their goodness;—still in the hand of the potter as the clay, and in the temple of their master as the cloud. It was not the mere bodily death that He conquered—that death had no sting. It was this spiritual death which He conquered, so that at last it should be swallowed up—mark the word—not in life; but in victory. As the dead body shall be raised to life, so also the defeated soul to victory, if only it has been fighting on its Master's side, has made no covenant with death; nor itself bowed its forehead for his seal. Blind from the prison-house, maimed from the battle, or mad from the tombs, their souls shall surely yet sit, astonished, at His feet Who giveth peace. —*Modern Painters*, vol. v., ch. xii., § 16.

Jer. xviii. 6.

2 Kings ix. 31.

For, exactly in proportion as the pride of life became more insolent, the fear of death became more servile; and the difference in the manner in which the men of early and later days adorned the sepulchre, confesses a still greater difference in their manner of regarding death. To those he came as the comforter and the friend, rest in his right hand, hope in his left; to these as the humiliator, the spoiler, and the avenger. And, therefore, we find the early tombs at once simple and lovely in adornment, severe and solemn in their expression; confessing the power, and accepting the peace, of death, openly and joyfully; and in all their symbols marking that the hope of resurrection lay only in Christ's righteousness; signed always with this simple utterance of the dead, 'I will lay me down in peace, and take my rest; for it is thou, Lord, only that makest me dwell in safety.'—*Stones of Venice*, vol. iii., ch. ii., § XLVI. [Psalm iv. 9.]

'Dew of the Morning.'

When you go out, delighted, into the dew of the morning, have you ever considered why it is so rich upon the grass;—why it is *not* upon the trees? It *is* partly on the trees, but yet your memory of it will be always chiefly of its gleam upon the lawn. On many trees you will find there is none at all. I cannot follow out here the many inquiries connected with this subject, but, broadly, remember the branched trees are fed chiefly by rain,—the unbranched ones by dew, visible or invisible; that is to say, at all events by moisture which they can gather for themselves out of the air; or else by streams and springs. Hence the division of the verse of the song of Moses: 'My doctrine shall drop as the rain; my speech shall distil as the dew: as the *small* rain upon the tender *herb*, as the showers upon the grass.'—*Proserpina*, ch. iii., § 22. [Deut. xxxii. 2.]

Dives and Lazarus.

It is one of the strange characters of the human mind, necessary indeed to its peace, but infinitely destructive of its power, that we never thoroughly feel the evils which are not actually set before our eyes. If, suddenly, in the midst of the enjoyments of the palate and lightnesses of heart of a London dinner-party, the walls of the chamber were parted, and through their gap, the nearest human beings who were famishing, and in

misery, were borne into the midst of the company—
feasting and fancy-free—if, pale with sickness, horrible
in destitution, broken by despair, body by body, they
were laid upon the soft carpet, one beside the chair of
every guest, would only the crumbs of the dainties be
cast to them—would only a passing glance, a passing
thought be vouchsafed to them? Yet the actual facts,
the real relations of each Dives and Lazarus, are not
altered by the intervention of the house wall between
the table and the sick-bed—by the few feet of ground
(how few!) which are indeed all that separate the merri-
ment from the misery.—*On the Old Road*, vol. i., part i.,
§ 270.

Divine Builder.

The glacier of the Col de Cervin lies as level as a
lake. This spur is one of the few points from which
the mass of the Mont Cervin is in anywise approachable.
It is a continuation of the masonry of the mountain
itself, and affords us the means of examining the character of its materials.

Few architects would like to build with them. The
slope of the rocks to the north-west is covered two feet
deep with their ruins, a mass of loose and slaty shale,
of a dull brick-red colour. . . . The rock is indeed
hard beneath, but still disposed in thin courses of these
cloven shales, so finely laid that they look in places
more like a heap of crushed autumn leaves than a rock;
and the first sensation is one of unmitigated surprise,
as if the mountain were upheld by miracle; but surprise
becomes more intelligent reverence for the great Builder,
when we find, in the middle of the mass of these dead
leaves, a course of living rock, of quartz as white as the
snow that encircles it, and harder than a bed of steel.

It is one only of a thousand iron bands that knit the
strength of the mighty mountain. Through the buttress
and the wall alike, the courses of its varied masonry are
seen in their successive order, smooth and true as if

laid by line and plummet,[1] but of thickness and strength continually varying, and with silver cornices glittering along the edge of each, laid by the snowy winds and carved by the sunshine,—stainless ornaments of the eternal temple, by which 'neither the hammer nor the axe, nor any tool, was heard while it was in building.'—*Stones of Venice*, vol. i., ch. v., §§ 3–5.

<small>1 Kings vi. 7.</small>

Divine Law.

When people read, 'The law came by Moses, but grace and truth by Christ,' do they suppose it means that the law was ungracious and untrue? The law was given for a foundation; the grace (or mercy) and truth for fulfilment;—the whole forming one glorious Trinity of judgment, mercy, and truth. And if people would but read the text of their Bibles with heartier purpose of understanding it, instead of superstitiously, they would see that throughout the parts which they are intended to make most personally their own (the Psalms) it is always the Law which is spoken of with chief joy. The Psalms respecting mercy are often sorrowful, as in thought of what it cost; but those respecting the law are always full of delight. David cannot contain himself for joy in thinking of it,—he is never weary of its praise:—'How love I thy law! it is my meditation all the day. Thy testimonies are my delight and my counsellors; sweeter, also, than honey and the honey-comb.' —*Modern Painters*, vol. v., Pt. vii., ch. iv., § 22.

<small>S. John i. 17.</small>
<small>Psalm cxix. 97.</small>
<small>Psalm xix. 10.</small>

Divine Power, in Active Life.

In general, active men, of strong sense and stern principle, do not care to see anything in a leaf, but vegetable tissue, and are so well convinced of useful moral truth, that it does not strike them as a new or notable thing when they find it in any way symbolized

---

[1] On the eastern side: violently contorted on the northern and western.

by material nature; hence there is a strong presumption, when first we perceive a tendency in any one to regard trees as living, and enunciate moral aphorisms over every pebble they stumble against, that such tendency proceeds from a morbid temperament, like Shelley's, or an inconsistent one, like Jaques's. But when the active life is nobly fulfilled, and the mind is then raised beyond it into clear and calm beholding of the world around us, the same tendency again manifests itself in the most sacred way: the simplest forms of nature are strangely animated by the sense of the Divine presence; the trees and flowers seem all, in a sort, children of God; and we ourselves, their fellows, made out of the same dust, and greater than they only in having a greater portion of the Divine power exerted on our frame, and all the common uses and palpably visible forms of things, become subordinate in our minds to their inner glory,—to the mysterious voices in which they talk to us about God, and the changeful and typical aspects by which they witness to us of holy truth, and fill us with obedient, joyful, and thankful emotion.—*Modern Painters*, vol. iii., ch. xvii., § 41.

Divine Service.

We say, 'Divine service will be "performed"' (that's our word—the form of it gone through) 'at so-and-so o'clock.' Alas; unless we perform Divine service in every willing act of life, we never perform it at all. The one Divine work—the one ordered sacrifice—is to do justice; and it is the last we are ever inclined to do. Anything rather than that! As much charity as you choose, but no justice. 'Nay,' you will say, 'charity is greater than justice.' Yes, it is greater; it is the summit of justice—It is the temple of which justice is the foundation. But you can't have the top without the bottom; you cannot build upon charity. You must build upon justice, for this main reason, that you have not, at first, charity to build with. It is the last reward of good work. Do justice to your brother (you can do that whether you love him or not), and you will come to love him. But do injustice to him, because you don't love him; and you will come to hate him.—*The Crown of Wild Olive*, § 39.

Dove of the Ark.

Of the splendour of your own true life, you are told, in the words which, **to-day, let me call,** as your **Fathers** did, words **of inspiration**—' Yet shall ye be as the wings of a dove, that is covered with silver wings and her feathers with gold.' . . . Psalm lxviii. 13.

Of the power of flight in these wings, and the tender purpose of their flight, you hear also in your Father's book. To the Church, flying from her enemies into desolate wilderness, there were indeed given two wings as of a great eagle. But the weary saint of God, looking forward to his home in calm of eternal peace, prays rather—' Oh that I had wings like a dove, for then should I flee away, and be at rest.' And Psalm lv. 6.
of these wings, and this mind of hers, this is what reverent science should teach you: first, with what parting of plume, and what soft pressure and rhythmic bearing of divided air, she reaches that miraculous swiftness of undubious motion, compared with which the tempest is slow, and the arrow uncertain; and secondly, what clue there is, visible, or conceivable to thought of man, by which, to her living conscience and errorless pointing of magnetic soul, her distant home is felt afar beyond the horizon, and the straight path, through concealing clouds, and over trackless lands, made plain to her desire, and her duty, by the finger of God.

And lastly, since in the tradition of the Old Covenant she was made the messenger of forgiveness to those eight souls saved through the baptism unto death, and in the Gospel of the New Covenant, under her image, was manifested the well-pleasing of God, in the fulfilment of all righteousness by Gen. viii. 11.
S. Mark i. 10.

His Son in the Baptism unto life,—surely alike all Christian people, old and young, should be taught to be gladdened by her sweet presence; and in every city and village in Christendom she should have such home as in Venice she has had for ages, and be, among the sculptured marbles of the temple, the sweetest sculpture; and, fluttering at your children's feet, their never-angered friend.—*On the Old Road*, vol. ii., §§ 281–83.

Dragon (Scriptural).

The reader may have heard, perhaps, in other books of Genesis than Hesiod's, of a Dragon being busy about a tree which bore apples, and of crushing the head of that dragon; but seeing how, in the Greek mind, this serpent was descended from the sea, he may, perhaps, be surprised to remember another verse, bearing also on the matter:—'Thou brakest the heads of the dragons in the waters;' and yet more surprised, going on with the Septuagint version, to find where he is being led: 'Thou brakest the head of the dragon, and gavest him to be meat to the Ethiopian people. Thou didst tear asunder the strong fountains and the storm-torrents; thou didst dry up the rivers of Etham,' πηγὰς καὶ χειμάρρους, the Pegasus fountains—' Etham on the edge of the wilderness.'—*Modern Painters*, vol. v., part ix., ch. x., § 11.

<small>Psalm lxxiv. 13, 14, 15.</small>

<small>Exod. xiii. 20.</small>

<small>Num. xxxiii. 6.</small>

It seems to me that just because we are intended, as long as we live, to be in a state of intense moral effort, we are *not* intended to be in intense physical or intellectual effort. Our full energies are to be given to the soul's work—to the great fight with the Dragon—the taking the kingdom of heaven by force.—*On the Old Road*, vol. i., part i., § 169.

<small>Rev. xx. 2.</small>

<small>S. Matt. xi. 12.</small>

Duty.

The greatest part of the good work of the world is done either in pure and unvexed instinct of duty, . . . or else, and better, it is cheerful and helpful doing of what the hand finds to do, in surety that at evening time, whatsoever is right the Master will give.—*Lectures on Art*, § 86.

Early Christianity.

In the early ages of Christianity, there was little care taken to analyse character. One momentous question was heard over the whole world,—Dost thou believe in the Lord with all thine heart? There was but one division among men,—the great unatoneable division between the disciple and adversary. The love of Christ was all, and in all; and in proportion [Col. iii. 11] to the nearness of their memory of His person and teaching, men understood the infinity of the requirements of the moral law, and the manner in which it alone could be fulfilled. The early Christians felt that virtue, like sin, was a subtle universal thing, entering into every act and thought, appearing outwardly in ten thousand diverse ways, diverse according to the separate framework of every heart in which it dwelt; but one and the same always in its proceeding from the love of God, as sin is one and the same in proceeding from hatred of God. And in their pure, early, and practical piety, they saw that there was no need for codes of morality, or systems of metaphysics. Their virtue comprehended everything, entered into everything; it was too vast and too spiritual to be defined; but there was no need of its definition. For through faith, working by love, they knew that all human excellence would [Gal. v. 6.] be developed in due order; but that, without faith, neither reason could define, nor effort reach, the lowest phase of Christian virtue. And therefore, when any of the Apostles have occasion to describe or enumerate any forms of vice or virtue by name, there is no attempt at system in their words. They use them hurriedly and energetically, heaping the thoughts one upon another, in order as far as possible to fill the reader's mind with a sense of the infinity both of crime and of righteousness.

Hear St. Paul describe sin: 'Being filled with all unrighteousness, fornication, wickedness, covetousness, maliciousness; full of envy, murder, debate, deceit, malignity; whisperers, backbiters, haters of God, despiteful, proud, boasters, inventors of evil things, disobedient to parents, without understanding, covenant breakers, without natural affection, implacable, unmerciful.' There is evidently here an intense feeling of the universality of sin; and in order to express it, the Apostle hurries his words confusedly together, little caring about their order, as knowing all the vices to be indissolubly connected one with another. It would be utterly vain to endeavour to arrange his expressions as if they had been intended for the ground of any system, or to give any philosophical definition of the vices. So also hear him speaking of virtue: 'Rejoice in the Lord. Let your moderation be known unto all men. Be careful for nothing, but in everything let your requests be made known unto God; and whatsoever things are honest, whatsoever things are just, whatsoever things are pure, whatsoever things are lovely, whatsoever things are of good report, if there be any virtue, and if there be any praise, think on these things.' Observe, he gives up all attempt at definition; he leaves the definition to every man's heart, though he writes so as to mark the overflowing fulness of his own vision of virtue. And so it is in all writings of the Apostles; their manner of exhortation, and the kind of conduct they press, vary according to the persons they address, and the feeling of the moment at which they write, and never show any attempt at logical precision. And, although the words of their Master are not thus irregularly uttered, but are weighed like fine gold, yet, even in His teaching, there is no detailed or organized system of morality; but the command only of that faith and love which were to embrace the whole being of man: 'On these two commandments hang all the law and the prophets.' Here and there an

Rom. i. 29, 30, 31.

Phil. iv. 4, 5, 6, 8.

S. Matt. xxii. 40.

incidental warning against this or that more dangerous form of vice or error. 'Take heed and beware of covetousness.' 'Beware of the leaven of the Pharisees;' here and there a plain example of the meaning of Christian love, as in the parables of the Samaritan and the Prodigal, and His own perpetual example: these were the elements of Christ's constant teaching; for the Beatitudes, which are the only approximation to anything like a systematic statement, belong to different conditions and characters of individual men, not to abstract virtues. And all early Christians taught in the same manner. They never cared to expound the nature of this or that virtue; for they knew that the believer who had Christ had all. Did he need fortitude? Christ was his rock: Equity? Christ was his righteousness: Holiness? Christ was his sanctification: Liberty? Christ was his redemption: Temperance? Christ was his ruler: Wisdom? Christ was his light: Truthfulness? Christ was the truth: Charity? Christ was love.—*Stones of Venice*, vol. ii., ch. viii., § XLV.

[margin: S. Luke xii. 15. S. Luke xii. 1. 1 Cor. x. 4; i. 30.]

Education.

Education is, indeed, of all differences not divinely appointed, an instant effacer and reconciler. Whatever is undivinely poor, it will make rich; whatever is undivinely maimed, and halt, and blind, it will make whole, and equal, and seeing. The blind and the lame are to it as to David at the siege of the Tower of the Kings, 'hated of David's soul.' But there are other divinely-appointed differences, eternal as the ranks of the everlasting hills, and as the strength of their ceaseless waters. And these, education does *not* do away with; but measures, manifests, and employs.

In the handful of shingle which you gather from the sea-beach, which the indiscriminate sea, with equality of fraternal foam, has only educated to be, every one,

[margin: 2 Sam v. 8.]

round, you will see little difference between the noble
and mean stones. But the jeweller's trenchant education of them will tell you another story. Even the
meanest will be better for it, but the noblest so much
better that you can class the two together no more.
The fair veins and colours are all clear now, and so
stern is nature's intent regarding this, that not only
will the polish show which is best, but the best will
take most polish. You shall not merely see they have
more virtue than the others, but see that more of virtue
more clearly; and the less virtue there is, the more
dimly you shall see what there is of it.

And the law about education, which is sorrowfullest
to vulgar pride, is this—that all its gains are at com-
pound interest; so that, as our work proceeds, every
hour throws us farther behind the greater men with
whom we began on equal terms.

Two children go to school hand in hand, and spell
for half-an-hour over the same page. Through all their
lives, never shall they spell from the same page more.
One is presently a page ahead,—two pages, ten pages,
—and evermore, though each toils equally, the interval
enlarges — at birth nothing, at death, infinite. — *Time
and Tide*, §§ 171, 172.

Egyptian Type of Servitude.

In the earliest and grandest shaft architecture which
we know, that of Egypt, we have no grouped arrangements, properly so called, but either single and smooth
shafts, or richly reeded and furrowed shafts, which represent the extreme conditions of a complicated group
bound together to sustain a single mass; and are indeed,
without doubt, nothing else than imitations of bundles of
reeds, or of clusters of the lotus: . . . the great Christian
truth of distinct services of the individual soul is typified
in the Christian shaft; and the old Egyptian servitude
of the multitudes, the servitude inseparable from the
children of Ham, is typified also in that ancient shaft

of the Egyptians which in its gathered strength of the river reeds, seems, as the sands of the desert drift over its ruin, to be intended to remind us for ever of the end of the association of the wicked. 'Can the rush grow up without mire, or the flag grow without water?—So are the paths of all that forget God; and the hypocrite's hope shall perish.'—*Stones of Venice*, vol. i., ch. viii., § XXIII. [Job viii. 11, 13.]

Elijah.

I must ask you to think with me to-day what is the meaning of the myth,—if you call it so, of the great prophet of the Old Testament, who is to be again sent before the coming of the day of the Lord. For truly, you will find that if any part of your ancient faith be true, it is needful for every soul which is to take up its cross, with Christ, to be also first transfigured in the light of Christ,—talking with Moses and with Elias. The contest of Moses is with the temporal servitude,—of Elijah, with the spiritual servitude, of the people; and the war of Elijah is with their servitude essentially to two Gods, Baal, or the Sun-God, in whose hand they thought was their life, and Baalzebub—the Fly-God,—of Corruption, in whose hand they thought was the arbitration of death. The entire contest is summed in the first assertion by Elijah, of his authority as the Servant of God, over those elemental powers by which the heart of Man, whether Jew or heathen, was filled with food and gladness. [Mal. iv. 5. S. Matt. xvii. 11. S. Matt. xvii. 3.]

And Elijah the Tishbite, who was of the inhabitants of Gilead, said unto Ahab, 'As the Lord God of Israel liveth, before whom I stand, there shall not be dew nor rain these years, but according to my word.' . . . [1 Kings xvii. 1.]

The whole confidence and glory of prayer is in its appeal to a Father who knows our necessities before we ask, who knows our thoughts before they rise in our hearts, and whose decrees, as unalterable in the eternal future as in the eternal past, yet in the close verity of visible fact, bend, like reeds, before the fore-ordained and faithful prayers of His children.

Of Elijah's contest on Carmel with that Sun-power in which, literally, you again now are seeking your life, you know the story, however little you believe it.

But of his contest with the Death-power, on the hill of Samaria, you read less frequently, and more doubt- fully. 'Oh, thou Man of God, the King hath said, Come down. And Elijah answered and said, If I be a man of God, let fire come down from Heaven, and consume thee, and thy fifty.' . . .

<small>2 Kings i. 9, 10.</small>

But note Elijah's message. 'Because thou hast sent to enquire of Baalzebub the God of Ekron, therefore, thou shalt not go down from the bed on which thou art gone up, but shalt surely die.'

<small>2 Kings i. 16.</small>

'Because thou hast sent to enquire': he had not sent to *pray* to the God of Ekron, only to *ask* of him. The priests of Baal *prayed* to Baal, but Ahaziah only *questions* the fly-god.—*On the Old Road*, vol. ii., §§ 285–87.

Emblems of the Bible.

You will assuredly admit this principle,—that whatever temporal things are spoken of in the Bible as emblems of the highest spiritual blessings, must be *good things* in themselves. You would allow that bread, for instance, would not have been used as an emblem of the word of life, unless it had been good, and necessary for man; nor water used as the emblem of sanctification, unless it also had been good and necessary for man. You will allow that oil, and honey, and balm are good, when David says, 'Let the righteous reprove me; it shall be an excellent oil;' or, 'How sweet are thy words unto my taste; yea, sweeter than honey to my mouth;' or when Jeremiah cries out in his weeping, 'Is there

<small>Psalm cxli. 5.</small>
<small>Psalm cxix. 103.</small>

no balm in Gilead? is there no physician there?' You would admit at once that the man who said there was no taste in the literal honey, and no healing in the literal balm, must be of distorted judgment, since God had used them as emblems of spiritual sweetness and healing. And how, then, will you evade the conclusion, that there must be joy, and comfort, and instruction in the literal beauty of architecture, when God, descending in His utmost love to the distressed Jerusalem, and addressing to her His most precious and solemn promises, speaks to her in such words as these: 'Oh, thou afflicted, tossed with tempest, and not comforted,'—What shall be done to her?—What brightest emblem of blessing will God set before her? 'Behold, I will *lay thy stones with fair colours*, and thy foundations with sapphires; and I will make thy *windows of agates*, and thy gates of carbuncles, and all thy borders of pleasant stones.' Nor is this merely an emblem of spiritual blessing; for that blessing is added in the concluding words, 'And all thy children shall be taught of the Lord, and great shall be the peace of thy children.' —*Lectures on Architecture and Painting*, § 56.

[margin: Jer. viii. 22. Isaiah liv. 11, 12. Isaiah liv. 13.]

England and her Great Men.

So far as in it lay, this century has caused every one of its great men, whose hearts were kindest, and whose spirits most perceptive of the work of God, to die without hope:—Scott, Keats, Byron, Shelley, Turner. Great England, of the Iron-heart now, not of the Lion-heart; for these souls of her children an account may perhaps be one day required of her.

She has not yet read often enough that old story of the Samaritan's mercy. He whom he saved was going down from Jerusalem to Jericho— to the accursed city (so the old Church used to understand it). He should not have left Jerusalem; it was his own fault that he went out into the desert, and fell

[margin: S. Luke x. 33.]

among the thieves, and was left for dead. Every one of these English children, in their day, took the desert by-path as he did, and fell among fiends — took to making bread out of stones at their bidding, and then died, torn and famished; careful England, in her pure, priestly dress, passing by on the other side. So far as we are concerned, that is the account *we* have to give of them.

So far as *they* are concerned, I do not fear for them; —there being one Priest Who never passes by. The longer I live, the more clearly I see how all souls are in His hand—the mean and the great. Fallen on the earth in their baseness, or fading as the mist of morning in their goodness;—still in the hand of the potter as the clay, and in the temple of their master as the cloud. It was not the mere bodily death that He conquered—that death had no sting. It was this spiritual death which He conquered, so that at last it should be swallowed up—mark the word— not in life; but in victory. As the dead body shall be raised to life, so also the defeated soul to victory, if only it has been fighting on its Master's side, has made no covenant with death; nor itself bowed its forehead for his seal. Blind from the prison-house, maimed from the battle, or mad from the tombs, their souls shall surely yet sit, astonished, at His feet Who giveth peace. —*Modern Painters*, vol. v., ch. xii., §§ 14–16.

[margin: Jer. xviii. 6.]
[margin: Isaiah xxv. 8.]

Errors.

There are few of the errors against which I have to warn my readers, into which I have not myself at some time fallen. Of which errors, the chief, and cause of all the rest, is the leaning on our own understanding; the thought that we can measure the hearts of our brethren, and judge of the ways of God. Of the hearts of men, noble, yet 'deceitful above all things, who can know them?'—*St. Mark's Rest*, § 67.

[margin: Jer. xvii. 9.]

Esdras.

It chanced, this morning, as I sat down to finish my preface, that I had, for my introductory reading, the fifth chapter of the second book of Esdras; in which, though often read carefully before, I had never enough noticed the curious verse 'Blood shall drop out of wood, and the stone shall give his voice, and the people shall be troubled.' Of which verse, so far as I can gather the meaning from the context, and from the rest of the chapter, the intent is, that in the time spoken of by the prophet, which, if not our own, is one exactly corresponding to it, the deadness of men to all noble things shall be so great, that the sap of trees shall be more truly blood, in God's sight, than their heart's blood; and the silence of men, in praise of all noble things, so great, that the stones shall cry out, in God's hearing, instead of their tongues; and the rattling of the shingle on the beach, and the roar of the rocks driven by the torrent, be truer Te Deum than the thunder of all their choirs. The writings of modern scientific prophets teach us to anticipate a day when even these lower voices shall be also silent; and leaf cease to wave, and stream to murmur, in the grasp of an eternal cold. But it may be, that rather out of the mouths of babes and sucklings a better peace may be promised to the redeemed Jerusalem; and the strewn branches, and low-laid stones, remain at rest at the gates of the city, built in unity with herself, and saying with her human voice, 'My King cometh.'—*Deucalion*, Intro., pp. 6, 7.

[2 Esdras v. 5.]
[Psalm viii. 2.]
[S. Matt. xxi. 16.]
[S. John xii. 15.]
[Zech. ix. 9.]
[S. Matt. xxi. 5.]

Eternal Charity.

'Charity never faileth; but whether there be prophecies they shall fail—tongues, they shall cease—knowledge, it shall vanish.' And the one message they bear to us is the commandment of the Eternal Charity. 'Thou shalt love the Lord thy God with *all* thine heart, and thy

[2 Cor. xiii. 8.]
[S. Matt. xxii. 37-39.]

neighbour as thyself.' As thyself—no more, even the dearest of neighbours. 'Therefore let every man see that he love his wife even as himself.' No more—else she has become an idol, not a fellow-servant; a creature between us and our Master.— *On the Old Road*, vol. i., part i., § 248.

<small>Eph. v. 33.</small>

Evangelists, The Four.

An Evangelion is the voice of the Messenger, saying, it is *here*.

And the four mystic Evangelists, under the figures of living creatures, are not types merely of the men that are to bring the Gospel message, but of the power of that message in all Creation—so far as it was, and is, spoken in all living things, and as the Word of God, which is Christ, was present, and not merely prophesied, in the Creatures of His hand. . . .

> 'QUÆQUE SUB OBSCURIS
> DE CRISTO DICTA FIGURIS
> HIS APERIRE DATUR
> ET IN HIS, DEUS IPSE NOTATUR.'

'Whatever things under obscure figures have been said of Christ, it is given to *these*' (creatures) 'to open; and in these, Christ himself is seen.'

A grave saying. Not in the least true of mere Matthew, Mark, Luke, and John. Christ was never seen *in* them, though told of by them. But, as the Word by which all things were made, He is seen in all things made, and in the Poiesis of them: and therefore, when the vision of Ezekiel is repeated to St. John, changed only in that the four creatures are to him more distinct—each with its single aspect, and not each fourfold,—they are full of eyes within, and rest not day nor night,—saying, 'Holy, Holy, Holy, Lord God Almighty, which art, and wast, and art to come.'

<small>Rev. iv. 8</small>

We repeat the words habitually, in our own most solemn religious service; but we repeat without noticing out of whose mouths they come. 'Therefore,' (we say, in much self-satisfaction,) 'with Angels and Archangels, and with all the Company of heaven,' (meaning each of us, I suppose, the select Company we expect to get into there,) 'we laud and magnify,' etc. But it ought to make a difference in our estimate of ourselves, and of our power to say, with our hearts, that God is Holy, if we remember that we join in saying so, not, for the present, with the Angels,—but with the Beasts.

Yet not with every manner of Beast; for afterwards, when all the Creatures in Heaven and Earth, and the Sea, join in the giving of praise, it is only these four who can say 'Amen.' _{Rev. v. 14.}

The Ox that treadeth out the corn; and the Lion that shall eat straw like the Ox, and lie down with the lamb; and the Eagle that fluttereth over her young; and the human creature that loves its mate, and its children. In these four is all the power and all the charity of earthly life; and in such power and charity 'Deus ipse notatur.' . . .

> 'SIC ACTUS CHRISTI
> DESCRIBUNT QUATUOR ISTI
> QUOD NEQUE NATURA
> LITER NENT, NEC UTRINQUE FIGURA.'

'Thus do these four describe the Acts of Christ. And weave his story, neither by natural knowledge, nor, contrariwise, by any figure.'

Compare now the two inscriptions. In the living creatures, Christ himself is seen by nature and by figure. But these four tell us his Acts, 'Not by nature—not by figure.' How then? You have had various 'lives of Christ.' But there is only one light by which you can read the life of Christ,—the light of the life you now lead in the flesh; and that not the natural, but the won life. 'Nevertheless, I live; yet not I, but Christ liveth in me.'—*St. Mark's Rest*, ch. viii., §§ 114, 121—7. _{Gal. ii. 20.}

Evil Spirits.

Without any discussion as to the personal existence or traditional character of evil spirits, you will find it a practical fact, that external temptations and inevitable trials of temper, have power against you which your health and virtue depend on your resisting; that, if not resisted, the evil energy of them will pass into your own heart, φρήν, or μῆνις; and that the ordinary and vulgarized phrase 'the Devil, or betraying Spirit, is *in him*,' is the most scientifically accurate which you can apply to any person so influenced. You will find also that, in the compass of literature, the casting out of, or cleansing from, such a state is best symbolized for you by the image of one who had been wandering wild and naked *among tombs*, sitting still, clothed, and in his right mind, and that in whatever literal or figurative sense you receive the Biblical statement of what followed, this is absolutely certain, that the herd of swine hastening to their destruction, in perfect sympathy with each other's fury, is the most accurate symbol ever given, in literature, of consummate ἀφροσύνη.—*Eagle's Nest*, § 69.

[S. Luke viii. 35.]

'Except ye be converted and become as little children.'

The first character of right childhood is that it is Modest. A well-bred child does not think it can teach its parents, or that it knows everything. It may think its father and mother know everything—perhaps that all grown-up people know everything; very certainly it is sure that *it* does not. And it is always asking questions, and wanting to know more. Well, that is the first character of a good and wise man at his work. To know that he knows very little;—to perceive that there are many above him wiser than he; and to be always asking questions, wanting to learn, not to teach. No one ever teaches well who wants to teach, or governs well who wants to govern; it is an old saying

(Plato's, but I know not if his, first) and as wise as old.

Then, the second character of right childhood is to be Faithful. Perceiving that its father knows best what is good for it, and having found always, when it has tried its own way against his, that he was right and it was wrong, a noble child trusts him at last wholly, gives him its hand, and will walk blindfold with him, if he bids it. And that is the true character of all good men also, as obedient workers, or soldiers under captains. They must trust their captains;—they are bound for their lives to choose none but those whom they *can* trust. Then, they are not always to be thinking that what seems strange to them, or wrong in what they are desired to do, *is* strange or wrong. They know their captain: where he leads they must follow,—what he bids, they must do; and without this trust and faith, without this captainship and soldiership, no great deed, no great salvation, is possible to man.

Then, the third character of right childhood is to be Loving. Give a little love to a child, and you get a great deal back. It loves everything near it, when it is a right kind of child; would hurt nothing, would give the best it has away, always if you need it; does not lay plans for getting everything in the house for itself: and, above all, delights in helping people; you cannot please it so much as by giving it a chance of being useful, in ever so humble a way.

And because of all these characters, lastly, it is Cheerful. Putting its trust in its father, it is careful for nothing—being full of love to every creature, it is happy always, whether in its play or its duty. Well, that's the great worker's character also. Taking no thought for the morrow; taking thought only for the duty of the day; trusting somebody else to take care of to-morrow; knowing indeed what labour is, but not what sorrow is; and always ready for play— S. Matt. vi. 34.

beautiful play. For lovely human play is like the play of the Sun. There's a worker for you. He, steady to his time, is set as a strong man to run his course, but also he *rejoiceth* as a strong man to run his course. See how he plays in the morning, with the mists below, and the clouds above, with a ray here, and a flash there, and a shower of jewels everywhere;— that's the Sun's play; and great human play is like his —all various—all full of light and life, and tender, as the dew of the morning.

<small>Psalm xix. 5.</small>

So then, you have the child's character in these four things—Humility, Faith, Charity and Cheerfulness. That's what you have got to be converted to. 'Except ye be converted and become as little children.'—You hear much of conversion nowadays: but people always seem to think they have got to be made wretched by conversion,—to be converted to long faces. No, friends, you have got to be converted to short ones; you have to repent into childhood, to repent into delight, and delightsomeness. . . . It is among children only, and as children only, that you will find medicine for your healing and true wisdom for your teaching. There is poison in the counsels of the *men* of this world; the words they speak are all bitterness, 'the poison of asps is under their lips,' but 'the sucking child shall play by the hole of the asp.' There is death in the looks of men. 'Their eyes are privily set against the poor:' they are as the uncharmable serpent, the cockatrice, which slew by seeing. But 'the weaned child shall lay his hand on the cockatrice' den.' There is death in the steps of men: 'their feet are swift to shed blood; they have compassed us in our steps like the lion that is greedy of his prey, and the young lion lurking in secret places;' but, in that kingdom, the wolf shall lie down with the lamb, and the fatling with the lion, and 'a little child shall

<small>S Matt. xviii. 3</small>

<small>Rom. iii. 13.</small>

<small>Isaiah xi. 8.</small>

<small>Psalm x. 8.</small>

<small>Isaiah xi. 8.</small>

<small>Rom. iii. 15.</small>

<small>Isaiah xi. 6.</small>

lead them.' There is death in the thoughts of men: the world is one wide riddle to them, darker and darker as it draws to a close; but the secret of it is known to the child, and the Lord of heaven and earth is most to be thanked in that 'He has hidden these things from the wise and prudent, and has revealed them unto babes.'—*Crown of Wild Olive*, §§ 47–51. _{S. Matt. xi. 25. S. Luke x. 21.}

Ezekiel's Vision, Altar-vault of St. Mark's.

Boy or girl, man or woman, of you, not one in a thousand, if one, has ever, I am well assured, asked what was the *use* of Ezekiel's Vision, either to Ezekiel, or to anybody else; any more than I used to think, myself, what St. Mark's was built for.

'As I was among the Captives by the River of Chebar, the Heavens were opened, and I saw visions of God.' _{Ezek. i. 1.}

(Fugitive at least,—and all *but* captive,—by the River of the deep stream,—the Venetians perhaps cared yet to hear what he saw.)

'In the fifth year of King Jehoiachin's captivity, the word of the Lord came *expressly* unto Ezekiel the Priest.'

(We also—we Venetians—have our Pontifices; we also our King. May we not hear?)

'And I looked, and, behold, a whirlwind came out of the north, and a fire infolding itself. Also in the midst thereof was [1] the likeness of Four living Creatures.

'And this was the aspect of them; the Likeness of a Man was upon them.

'And every one had four faces, and every one four wings. And they had the hands of a Man under their wings. And their wings were stretched upward, two wings of every one were joined one to another, and two covered their bodies. And when they went, I heard the noise of their wings, like the noise of great

---

[1] What alterations I make are from the Septuagint.

waters, as the voice of the Almighty, the voice of speech, the noise of an Host.'

(To us in Venice, is not the noise of the great waters known—and the noise of an Host? May we hear also the voice of the Almighty?)

'And they went every one straight forward. Whither the Spirit was to go, they went. And this was the likeness of their faces: they four had the face of a Man' (to the front), 'and the face of a Lion on the right side, and the face of an Ox on the left side, and' (looking back) 'the face of an Eagle.'

The face of Man; and of the wild beasts of the earth, and of the tame, and of the birds of the air. This was the Vision of the Glory of the Lord.

'And as I beheld the living creatures, behold, *one* wheel upon the earth, by the living creatures, with *his* four faces, . . . and their aspect, and their work, was as a wheel in the midst of a wheel.'

Crossed, that is, the meridians of the four quarters of the earth. (See Holbein's drawing of it in his Old Testament series.)

'And the likeness of the Firmament upon the heads of the living creatures was as the colour of the terrible crystal.

'And there was a voice from the Firmament that was over their heads, when they stood, *and had let down* their wings.

'And above the Firmament that was over their heads was the likeness of a Throne; and upon the likeness of the Throne was the likeness of the Aspect of a Man above, upon it.

'And from His loins round about I saw as it were the appearance of fire; and it had brightness round about, as the bow that is in the cloud in the day of rain. This was the appearance of the likeness of the Glory of the Lord. And when I saw it, I fell upon my face.'

Can any of us do the like—or is it worth while?

... Or is there, nowadays, no more anything for *us* to be afraid of, or to be thankful for, in all the wheels, and flame, and light, of earth and heaven?

This that follows, after the long rebuke, is their Evangelion. This the sum of the voice that speaks in them. 'Therefore say, Thus saith the Lord, Though I have cast them far off among the heathen, yet will I be to them as a little sanctuary in the places whither they shall come. Ezek. xi. 16.

'And I will give them one heart; and I will put a new spirit within them; and I will take the stony heart out of their flesh, and will give them a heart of flesh. That they may walk in my statutes, and keep mine ordinances and do them, and they shall be my people, and I will be their God. Ezek. xi. 19, 20.

'Then did the Cherubims lift up their wings, and the wheels beside them, and the glory of the God of Israel was over them above.' Ezek. xi. 22.

That is the story of the Altar-vault of St. Mark's, of which though much was gone, yet, when I was last in Venice, much was left, wholly lovely and mighty. The principal figure of the Throned Christ was indeed for ever destroyed by the restorer; but the surrounding Prophets, and the Virgin in prayer, at least retained so much of their ancient colour and expression as to be entirely noble,—if only one had nobility enough in one's own thoughts to forgive the failure of any other human soul to speak clearly what it had felt of most divine.—*St. Mark's Rest*, §§ 115–18.

Faith.

Faith, whether we receive it in the sense of adherence to resolution, obedience to law, regardfulness of promise, in which from all time it has been the test, as the shield, of the true being and life of man; or in the still higher sense of trustfulness in the presence, kindness, and word of God, in which form it has been exhibited under the Christian dispensation. For, whether in one or other form,—whether the faithfulness of men whose path is chosen and portion fixed, in the following and receiving of that path and portion, as in the Thermopylæ camp; or the happier faithfulness of children in the good giving of their Father, and of subjects in the conduct of their King, as in the 'Stand still and see the salvation of God' of the Red Sea shore, there is rest and peacefulness, the 'standing still,' in both, the quietness of action determined, of spirit unalarmed, of expectation unimpatient: beautiful even when based only, as of old, on the self-command and self-possession, the persistent dignity or the uncalculating love, of the creature; but more beautiful yet when the rest is one of humility instead of pride, and the trust no more in the resolution we have taken, but in the hand we hold.—*Modern Painters*, vol. ii., sec. i., ch. vii., § 4.

<small>Exod. xiv. 13.</small>

Fear of God.

Among the children of God, while there is always that fearful and bowed apprehension of His majesty, and that sacred dread of all offence to Him, which is called the Fear of God, yet of real and essential fear there is not any, but clinging of confidence to Him as their Rock, Fortress, and Deliverer; and perfect love, and casting out of fear; so that it is not possible that, while the mind is rightly bent on Him, there should be dread of anything either earthly or supernatural; and the more dreadful seems the height of His majesty, the less fear they feel that dwell in the shadow of it ('Of whom shall I be afraid?'), so that they are as David was, 'devoted to His fear'; whereas, on the other hand, those who, if they may help it, never conceive of God, but thrust away all thought and memory of Him, and in His real terribleness and omnipresence fear him not nor know Him, yet are by real, acute, piercing, and ignoble fear, haunted for evermore.—*Modern Painters*, vol. ii., sec. i., ch. xiv., § 27.

<small>2 Sam. xxii. 2
S. John iv. 18.
Psalm xxvii. 1.
Psalm cxix. 38.</small>

Firmament.

I understand the making of the firmament to signify that, so far as man is concerned, most magnificent ordinance of the clouds;—the ordinance, that as the great plain of waters was formed on the face of the earth, so also a plain of waters should be stretched along the height of air, and the face of the cloud answer the face of the ocean; and that this upper and heavenly plain should be of waters, as it were, glorified in their nature, no longer quenching the fire, but now bearing fire in their own bosoms; no longer murmuring only when the winds raise them or rocks divide, but answering each other with their own voices from pole to pole; no longer restrained by established shores, and guided through unchanging channels, but going forth at their pleasure like the armies of the angels, and choosing their encampments upon the heights of the hills; no longer hurried downwards for ever, moving but to fall, nor lost in the lightless accumulation of the abyss, but covering the east and west with the waving of their wings, and robing the gloom of the farther infinite with a vesture of divers colours, of which the threads are purple and scarlet, and the embroideries flame.

This, I believe, is the ordinance of the firmament; and it seems to me that in the midst of the material nearness of these heavens God means us to acknowledge His own immediate presence as visiting, judging, and blessing us. 'The earth shook, the heavens also dropped, at the presence of God.' 'He doth set His bow in the cloud,' and thus renews, in the sound of every drooping swathe of rain, His promises of everlasting love. 'In them hath He set a *tabernacle* for the sun;' whose burning ball, which without the firmament would be seen but as an intolerable and scorching circle in the blackness of vacuity, is by that firmament surrounded with gorgeous service, and tempered by mediatorial ministries; by the firmament of clouds the golden

Psalm lxviii. 8.

Gen. ix. 13.

Psalm xix. 4.

pavement is spread for his chariot wheels at morning; by the firmament of clouds the temple is built for his presence to fill with light at noon; by the firmament of clouds the purple veil is closed at evening round the sanctuary of his rest; by the mists of the firmament his implacable light is divided, and its separated fierceness appeased into the soft blue that fills the depth of distance with its bloom, and the flush with which the mountains burn as they drink the overflowing of the dayspring. And in this tabernacling of the unendurable sun with men, through the shadows of the firmament, God would seem to set forth the stooping of His own majesty to men, upon the *throne* of the firmament. As the Creator of all the worlds, and the Inhabiter of eternity, we cannot behold Him; but, as the Judge of the earth and the Preserver of men, those heavens **S. Matt.** are indeed His dwelling-place. 'Swear not, **v. 34, 35.** neither by heaven, for it is God's throne; nor by the earth, for it is His footstool.' And all those passings to and fro of fruitful shower and grateful shade, and all those visions of silver palaces built about the horizon, and voices of moaning winds and threatening **S. Matt.** thunders, and glories of coloured robe and **vi. 9.** cloven ray, are but to deepen in our hearts the **S. Luke** acceptance, and distinctness, and dearness of **xi. 2.** the simple words, 'Our Father, which art in heaven.'—*Modern Painters*, vol. iv., ch. vi., §§ 8, 9.

Forgiveness.

Mercy—misericordia: it does not in the least mean forgiveness of sins,—it means pity of sorrows. In that very instance which the Evangelicals are so fond of quoting—the adultery of David—it is not the Passion for which he is to be judged, but the *want* of Passion, —the want of Pity. *This* he is to judge himself for, by **2 Sam.** his own mouth:—'As the Lord liveth, the **xii. 5, 6.** man that hath done this thing shall surely die, —because he hath done this thing, and because he had *no pity.*' And you will find, alike throughout the record of the Law and the promises of the Gospel, that there is, indeed, forgiveness with God, and Christ, for the passing sins of the hot heart, but none for the eternal and inherent sin of the cold. 'Blessed are the merciful, for they shall obtain mercy;'—find it you written anywhere that the *un*merciful shall? 'Her sins, which are many, are forgiven, for she loved much.' But have you record of any one's sins being forgiven who loved not at all?—*Fors Clavigera*, Letter XLII. S. Matt. v. 7. S. Luke, vii. 47.

Garden of Eden, The.

'To dress it and to keep it.'   Gen. ii. 15.

That, then, was to be our work. Alas! what work have we set ourselves upon instead! How have we ravaged the garden instead of kept it — feeding our war-horses with its flowers, and splintering its trees into spear-shafts.

'And at the East a flaming sword.'   Gen. iii. 24.

Is its flame quenchless? and are those gates that keep the way indeed passable no more? Or is it not rather that we no more desire to enter? For what can we conceive of that first Eden which we might not yet win back, if we chose? It was a place full of flowers, we say. Well: the flowers are always striving to grow wherever we suffer them; and the fairer, the closer. There may, indeed, have been a Fall of Flowers, as a Fall of Man; but assuredly creatures such as we are can now fancy nothing lovelier than roses and lilies, which would grow for us side by side, leaf overlapping leaf, till the Earth was white and red with them, if we cared to have it so. And Paradise was full of pleasant shades and fruitful avenues. Well: what hinders us from covering as much of the world as we like with pleasant shade, and pure blossom, and goodly fruit? Who forbids its valleys to be covered over with corn till they laugh and sing? Who prevents its dark forests, ghostly and uninhabitable, from being   Psalm lxv. 13.

changed into infinite orchards, wreathing the hills with frail-floreted snow, far away to the half-lighted horizon of April, and flushing the face of all the autumnal earth with glow of clustered food? But Paradise was a place of peace, we say, and all the animals were gentle servants to us. Well: the world would yet be a place of peace if we were all peacemakers, and gentle service should we have of its creatures if we gave them gentle mastery. But so long as we make sport of slaying bird and beast, so long as we choose to contend rather with our fellows than with our faults, and make battlefields of our meadows instead of pasture—so long, truly, the Flaming Sword will still turn every way, and the gates of Eden remain barred close enough, till we have sheathed the sharper flame of our own passions, and broken down the closer gates of our own hearts. I have been led to see and feel this more and more, as I considered the service which the flowers and trees, which man was at first appointed to keep, were intended to render to him in return for his care; and the services they still render to him, as far as he allows their influence, or fulfils his own task towards them.—*Modern Painters*, vol. v. Pt. vi. ch. i., §§ 1, 2.

<small>Gen. iii. 24.</small>

When we speak carelessly of the traditions respecting the Garden of Eden, (or in Hebrew, remember, Garden of Delight) we are apt to confuse Milton's descriptions with those in the book of Genesis. Milton fills his Paradise with flowers; but no flowers are spoken of in Genesis. We may indeed conclude that in speaking of every herb of the field, flowers are included. But they are not named. The things that are *named* in the Garden of Delight are trees only. The words are, 'every tree that was pleasant to the sight and good for food;' and as if to mark the idea more strongly for us in the Septuagint, even the ordinary Greek word for tree is not used, but the word ξυλον,—literally, every 'wood,' every piece of *timber* that was pleasant or good. They are indeed the 'vivi travi,'—living rafters, of Dante's

<small>Gen. ii. 9.</small>

Apennine. Do you remember how those trees were said to be watered? Not by the four rivers only. The rivers could not supply the place of rain. No rivers do; for in truth they are the refuse of rain. No storm-clouds were there, hidings of the blue by darkening veil; but there went up a *mist* from the earth, and watered the face of the ground,—or, as in Septuagint and Vulgate, 'There went forth a fountain from the earth, and gave the earth to drink.' _{Gen. ii. 6.}

And now, lastly, we continually think of that Garden of Delight, as if it existed, or could exist, no longer; wholly forgetting that it is spoken of in Scripture as perpetually existent; and some of its fairest trees as existent also, or only recently destroyed. When Ezekiel is describing to Pharaoh the greatness of the Assyrians, do you remember what image he gives of them? 'Behold, the Assyrian was a cedar in Lebanon, with fair branches; and his top was among the thick boughs; the waters nourished him, and the deep brought him up, with her rivers running round about his plants. Under his branches did all the beasts of the field bring forth their young; and under his shadow dwelt all great nations.' _{Ezek. xxxi. 3, 4, 6.}

Now hear what follows. 'The cedars *in the Garden of God* could not hide *him*. The fir trees were not like his boughs, and the chestnut trees were not like his branches: nor any tree in the Garden of God was like unto him in beauty.' _{Ezek. xxxi. 8.}

So that you see, whenever a nation rises into consistent, vital, and, through many generations, enduring power, *there* is still the Garden of God; still it is the water of life which feeds the roots of it; and still the succession of its people is imaged by the perennial leafage of trees of Paradise. Could this be said of Assyria, and shall it not be said of England? How much more, of lives such as ours should be,—just, laborious, united in aim, beneficent in fulfilment,—may the image be used of the leaves of the trees of Eden! _{Rev. xxii. 1, 2.}

Other symbols have been given often to show the evanescence and slightness of our lives—the foam upon the water, the grass on the housetop, the vapour that vanishes away; yet none of these are images of true human life. That life, when it is real, is *not* evanescent; is *not* slight; does *not* vanish away. Every noble life leaves the fibre of it interwoven for ever in the work of the world; by so much, evermore, the strength of the human race has gained; more stubborn in the root, higher towards heaven in the branch; and 'as a teil tree, and as an oak,—whose substance is in them when they cast their leaves,—so the holy seed is in the midst thereof.'

<small>Isaiah vi. 13.</small>

Only remember on what conditions. In the great Psalm of life, we are told that everything that a man doeth shall prosper, so only that he delight in the law of his God, that he hath not walked in the counsel of the wicked, nor sat in the seat of the scornful. Is it among these leaves of the perpetual Spring,—helpful leaves for the healing of the nations,—that we mean to have our part and place, or rather among the ' brown skeletons of leaves that lag, the **forest** brook along'? For other leaves there are, and other streams that water them,—not water of life, but water of Acheron. Autumnal leaves there are that strew the brooks, in Vallombrosa. Remember you how the name of the place was changed: ' Once called "Sweet water" (Aqua bella), now, the Shadowy Vale.' Portion in one or other name we must choose, all of us,—with the living olive, by the living fountains of waters, or with the wild fig trees, whose leafage of human soul is strewed along the brooks of death, in the eternal Vallombrosa.—*Proserpina*, ch. iii., §§ 29-32.

<small>Psalm i. 1, 2.</small>

<small>Rev. xxii. 2.</small>

Gift of God's Unchangeable Mercy, The.

David, ruddy and of a fair countenance, with the brook stone of deliverance in his hand, is not more ideal than David leaning on the old age

<small>1 Sam. xvii. 42.</small>

of Barzillai, returning chastened to his kingly home.
And they who are as the angels of God in hea- 2 Sam.
ven, yet cannot be conceived as so assimilated xix. 31-39.
that their different experiences and affections upon
earth shall then be forgotten and effectless; the child
taken early to his place cannot be imagined to wear
there such a body, nor to have such thoughts, as the
glorified apostle who has finished his course and kept
the faith on earth. And so whatever perfections and
likeness of love we may attribute to either the tried or
the crowned creatures, there is the difference of 1 Cor.
the stars in glory among them yet; differences xv. 41.
of original gifts, though not of occupying till their Lord
come, different dispensations of trial and of trust, of
sorrow and support, both in their own inward, variable
hearts, and in their positions of exposure or of peace,
of the gourd shadow and the smiting sun, of Jonah
calling at heat of day or eleventh hour, of the iv. 6-8.
house unroofed by faith, or the clouds opened S. Mark.
by revelation; differences in warning, in ii. 4.
mercies, in sicknesses, in signs, in time of calling to
account; alike only they all are, by that which S. Matt.
is not of them, but the gift of God's unchange- xx. 14.
able mercy. 'I will give unto this last even as unto
thee.'—*Modern Painters*, vol. ii., sec. i., ch. xiv., § 10.

Gift of Rain.

Whenever a nation is in its right mind, it always has
a deep sense of divinity in the gift of rain from heaven,
filling its heart with food and gladness; and all the
more when that gift becomes gentle and perennial in the
flowing of springs. It literally is not possible that any
fruitful power of the Muses should be put forth upon a
people which disdains their Helicon; still less is Gen.
it possible that any Christian nation should grow xxii. 10, 11.
up 'tanquam lignum quod plantatum est secus Gen.
decursus aquarum,' which cannot recognize the xxix. 2.
lesson meant in their being told of the places where

Rebekah was met;—where Rachel,—where Zipporah,— and she who was asked for water under Mount Gerizim by a Stranger, weary, who had nothing to draw with.—*Lectures on Art*, § 118.

<small>Exod. ii. 15, 16; S. John iv. 6, 7.</small>

Gifts to the Church.

It is not the church we want, but the sacrifice; not the emotion of admiration, but the act of adoration; not the gift, but the giving. And see how much more charity the full understanding of this might admit, among classes of men of naturally opposite feelings; and how much more nobleness in the work. There is no need to offend by importunate, self-proclaimant splendour. Your gift may be given in an unpresuming way. Cut one or two shafts out of a porphyry whose preciousness those only would know who would desire it to be so used; add another month's labour to the under-cutting of a few capitals, whose delicacy will not be seen nor loved by one beholder of ten thousand; see that the simplest masonry of the edifice be perfect and substantial; and to those who regard such things, their witness will be clear and impressive; to those who regard them not, all will at least be inoffensive. But do not think the feeling itself a folly, or the act itself useless. Of what use was that dearly bought water of the well of Bethlehem, with which the King of Israel slaked the dust of Adullam? yet was it not thus better than if he had drunk it? Of what use was that passionate act of Christian sacrifice, against which, first uttered by the false tongue, the very objection we would now conquer took a sullen tone for ever? So also let us not ask of what use our offering is to the church: it is at least better for *us* than if it had been retained for ourselves. It may be better for others also: there is, at any rate, a chance of this; though we must always fearfully and widely shun the thought that the magnificence of the temple can materially add to the efficiency of the worship or to the

<small>1 Chron. xi. 17, 18.</small>

<small>S. John xii. 5.</small>

power of the ministry. Whatever we do, or whatever we offer, let it not interfere with the simplicity of the one, or abate, as if replacing, the zeal of the other. . . .

God never forgets any work or labour of love; and whatever it may be of which the first and best portions or powers have been presented to Him, He will multiply and increase sevenfold.—*Seven Lamps of Architecture*, ch. i., §§ viii., ix.

Glory of God.

Man's use and function (and let him who will not grant me this, follow me no farther, for this I purpose always to assume) are, to be the witness of the glory of God, and to advance that glory by his reasonable obedience and resultant happiness.

Whatever enables us to fulfil this function is, in the pure and first sense of the word, Useful to us: pre-eminently, therefore, whatever sets the glory of God more brightly before us. But things that only help us to exist are, (*only*) in a secondary and mean sense, useful; or rather, if they be looked for alone, they are useless, and worse, for it would be better that we should not exist, than that we should guiltily disappoint the purposes of existence.

And yet people speak in this working age, when they speak from their hearts, as if houses and lands, and food and raiment were alone useful, and as if Sight, Thought, and Admiration were all profitless, so that men insolently call themselves Utilitarians, who would turn, if they had their way, themselves and their race into vegetables; men who think, as far as such can be said to think, that the meat is more than the life, and the raiment than the body, who look to the earth as a stable, and to its fruit as fodder; vine-dressers and husbandmen, who love the corn they grind, and the grapes they crush, better than the gardens of the angels upon the slopes of Eden; hewers of wood and drawers of water, who think that it is to give them wood to hew and water to draw, that the S. Matt. vi. 25. S. Luke xii. 23. Josh. ix. 21.

pine-forests cover the mountains like the shadow of God, and the great rivers move like His eternity. And so comes upon us that Woe of the preacher, that though God 'hath made everything beautiful in His time, also He hath set the world in their heart, so that no man can find out the work that God maketh from the beginning to the end.'—*Modern Painters*, vol. ii., sec. i., ch. i., §§ 4, 5.

<small>Eccle. iii. 11.</small>

God of Light.

Do you think the words, 'Light of the World' mean only 'Teacher or Guide of the World'? When the Sun of Justice is said to rise with health in its wings, do you suppose the image only means the correction of error? Or does it even mean so much? The Light of Heaven is needed to do that perfectly. But what we are to pray for is the Light of the *World;* nay, the Light 'that lighteth *every man that cometh into the world.*'

<small>S. John viii. 12; ix. 5.</small>
<small>Mal. iv. 2.</small>
<small>S. John i. 9.</small>

You will find that it is no metaphor—nor has it ever been so.

To the Persian, the Greek, and the Christian, the sense of the power of the God of Light has been one and the same. That power is not merely in teaching or protecting, but in the enforcement of purity of body, and of equity or justice in the heart; and this, observe, not heavenly purity, nor final justice; but, now, and here, actual purity in the midst of the world's foulness,—practical justice in the midst of the world's iniquity. And the physical strength of the organ of sight,—the physical purity of the flesh, the actual love of sweet light and stainless colour,—are the necessary signs, real, inevitable, and visible, of the prevailing presence, with any nation, or in any house, of the 'Light that lighteth every man that cometh into the world.'—*Eagle's Nest*, §§ 115–16.

God speaking to Man.

The greater number of the words which are recorded in Scripture, as directly spoken to men by the lips of the Deity, are either simple revelations of His law, or special threatenings, commands, and promises relating to special events. But two passages of God's speaking, one in the Old and one in the New Testament, possess, it seems to me, a different character from any of the rest, having been uttered, the one to effect the last necessary change in the mind of a man whose piety was in other respects perfect; and the other, as the first statement to all men of the principles of Christianity by Christ Himself—I mean the 38th to 41st chapters of the book of Job, and the Sermon on the Mount. Now the first of these passages is, from beginning to end, nothing else than a direction of the mind which was to be perfected to humble observance of the works of God in nature. And the other consists only in the inculcation of *three* things: 1st, right conduct; 2nd, looking for eternal life; 3rd, trusting God, through watchfulness of His dealings with His creation: and the entire contents of the book of Job, and of the Sermon on the Mount, will be found resolvable simply into these three requirements from all men,—that they should act rightly, hope for heaven, and watch God's wonders and work in the earth; the right conduct being always summed up under the three heads of *justice, mercy*, and *truth*, and no mention of any doctrinal point whatsoever occurring in either piece of divine teaching.—*Modern Painters*, vol. iii., ch. xvii., § 33.

God's Communications of Truth to Men.

It is to be noted that it is neither by us ascertainable what moments of pure feeling or aspiration may occur to men of minds apparently cold and lost, nor by us to be pronounced through what instruments, and in what strangely occurrent voices, God may choose to communicate good to men. It seems to me that much of what is great, and to all men beneficial, has been wrought by those who neither intended nor knew the good they did; and that many mighty harmonies have been discoursed by instruments that had been dumb or discordant, but that God knew their stops. The Spirit of Prophecy consisted with the avarice of Balaam, and the disobedience of Saul. Could we spare from its page that parable, <small>Num. xxiv. 4-16.</small> which he said, who saw the vision of the Almighty, falling into a trance; but having his eyes open; though we know that the sword of his punishment was then sharp in its sheath beneath him <small>2 Sam. i. 21.</small> in the plains of Moab? or shall we not lament with David over the shield, cast away on the Gilboa mountains, of him to whom God gave *another heart* that day, when he turned his back to go from Samuel? It is not our part to look hardly, nor to look always, to the character or the deeds of men, but to accept from all of them, and to hold fast, that which we can prove good, and feel to be ordained for us. We know that whatever good there is in them is itself divine; and wherever we see the virtue of ardent labour and self-surrendering to a single purpose, wherever we find constant reference made to the written scripture of natural beauty, this at least we know is great and good; this we know is not granted by the counsel of God without purpose, nor maintained without result: their interpretation we may accept, into their labour we may enter, but they themselves must look to it, if what they do has no intent of good, nor any reference to the Giver of all gifts. Selfish in their industry, unchastened in their wills, ungrateful for the Spirit that is upon them, <small>S. James iii. 4.</small> they may yet be helmed by that Spirit whithersoever the Governor listeth; involuntary instruments they may become of others' good; unwillingly they may bless Israel, doubtingly discomfort Amalek; but short-coming there will be of their glory, and sure, of their punishment.—*Modern Painters*, vol. ii., sec. i., ch. xv., § 8.

Good and Evil.

Where chiefly the beauty of God's working was manifested to men, warning was also given, and that to the full, of the enduring of His indignation against sin. It seems one of the most cunning and frequent of self-deceptions to turn the heart away from this warning, and refuse to acknowledge anything in the fair scenes of the natural creation but beneficence. Men in general lean towards the light, so far as they contemplate such things at all, most of them passing 'by on the other side,' either in mere plodding pursuit of their own work, irrespective of what good or evil is around them, or else in selfish gloom, or selfish delight, resulting from their own circumstances at the moment. Of those who give themselves to any true contemplation, the plurality, being humble, gentle, and kindly hearted, look only in nature for what is lovely and kind; partly, also, God gives the disposition to every healthy human mind in some degree to pass over or even harden itself against evil things, else the suffering would be too great to be borne; and humble people, with a quiet trust that everything is for the best, do not fairly represent the facts to themselves, thinking them none of their business. So, what between hard-hearted people, thoughtless people, busy people, humble people, and cheerfully-minded people,—giddiness of youth, and preoccupations of age,—philosophies of faith, and cruelties of folly,—priest and Levite, masquer and merchantman, all agreeing to keep their own side of the way,—the evil that God sends to warn us gets to be forgotten, and the evil that He sends to be mended by us gets left unmended. And then, because people shut their eyes to the dark indisputableness of the facts in front of them, their Faith, such as it is, is shaken or uprooted by every darkness in what is revealed to them. In the present day it is not easy to find a well-meaning man among our more earnest thinkers, who will not take upon himself to dispute the whole system of redemption, because

S. Luke x. 31, 32.

he cannot unravel the mystery of the punishment of sin. But can he unravel the mystery of NO sin? . . .

We cannot reason of these things. But this I know—and this may by all men be known—that no good or lovely thing exists in this world without its correspondent darkness; and that the universe presents itself continually to mankind under the stern aspect of warning, or of choice, the good and the evil set on the right hand and the left.—*Modern Painters*, vol. iv., ch. xix., §§ 32, 33.

I understand not the most dangerous, because most attractive form of modern infidelity, which, pretending to exalt the beneficence of the Deity, degrades it into a reckless infinitude of mercy, and blind obliteration of the work of sin: and which does this chiefly by dwelling on the manifold appearances of God's kindness on the face of creation. Such kindness is indeed everywhere and always visible; but not alone. Wrath and threatening are invariably mingled with the love; and in the utmost solitudes of nature, the existence of Hell seems to me as legibly declared by a thousand spiritual utterances, as that of Heaven. It is well for us to dwell with thankfulness on the unfolding of the flower, and the falling of the dew, and the sleep of the green fields in the sunshine; but the blasted trunk, the barren rock, the moaning of the bleak winds, the roar of the black, perilous, merciless whirlpools of the mountain streams, the solemn solitudes of moors and seas, the continual fading of all beauty into darkness, and of all strength into dust, have these no language for us? We may seek to escape their teaching by reasonings touching the good which is wrought out of all evil; but it is vain sophistry. The good succeeds to the evil as day succeeds the night, but so also the evil to the good. Gerizim and Ebal, birth and death, light and darkness, heaven and hell, divide the existence of man, and his Futurity.—*Stones of Venice*, vol. iii., ch. iii., § XLII.

<small>Deut. xi. 29.</small>

Goodwill to men.

In the passage, so often read by us, which announces the advent of Christianity as the dawn of peace on earth, we habitually neglect great part of the promise, owing to the false translation of the second clause of the sentence. I cannot understand how it should be still needful to point out to you here in Oxford that neither the Greek words 'ἐν ἀνθρώποις εὐδοκία,' nor those of the Vulgate, 'in terra pax hominibus bonæ voluntatis,' in the slightest degree justify our English words, 'good will to men.' Of God's goodwill to men, and to all creatures, for ever, there needed no proclamation by angels. But that men should be able to please *Him*,—that their wills should be made holy, and they should not only possess peace in themselves, but be able to give joy to their God, in the sense in which He afterwards is pleased with His own baptized Son;—this was a new thing for angels to declare, and for shepherds to believe.

And the error was made yet more fatal by its repetition in a passage of parallel importance,—the thanksgiving, namely, offered by Christ, that His Father, while He had hidden what it was best to know, not from the wise and prudent, but from some among the wise and prudent, and had revealed it unto babes; not 'for so it seemed good' in His sight, but 'that these might be well pleasing in his sight,'— namely, that the wise and simple might equally live in the necessary knowledge, and enjoyed presence, of God. And if, having accurately read these vital passages, you then as carefully consider the tenour of the two songs of human joy in the birth of Christ, the Magnificat, and the Nunc Dimittis, you will find the theme of both to be, not the newness of blessing, but the equity which disappoints the cruelty and humbles the strength of men; which scatters the proud in the imagination of their hearts; which fills the hungry with good things; and is not only the glory of Israel, but the light of the Gentiles.—*Val d'Arno*, §§ 253-54.

S. Matt. xi. 25, 26.
S. Luke x. 21.
Heb. xiii. 21.
S. Luke i. 51.
S. Luke ii. 32.

Gospel, or Divine Facts.

What the natural or divine facts of the universe *are;* what God is, or what His work has been, or shall be, no man has ever yet known, nor has any wise man ever attempted, but as a child, to discover. But the utmost reach both towards the reality and the love of all things yet granted to human intellect, has been granted to the thinkers and the workmen who have trusted in the teaching of Christ, and in the spiritual help of the mortals who have tried to serve Him. And the strength, and joy, and height of achievement, of any group or race of mankind has, from the day of Christ's nativity to this hour, been in exact proportion to their power of apprehending, and honesty in obeying the truth of His Gospel.—*Stones of Venice*, vol. iii., ch. v., § VII.

Gospel Teaching.

Are you not bid to go into *all* the world and preach it to every creature? (I should myself think the clergyman most likely to do good who accepted the πάσῃ τῇ κτίσει so literally as at least to sympathize with St. Francis' sermon to the birds, and to feel that feeding either sheep or fowls, or unmuzzling the ox, or keeping the wrens alive in the snow, would be received by their Heavenly Feeder as the *perfect* fulfilment of His 'Feed my sheep' in the higher sense.)[1] . . .

<small>S. John xxi. 16, 17.</small>

I want only to put the sterner question before your council, *how* this Gospel is to be preached either 'πανταχοῦ' or to 'πάντα τά ἔθνη,' if first its preachers have not determined quite clearly what it *is?* And might not such definition, acceptable to the entire body of the Church of Christ, be arrived at by merely explaining, in their completeness and life, the terms of the Lord's Prayer—the first words taught to children all over the Christian world? . . . My meaning, in saying that the Lord's Prayer might be made a

<small>S. Matt. vi. 9.</small>

---

[1] 'Arrows of the Chase,' ii., 209, 184.

foundation of Gospel-teaching, was not that it contained all that Christian ministers have to teach; but that it contains what all Christians are agreed upon as first to be taught; and that no good parish-working pastor in any district of the world but would be glad to take his part in making it clear and living to his congregation. And the first clause of it, of course rightly explained, gives us the ground of what is surely a mighty part of the Gospel—its 'first and great commandment,' namely, that we have a Father whom we *can* love, and are required to love, and to desire to be with Him in Heaven, wherever that may be. And to declare that we have such a loving Father, whose mercy is over *all* His works, and whose will and law is [Psalm cxlv. 9.] so lovely and lovable that it is sweeter than honey, and more precious than gold, to those [Psalm xix. 10.] who can 'taste' and 'see' that the Lord is Good—this, surely, is a most pleasant and [Psalm xxxiv. 8.] glorious good message and *spell* to bring to men—as distinguished from the evil message and accursed spell that Satan has brought to the nations of the world instead of it, that they have no Father, but only 'a consuming fire' ready to devour them, unless they are delivered from its raging flame by some [Heb. xii. 29.] scheme of pardon for all, for which they are to be thankful, not to the Father, but to the Son. Supposing this first article of the true Gospel agreed to, how would the blessing that closes the epistles of that Gospel become intelligible and living, instead of dark and dead: 'The grace of Christ, and the *love* of God, and the fellowship of the Holy Ghost,' [2 Cor. xiii. 14.] —the most *tender* word being that used of the Father?—*On the Old Road*, vol. ii., §§ 227-29.

"Grass of the Field."

Gather a single blade of grass, and examine for a minute, quietly, its narrow sword-shaped strip of fluted green. Nothing, as it seems there, of notable goodness or beauty. A very little strength, and a very little tallness, and a few delicate long lines meeting in a point,—not a perfect point neither, but blunt and unfinished, by no means a creditable or apparently much cared-for example of Nature's workmanship; made, as it seems, <small>S. Luke xii. 28.</small> only to be trodden on to-day, and to-morrow to be cast into the oven; and a little pale and hollow stalk, feeble and flaccid, leading down to the dull brown fibres of roots. And yet, think of it well, and judge whether of all the gorgeous flowers that beam in summer air, and of all strong and goodly trees, pleasant to the eyes or good for food,—stately palm and pine, strong ash and oak, scented citron, burdened vine,—there be any by man so deeply loved, by God so highly graced, as that narrow point of feeble green. It seems to me not to have been without a peculiar significance, that our Lord, when about to work the miracle which, of all that He showed, appears to have been felt by the multitude as the most impressive,—the miracle of the loaves,—commanded the people to sit down by com- <small>S. Mark vi. 39.</small> panies 'upon the green grass.' He was about to feed them with the principal produce of earth and the sea, the simplest representations of the food of mankind. He gave them the *seed* of the herb; He bade them sit down upon the herb itself, which was as great a gift, in its fitness for their joy and rest, as its perfect fruit, for their sustenance; thus, in this single order and act, when rightly understood, indicating for evermore how the Creator had entrusted the comfort, consolation, and sustenance of man, to the simplest and most despised of all the leafy families of the earth. And well does it fulfil its mission. Consider what we owe merely to the meadow grass, to the covering of the dark ground by that glorious enamel, by the companies of those soft, and countless, and peaceful spears. . . . Look up towards the higher hills, where the waves of everlasting green roll silently into their long inlets among the shadows of the pines, and we may, perhaps, at last know the meaning of those quiet words of the 147th Psalm, 'He maketh grass to grow upon the mountains.' . . .

From Isaiah xl. 6, we find the grass and flowers are types, in their passing, of the passing of human life, and, in their excellence, of the excellence of human life; and this in twofold way; first, by their Beneficence, and then, by their Endurance:—the grass of the earth, in giving the seed of corn, and in its beauty under tread of foot and stroke of scythe; and the grass of the waters, in giving its freshness to our rest, and in its bending before the wave.

So also in Isaiah xxxv. 7, the prevalence of righteousness and peace over all evil is thus foretold. 'In the habitation of dragons, where each lay, shall be *grass* with *reeds* and *rushes*.'—*Modern Painters*, vol. iii., ch. xiv., §§ 51–53.

Grass Reeds and Rushes.

But understood in the broad human and Divine sense, the '*herb* yielding seed' (as opposed to the fruit-tree yielding fruit) includes a third family of plants, and fulfils a third office to the human race. It includes the great family of the lints and flaxes, and fulfils thus the *three* offices of giving food, raiment, and rest. Follow out this fulfilment; consider the association of the linen garment and the linen embroidery, with the priestly office, and the furniture of the Tabernacle; and consider how the rush has been, in all time, the first natural carpet thrown under the human foot. Then next observe the three virtues definitely set forth by the three families of plants; not arbitrarily or fancifully associated with them, but in all the three cases marked for us by Scriptural words: [Gen. i. 11.]

1st. Cheerfulness, or joyful serenity; in the grass for food and beauty.—'Consider the lilies of the field, how they grow; they toil not, neither do they spin.' [S. Matt. vi. 28.]

2nd. Humility; in the grass for rest.—'A bruised reed shall He not break.' [Isaiah xlii. 3. S. Matt. xii. 20.]

3rd. Love; in the grass for clothing (because

of its swift kindling).—'The smoking flax shall He not quench.' And then, finally, observe the confirmation of these last two images in, I suppose, the most important prophecy, relating to the future state of the Christian Church, which occurs in the Old Testament, namely, that contained in the closing chapters of Ezekiel. The measures of the Temple of God are to be taken; and because it is only by charity and humility that those measures ever can be taken, the angel has 'a line of *flax* in his hand, and a measuring *reed*.' The use of the line was to measure the land, and of the reed to take the dimensions of the buildings; so the buildings of the church, or its labours, are to be measured by *humility*, and its territory or land, by *love*.—*Modern Painters*, vol. iii., ch. xiv., § 53.

<small>Isaiah xlii. 3.
S. Matt. xii. 20.
Ezek. xl. 3.</small>

Happiness.

Now in what are you rightly happy? Not in thinking of what you have done yourself; not in your own pride; not your own birth; not in your own being, or your own will, but in looking at God; watching what He does; what He is; and obeying His law, and yielding yourself to His will.—*Stones of Venice*, vol. i., ch. xx., § XVI.

I do verily believe that it [the world] will come, finally, to understand that God paints the clouds and shapes the moss-fibres, that men may be happy in seeing Him at His work, and that in resting quietly beside Him, and watching His working, and—according to the power He has communicated to ourselves, and the guidance He grants,—in carrying out His purposes of peace and charity among all His creatures, are the only real happinesses that ever were, or will be, possible to mankind.—*Modern Painters*, vol. iii., ch. xvii., § 38.

Heathen Creed.

The creed of the philosophers or sages varied according to the character and knowledge of each;—their relative acquaintance with the secrets of natural science—their intellectual and sectarian egotism—and their mystic or monastic tendencies, for there is a classic as well as a mediæval monasticism. They ended in losing the life of Greece in play upon words; but we owe to their early thought some of the soundest ethics, and the foundation of the best practical laws, yet known to mankind.

Such was the general vitality of the heathen creed in its strength. Of its direct influence on conduct, it is, as I said,-impossible for me to speak now; only, remember always, in endeavouring to form a judgment of it, that what of good or right the heathens did, they did looking for no reward. The purest forms of our own religion have always consisted in sacrificing less things to win greater;—time, to win eternity,—the world, to win the skies. The order, 'sell that thou hast,' is not given without the promise,— 'thou shalt have treasure in heaven;' and well for the modern Christian if he accepts the alternative as his Master left it—and does not practically read the command and promise thus: 'Sell that thou hast in the best market, and thou shalt have treasure in eternity also.' But the poor Greeks of the great ages expected no reward from heaven but honour, and no reward from earth but rest;—though, when, on those conditions, they patiently, and proudly, fulfilled their task of the granted day, an unreasoning instinct of an immortal benediction broke from their lips in song: and they, even they, had sometimes a prophet to tell them of a land 'where there is sun alike by day, and alike by night—where they shall need no more to trouble the earth by strength of hands for daily bread—but the ocean breezes blow around the blessed islands, and golden flowers burn on their bright trees for evermore.'—*Queen of the Air*, §§ 49, 50.

[S. Luke xviii. 22.]
[S. Matt. xix. 21.]

Heavens, The.

When the earth had to be prepared for the habitation of man, a veil, as it were, of intermediate being was spread between him and its darkness, in which were joined, in a subdued measure, the stability and insensibility of the earth, and the passion and perishing of mankind.

But the heavens, also, had to be prepared for his habitation.

Between their burning light,—their **deep** vacuity, and man, as between the earth's gloom of iron substance, **and** man, a veil had to be spread of intermediate being;— which should appease the unendurable glory to the level of human feebleness, and sign the changeless motion of the heavens with a semblance of human vicissitude. Between the earth and man arose the leaf. Between the heaven and man came **the cloud.** His life being partly as the falling leaf, and partly **as the flying** vapour.

Has the reader any distinct **idea** of what clouds **are?** . . . So far from it, I rather believe that some of the mysteries of the clouds never will be understood by us at all. 'Knowest thou the balancings of the clouds?' Is the **answer ever to** be one of pride? 'The wondrous **works of Him** which is *perfect* in knowledge?' Is *our* knowledge ever to be so?—*Modern Painters*, vol. v., part vii., ch. i., §§ 1–3.

<small>Job xxxvii. 16</small>

'Heavens declare the Glory of God,' 'The.'

The first thing that children should be taught about their Bibles is, to distinguish clearly between words that they understand and words that they do not; and to put aside the words they do not understand, and verses connected with them, to be asked about, or for a future time; and never to think they are reading the Bible when they are merely repeating phrases of an unknown tongue.

Let us try, by way of example, this nineteenth **Psalm, and** see what plain meaning is uppermost in it.

'The heavens declare **the** glory of God.'

What are the heavens?

Now there can be no question that in the minds of the sacred writers, it stood naturally for the entire system of cloud, and of space beyond it, conceived by them as a vault set with stars. But there can, also, be no question, that the firmament, which is said to have been 'called' heaven, at the creation, expresses, in all definite use of the word, the system of clouds, as spreading the power of the water over the earth; hence the constant expressions dew of heaven, rain of heaven, etc., where heaven is used in the singular; while 'the heavens' when used plurally, and especially when in distinction, as here, from the word 'firmament,' remained expressive of the starry space beyond.

A child might therefore be told (surely, with advantage), that our beautiful word Heaven may possibly have been formed from a Hebrew word, meaning 'the high place;' that the great warrior Roman nation, camping much out at night, generally overtired and not in moods for thinking, are believed by many people to have seen in the stars only the likeness of the glittering studs of their armour, and to have called the sky 'The bossed, or studded'; but that others think those Roman soldiers on their night-watches had rather been impressed by the great emptiness and void of night, and by the far-coming of sounds through its darkness, and had called the heaven, 'The Hollow place.' Finally, I should tell the children, showing them first the setting of a star, how the great Greeks had found out the truest power of the heavens, and had called them, 'The Rolling.' But whatever different nations had called them, at least I would make it clear to the child's mind that in this nineteenth Psalm, their whole power being intended, the two words are used which express it; the Heavens, for the great vault or void, with all its planets, and stars, and ceaseless march of orbs innumerable; and the Firmament, for the ordinance of the clouds.

These heavens, then, 'declare the *glory* of God;'

that is, the light of God, the eternal glory, stable, and changeless. As their orbs fail not—but pursue their course for ever, to give light upon the earth—so God's glory surrounds man for ever—changeless, in its fulness insupportable—infinite.

'And the firmament sheweth His *handywork.*'

The clouds, prepared by the hands of God for the help of man, varied in their ministration—veiling the inner splendour—show, not His eternal glory, but His daily handiwork. So He dealt with Moses. I will cover thee 'with my hand' as I pass by. Compare Job xxxvi. 24 : 'Remember that thou magnify His work, which men behold. Every man may see it.' Not so the glory—that only in part; the courses of these stars are to be seen imperfectly, and but by few. But this firmament, 'every man may see it, man may behold it afar off.' 'Behold, God is great, and we know Him not. For He maketh small the drops of water: they pour down rain according to the vapour thereof.'

<small>Exod. xxxiii. 22.</small>

<small>Job xxxvi. 26.</small>

'Day unto day uttereth speech, and night unto night sheweth knowledge. They have no speech nor language, yet without these their voice is heard. Their rule is gone out throughout the earth, and their words to the end of the world.'

Note that. Their rule throughout the earth, whether inhabited or not—their law of light is thereon; but their words, spoken to human souls, to the end of the inhabited world.

'In them hath he set a tabernacle for the sun,' etc. Literally, a tabernacle, or curtained tent, with its veil and its hangings; also of the colours of His desert tabernacle—blue, and purple, and scarlet.

<small>Exod. xxxv. 6.</small>

Thus far the Psalm describes the manner of this great heaven's message.

Thenceforward it comes to the matter of it.

Observe, you have the two divisions of the declaration. The heavens (compare Psalm viii.) declare the eternal glory of God before men, and the firmament the daily mercy of God towards men. And the eternal glory is in this—that the law of the Lord is perfect, and His testimony sure, and His statutes right.

And the daily mercy in this—that the commandment of the Lord is pure, and His fear is clean, and His judgments true and righteous.

There are three oppositions :—

Between law and commandment.

Between testimony and fear.

Between statute and judgment.

i. Between law and commandment.

The law is fixed and everlasting; uttered once, abiding for ever, as the sun, it may not be moved. It is 'perfect, converting the soul': the whole question about the soul being, whether it has been turned from darkness to light, acknowledged this law or not,—whether it is godly or ungodly? But the commandment is given momentarily to each man, according to the need. It does not convert: it guides. It does not concern the entire purpose of the soul: but it enlightens the eyes, respecting a special act. The law is, 'Do this always;' the commandment, 'Do *thou* this *now*:' often mysterious enough, and through the cloud; chilling, and with strange rain of tears; yet always pure (the law converting, but the commandment cleansing): a rod not for guiding merely, but for strengthening, and tasting honey with. 'Look how mine eyes have been enlightened, because I tasted a little of this honey.' [1 Sam. xiv. 29.]

ii. Between testimony and fear.

The testimony is everlasting: the true promise of salvation. Bright as the sun beyond all the earth-cloud, it makes wise the simple; all wisdom being assured in perceiving it and trusting it; all wisdom brought to nothing which does not perceive it.

But the fear of God is taught through special encouragement and special withdrawal of it, according to each man's need—by the earth-cloud—smile and frown alternately: it also, as the commandment, is clean, purging, and casting out all other fear, it only remaining for ever.

iii. Between statute and judgment.

The statutes are the appointments of the Eternal justice; **fixed** and **bright**, and constant as the stars; **equal and** balanced as their **courses.** They 'are right, rejoicing the heart.' But the judgments are special judgments of given acts of men. 'True,' that is to say, fulfilling the warning or promise given to each man; 'righteous altogether,' that is, done or executed in truth and righteousness. The statute is right, in appointment. The judgment righteous altogether, in appointment and fulfilment;—yet not always rejoicing the heart.

Then, respecting all these, comes the expression of passionate desire, and **of joy;** that also divided with respect to each. The glory of God, eternal in the Heavens, is future, 'to be *desired* more than gold, than much fine gold'—treasure in the heavens that faileth not. But the present guidance and teaching of God **are on** earth; they are now possessed, sweeter than all earthly food—'sweeter than honey and the honeycomb. Moreover by **them**' (the law **and the** testimony) 'is Thy servant warned'—warned of the ways of death and life. 'And in keeping them' (the commandments and the judgments) 'there is great reward:' pain now, and bitterness of tears, but reward unspeakable.

Thus far the psalm has been descriptive and interpreting. It ends in prayer.

'Who can understand his errors?' (wanderings from the perfect law.) 'Cleanse Thou me from secret faults'; from all that I have done against Thy will, and far from Thy way, in the darkness. 'Keep back Thy servant from presumptuous sins' (sins against the commandment), against Thy will when it is seen and direct, pleading with heart and conscience. 'So shall I be

undefiled, and innocent from the great transgression'—
the transgression that crucifies afresh.

'Let the words of my mouth (for I have set them to
declare Thy law), and the meditation of my heart (for I
have set it to keep Thy commandments), be acceptable in
Thy sight,' whose glory is my strength, and whose work,
my redemption;' 'my Strength, and my Redeemer.'—
Modern Painters, vol. v., part vii., ch. iv., §§ 26-35.

Helpfulness.

Dwell a little on this word 'Help.' It is a grave one.
In substance which we call 'inanimate,' as of clouds, or
stones, their atoms may cohere to each other, or consist
with each other, but they do not help each other. The
removal of one part does not injure the rest.

But in a plant, the taking away of any one part
does injure the rest. Hurt or remove any portion of
the sap, bark, or pith, the rest is injured. If any part
enters into a state in which it no more assists the rest,
and has thus become 'helpless,' we call it also 'dead.'

The power which causes the several portions of the
plant to help each other, we call life. Much more is
this so in an animal. We may take away the branch of
a tree without much harm to it; but not the animal's
limb. Thus, intensity of life is also intensity of helpfulness—completeness of depending of each part on all the
rest. The ceasing of this help is what we call corruption; and in proportion to the perfectness of the help,
is the dreadfulness of the loss. The more intense the
life has been, the more terrible is its corruption. . . .

Though atoms of inanimate substance could not
help each other, they could 'consist' with each other.
'Consistence' is their virtue. Thus the parts of a
crystal are consistent, but of dust, inconsistent. Orderly
adherence, the best help its atoms can give, constitutes
the nobleness of such substance.

Life and consistency, then, both expressing one character (namely, helpfulness of a higher or lower order),

the Maker of all creatures and things, 'by whom all creatures live, and all things consist,' is essentially and for ever the **Helpful One**, or in softer Saxon, the 'Holy' One. The word has no other ultimate meaning: Helpful, harmless, undefiled: 'living' or 'Lord of life.'

Col. i. 17.

The idea is clear and mighty in the cherubim's cry: 'Helpful, Helpful, Helpful, Lord God of Hosts;' *i.e.*, of all the hosts, armies, and creatures of the earth. A pure or holy **state** of anything, therefore, is that in which all its parts are helpful or consistent. They may or may not be homogeneous. The highest or organic purities are composed of many elements in an entirely helpful state. The highest and first law of the universe—and the other name of life is, therefore, 'help.' The other name of death is 'separation.' Government and co-operation are in all things and eternally the laws of life. Anarchy and competition, eternally, and in all things, the laws of death.— *Modern Painters*, vol. v., part viii., ch. i., §§ 4-6.

Rev. iv. 7.

'Herb for the Service of Man.'

That sentence of Genesis, 'I have given thee every green herb for meat,' like all the rest of the book, has a profound symbolical as well as a literal meaning. It is not merely the nourishment of the body, but the food of the soul, that is intended. The green herb is, of all nature, that which is most essential to the healthy spiritual life of man. Most of us do not need fine scenery; the precipice and the mountain peak are not intended to be seen by all men, —perhaps their power is greatest over those who are unaccustomed to them. But trees and fields and flowers were made for all, and are necessary for all. God has connected the labour which is essential to the bodily sustenance with the pleasures which are healthiest for the heart; and while He made the ground stubborn, He made its herbage fragrant, and its blossoms fair.

Gen. i. 30.

The proudest architecture that man can build has no higher honour than to bear the image and recall the memory of that grass of the field which is, at once, the type and the support of his existence; the goodly building is then most glorious when it is sculptured into the likeness of the leaves of **Paradise; and the** great Gothic spirit, as we showed it to be noble in its disquietude, is also noble in its hold of nature; it is, indeed, like the dove of Noah, in that she found no rest upon the face of the waters,—but like her in this also, 'LO, IN HER MOUTH WAS AN OLIVE BRANCH PLUCKED OFF.'—*Stones of Venice*, vol. ii., ch. vi., § LXXI [Gen. viii. 9. Gen. viii. 11.]

Hills, Mission of the.

The feeding of the rivers and the purifying of the winds are the least of the services appointed to the hills. To fill the thirst of the human heart for the beauty of God's working,—to startle its lethargy with the deep and pure agitation of astonishment,—are their higher missions. They are as a great and noble architecture; first giving shelter, comfort, and rest; and covered also with mighty sculpture and painted legend. It is impossible to examine in their connected system the features of even the most ordinary mountain scenery, without concluding that it has been prepared in order to unite as far as possible, and in the closest compass, every means of delighting and sanctifying the heart of man. 'As far as *possible*'; that is, as far as is consistent with the fulfilment of the sentence of condemnation on the whole earth. Death must be upon the hills; and the cruelty of the tempests smite them, and the briar and thorn spring up upon them: but they so smite, as to bring their rocks into the fairest forms; and so spring, as to make the very desert blossom as the rose.—*Modern Painters*, vol. iv., ch. vii., § 4. [Isaiah xxxv. 1]

Hills, Sanctity of.

There was an idea of sanctity attached to rocky wilderness, because it had always been among hills that the Deity had manifested Himself most intimately to men, and to the hills that His saints had nearly always retired for meditation, for especial communion with Him, and to prepare for death. Men acquainted with the history of Moses, alone at Horeb, or with Israel at Sinai,—of Elijah by the brook Cherith, and in the Horeb cave; of the deaths of Moses and Aaron on Hor and Nebo; of the preparation of Jephthah's daughter for her death among the Judæa mountains; of the continual retirement of Christ Himself to the mountains for prayer, His temptation in the desert of the Dead Sea, His sermon on the hills of Capernaum, His transfiguration on Mount Hermon, and His evening and morning walks over Olivet for the four or five days preceding His crucifixion, —were not likely to look with irreverent or unloving eyes upon the blue hills that girded their golden horizon, or drew down upon them the mysterious clouds out of the height of the darker heaven. But with this impression of their greater sanctity was involved also that of a peculiar terror. In all this,—their haunting by the memories of prophets, the presences of angels, and the everlasting thoughts and words of the Redeemer,—the mountain ranges seem separated from the active world, and only to be fitly approached by hearts which were condemnatory of it. Just in so much as it appeared necessary for the noblest men to retire to the hill recesses before their missions could be accomplished, or their spirits perfected, in so far did the daily world seem by comparison to be pronounced profane and dangerous; and to those who loved that world, and its work, the mountains were thus voiceful with perpetual rebuke, and necessarily contemplated with a kind of pain and fear. . . . It was

Margin references:
Exod. iii. 12.
Deut. xxxiii. 2.
1 Kings xvii. 5.
Deut. xxxiv. 5.
Num. xx. 28.
Judges xi. 37.
S. Matt. iv. 1-4; v.-vii. 27; xvii. 1, 2.
S. Luke ix. 28-36.
S. Matt. xxvi. 30.
S. Luke xxii. 39.

only for their punishment, or in their despair, that men consented to tread the crocused slopes of the Chartreuse, or the soft glades and dewy pastures of Vallombrosa.—*Modern Painters*, vol. iii., ch. xiv., § 10.

Holiness of Colour.
The early religious painting of the Flemings is as brilliant in hue as it is holy in thought. . . . The builders of our great cathedrals veiled their casements and wrapped their pillars with one robe of purple splendour. The builders of the luxurious Renaissance left their palaces filled only with cold white light, and in the paleness of their native stone.

Nor does it seem difficult to discern a noble reason for this universal law. In that heavenly circle which binds the statutes of colour upon the front of the sky, when it became the sign of the covenant of peace, the pure hues of divided light were sanctified to the human heart for ever; nor this, it would seem, by mere arbitrary appointment, but in consequence of the fore-ordained and marvellous constitution of those hues into a sevenfold, or, more strictly still, a threefold order, typical of the Divine nature itself. Observe also, the name Shem, or Splendour, given to that son of Noah in whom this covenant with mankind was to be fulfilled, and see how that name was justified by every one of the Asiatic races which descended from him. Not without meaning was the love of Israel to his chosen son expressed by the coat 'of many colours;' not without deep sense of the sacredness of that symbol of purity did the lost daughter of David tear it from her breast:— 'With such robes were the king's daughters that were virgins apparelled.' We know it to have been by Divine command that the Israelite, rescued from servitude, veiled the tabernacle with its rain of purple and scarlet, while the under sunshine flashed through the fall of the colour from its tenons of gold: but was it less by Divine guidance that the

Gen. xxxvii. 3.

2 Sam. xiii. 18.

Exodus xxxvi. 35.

Mede, as he struggled out of anarchy, encompassed his king with the sevenfold burning of the battlements of Ecbatana?—of which one circle was golden like the sun, and another silver like the moon; and then came the great secret chord of colour, blue, purple, and scarlet; and then a circle white like the day, and another dark, like night; so that the city rose like a great mural rainbow, a sign of peace amidst the contending of lawless races, and guarded, with colour and shadow, that seemed to symbolize the great order which rules over Day, and <small>Daniel vi. 8, 12.</small> Night, and Time, the first organization of the mighty statutes—the law of the Medes and Persians, that altereth not.—*Stones of Venice*, vol. ii., ch. v., §§ XXXII., XXXIII.

Holy Ghost, Sin against the.

All of you who have ever read your Gospels carefully must have wondered, sometimes, what could be the <small>S. Matt. xii. 32.</small> meaning of those words,—'If any speak against the Son of Man it shall be forgiven; but if against the Holy Spirit, it shall not be forgiven, neither in this world nor in the next.'

The passage may have many meanings which I do not know; but one meaning I know positively, and I tell you so just as frankly as I would that I knew the meaning of a verse in Homer. Those of you who still go to chapel say every day your creed; and, I suppose, too often, less and less every day believing it. Now, you may cease to believe two articles of it, and,—admitting Christianity to be true,—still be forgiven. But I can tell you—you must *not* cease to believe the third! You begin by saying that you believe in an Almighty Father. Well, you may entirely lose the sense of that Fatherhood, and yet be forgiven. You go on to say that you believe in a Saviour Son. You may entirely lose the sense of that Sonship, and yet be forgiven.

But the third article—disbelieve if you dare! 'I believe in the Holy Ghost, the Lord and Giver of life.'

Disbelieve that; and your own being is degraded into the state of dust driven by the wind; and the elements of dissolution have entered your very heart and soul.

All nature, with one voice—with one glory,—is set to teach you reverence for the life communicated to you from the Father of Spirits. The song of birds, and their plumage; the scent of flowers, their colour, their very existence, are in direct connection with the mystery of that communicated life: and all the strength, and all the arts of men, are measured by, and founded upon, their reverence for the passion, and their guardianship of the purity, of Love.—*The Eagle's Nest*, § 169.

Holy Life, A.

Fra Angelico was a man of (humanly speaking) *perfect* piety—humility, charity, and faith—that he never employed his art but as a means of expressing his love to God and man, and with the view, single, simple, and straightforward, of glory to the Creator, and good to the Creature. Every quality or subject of art by which these ends were not to be attained, or to be attained secondarily only, he rejected; from all study of art, as such, he withdrew; whatever might merely please the eye, or interest the intellect, he despised, and refused; he used his colours and lines, as David his harp, after a kingly fashion, for purposes of praise and not of science. To this grace and gift of holiness were added, those of a fervent imagination, vivid invention, keen sense of loveliness in lines and colours, unwearied energy, and to all these gifts the crowning one of quietness of life and mind.—*On the Old Road*, vol. i., part i., § 90.

Angelico in perpetual peace. Not seclusion from the world. No shutting out of the world is needful for him. . . . The little cell was as one of the houses of heaven prepared for him by his Master. 'What need had it to be elsewhere? Was not the Val D'Arno, with its olive woods in white blossom, paradise enough for a poor monk? or could Christ be indeed in heaven more than here? Was He not always with him? Could he breathe or see, but that Christ breathed beside him, and looked into his eyes? Under every cypress avenue the angels walked; he had seen their white robes, whiter than the dawn, at his bedside, as he awoke in early summer. They had sung with him, one on each side, when his voice failed for joy at sweet vesper and matin time; his eyes were blinded by their wings in the sunset, when it sank behind the hills of Luni.'—*Modern Painters*, vol. v., part ix., ch. viii., § 13.

Homes.

When men do not love their hearths, nor reverence their thresholds, it is a sign that they have dishonoured both, and that they have never acknowledged the true universality of that Christian worship which was indeed to supersede the idolatry, but not the piety of the pagan. Our God is a household God, as well as a heavenly one; He has an altar in every man's dwelling; let men look to it when they rend it lightly and pour out its ashes.— *Seven Lamps of Architecture*, ch. vi., § 4.

So far as it is a sacred place, a vestal temple, a temple of the hearth watched over by Household Gods, before whose faces none may come but those whom they can receive with love,—so far as it is this, and roof and fire are types only of a nobler shade and light,— shade as of the rock in a weary land, and light as of the Pharos in the stormy sea:—so far it vindicates the name, and fulfils the praise, of Home.—*Sesame and Lilies*, § 68.

<small>Isaiah xxxii. 2.</small>

Hope.

We usually paint Hope as young, and joyous. Veronese knows better. That young hope is vain hope—passing away in rain of tears; but the Hope of Veronese is aged, assured, remaining when all else has been taken away. 'For tribulation worketh patience, and patience experience, and

<small>Rom. v. 3, 4, 5.</small>

experience hope;' and *that* hope maketh not ashamed. —*Modern Painters*, vol. v., part ix., ch. iii., § 20.

Of all the virtues, this is the most distinctively Christian (it could not, of course, enter definitely into any Pagan scheme); and above all others, it seems to me the *testing* virtue,—that by the possession of which we may most certainly determine whether we are Christians or not; for many men have charity, that is to say general kindness of heart, or even a kind of faith, who have not any habitual *hope* of, or longing for, heaven.—*Stones of Venice*, vol. ii. ch. viii., § LXXXV.

Hope of the Resurrection.

This is the root of all life and all rightness in Christian harmony, whether of word or instrument; and so literally, that in precise manner as this hope disappears, the power of song is taken away, and taken away utterly. When the Christian falls back out of the bright hope of the Resurrection, even the Orpheus song is forbidden him. Not to have known the hope is blameless: one may sing, unknowing, as the swan, or Philomela. But to have known and fall away from it, and to declare that the human wishes, which are summed in that one— 'Thy kingdom come'—are vain! The Fates ordain there shall be no singing after that denial. S. Matt. vi. 10.

For observe this, and earnestly. The old Orphic song, with its dim hope of yet once more Eurydice,— the Philomela song—granted after the cruel silence,— the Halcyon song—with its fifteen days of peace, were all sad, or joyful only in some vague vision of conquest over death.—*On the Old Road*, vol. ii., §§ 45, 46.

Human Heart, The.

'A good man, out of the good treasure of his heart, bringeth forth that which is good; and an evil man, out of the evil treasure, bringeth forth that which is evil.' 'They on the rock are they which, in an S. Luke v. 45.

honest and good heart, having heard the word keep it.'
'Delight thyself in the Lord, and He shall give thee the desires of thine heart.' 'The wicked have bent their bow, that they may privily shoot at him that is upright in heart.' And so on; they are countless, to the same effect. And, for all of us, the question is not at all to ascertain how much or how little corruption there is in human nature; but to ascertain whether, out of all the mass of that nature, we are of the sheep or the goat breed; whether we are people of upright heart, being shot at, or people of crooked heart, shooting. And, of all the texts bearing on the subject, this, which is a quite simple and practical order, is the one you have chiefly to hold in mind. 'Keep thy heart with all diligence, for out of it are the issues of life.'—*Ethics of the Dust*, p. 101.

S. Luke viii. 13-15.
Psalm xxxvii. 4.
Prov. iv. 23.

Human Nature.

Human nature is a noble and beautiful thing; not a foul nor a base thing. All the sin of men I esteem as their disease, not their nature; as a folly which may be prevented, not a necessity which must be accepted. And my wonder, even when things are at their worst, is always at the height which this human nature can attain. Thinking it high, I find it always a higher thing than I thought it; while those who think it low, find it, and will find it, always, lower than they thought it: the fact being, that it is infinite, and capable of infinite height and infinite fall; but the nature of it—and here is the faith which I would have you hold with me—the *nature* of it is in the nobleness, not in the catastrophe. . . .

You have had false prophets among you,—for centuries you have had them,—solemnly warned against them though you were; false prophets, who have told you that all men are nothing but fiends or wolves, half beast, half devil. Believe that, and indeed you may sink to that. But refuse that, and have faith that

God 'made you upright,' though *you* have sought out many inventions; so, you will strive daily to become more what your Maker meant and means you to be, and daily gives you also the power to be,—and you will cling more and more to the nobleness and virtue that is in you, saying, ' My righteousness I hold fast, and will not let it go.'—*Crown of Wild Olive*, §§ 106, 107.

^{Job xxvii. 6.}

Humility.

This, it seems to me, is the principal lesson we are intended to be taught by the book of Job; for there God has thrown open to us the heart of a man most just and holy, and apparently perfect in all things possible to human nature except humility. For this he is tried: and we are shown that no suffering, no self-examination however honest, however stern, no searching out of the heart by its own bitterness, is enough to convince man of his nothingness before God; but that the sight of God's creation will do it. For, when the Deity Himself has willed to end the temptation, and to accomplish in Job that for which it was sent, He does not vouchsafe to reason with him, still less does He overwhelm him with terror, or confound him by laying open before his eyes the book of his iniquities. He opens before him only the arch of the dayspring, and the fountains of the deep; and amidst the covert of the reeds, and on the heaving waves, He bids him watch the kings of the children of pride,—' Behold now Behemoth, which I made with thee.' And the work is done. *Stones of Venice*, vol. iii., ch. ii., § XXXI.

^{Job xl. 15.}

Idleness.

There are no chagrins so venomous as the chagrins of the idle; there are no pangs so sickening as the satieties of pleasure. Nay, the bitterest and most enduring sorrow may be borne through the burden and heat of day bravely to the due time of death, by a true worker. And, indeed, it is this very dayspring and fount of peace in the bosoms of the labouring poor which has till now rendered their oppression possible. Only the idle among *them* revolt against their state;—the brave workers die passively, young and old—and make no sign. It is for you to pity them, for you to stand with them, for you to cherish, and save.—*Fors Clavigera*, Letter XCIII.

<small>S. Matt. xx. 12.</small>
<small>S. Luke i. 78.</small>

Idolatry.

Idolatry is, both literally and verily, not the mere bowing down before sculptures, but the serving or becoming the slave of any images or imaginations which stand between us and God, and it is otherwise expressed in Scripture as 'walking after the *Imagination*' of our own hearts. And observe also that while, at least on one occasion, we find in the Bible an indulgence granted to the mere external and literal violation of the second commandment, 'When I bow myself in the house of Rimmon, the Lord pardon thy servant in this thing,' we find no indulgence in any instance, or in the slightest degree, granted to 'covetousness, which is idolatry' (Col. iii. 5; no casual association of terms, observe, but again energetically repeated in Ephesians v. 5, 'No covetous man, who is an idolater, hath any inheritance in the kingdom of Christ'); nor any to that denial of God, idolatry in one of its most subtle forms, following so often on the possession of that wealth against which Agur prayed so earnestly, 'Give me neither poverty nor riches, lest I be full and deny thee, and say, "Who is the Lord?"'

<small>Jer. xxiii. 17.</small>
<small>2 Kings v. 18.</small>
<small>Prov. xxx. 8.</small>

And in this sense, which of us is not an idolater? Which of us has the right, in the fulness of that better knowledge, in spite of which he nevertheless is not yet separated from the service of this world, to speak scornfully of any of his brethren, because, in a guiltless ignorance, they have been accustomed to bow their knees before a statue? Which of us shall say that there may not be a spiritual idolatry in our own apparent worship?

For indeed it is utterly impossible for one man to judge of the feeling with which another bows down before an image. From that pure reverence in which Sir Thomas Browne wrote, 'I can dispense with my hat at the sight of a cross, but not with a thought of my Redeemer,' to the worst superstition of the most ignorant Romanist, there is an infinite series of subtle transitions; and the point where simple reverence and the use of the image merely to render conception more vivid, and feeling more intense, change into definite idolatry by the attribution of Power to the image itself, is so difficultly determinable that we cannot be too cautious in asserting that such a change has actually taken place in the case of any individual. Even when it is definite and certain, we shall oftener find it the consequence of dulness of intellect than of real alienation of heart from God; and I have no manner of doubt that half of the poor and untaught Christians who are this day lying prostrate before crucifixes, Bambinos, and Voltos Santos, are finding more acceptance with God than many Protestants who idolise nothing but their own opinions or their own interests. I believe that those who have worshipped the thorns of Christ's crown will be found at last to have been holier and wiser than those who worship the thorns of the world's service, and that to adore the nails of the cross is a less sin than to adore the hammer of the workman.

But, on the other hand, though the idolatry of the lower orders in the Romish Church may thus be frequently excusable, the ordinary subterfuges by which it is defended are not so. It may be extenuated, but cannot be denied; and the attribution of power to the image, in which it consists, is not merely a form of popular feeling, but a tenet of priestly instruction, and may be proved, over and over again, from any book of the Romish Church services.—*Stones of Venice*, vol. ii. Appendix 10.

The essence of evil idolatry begins only in the idea or belief of a real presence of any kind, in a thing in which there is no such presence. I need not say that the harm of the idolatry must depend on the certainty of the negative. If there be a real presence in a pillar of cloud, in an unconsuming flame, or in a still small voice, it is no sin to bow down before these.—*Aratra Pentelici*, §§ 45, 46.

<small>Exodus xiii. 21; iii. 2.</small>
<small>1 Kings xix. 12.</small>

'**Imagination of the Heart.**'

First, consider what are the legitimate uses of the imagination, that is to say, of the power of perceiving, or conceiving with the mind, things which cannot be perceived by the senses.

Its first and noblest use is, to enable us to bring sensibly to our sight the things which are recorded as belonging to our future state, or as invisibly surrounding us in this. It is given us, that we may imagine the cloud of witnesses in heaven and earth, and see, as if they were now present, the souls of the righteous waiting for us; that we may conceive the great army of the inhabitants of heaven, and discover among them those whom we most desire to be with for ever; that we may be able to vision forth the ministry of angels beside us, and see the chariots of fire on the mountains that gird us round; but, above all, to call up the scenes and facts in which we are commanded to believe, and be present, as if in the body, at every recorded event of the history of the Redeemer.—*Modern Painters*, vol. iii., ch. iv., § 5.

<small>Hebrews xii. 1.</small>

Infallibility of the Church.

Observe, St. Paul, and the rest of the Apostles, write nearly all their epistles to the Invisible Church :—those epistles are headed, Romans, 'To the beloved of God, called to be saints;' 1 Corinthians, 'To them that are sanctified in Christ Jesus;' 2 Corinthians, 'To the saints in all Achaia;' Ephesians, 'To the saints which are at Ephesus, and to the faithful in Christ Jesus;' Philippians, 'To all the saints which are at Philippi;' Colossians, 'To the saints and faithful brethren which are at Colosse;' 1 and 2 Thessalonians, 'To the Church of the Thessalonians, which is in God the Father, and the Lord Jesus;' 1 and 2 Timothy, 'To his own son in the faith;' Titus, to the same; 1 Peter, 'To the Strangers, Elect according to the foreknowledge of God;' 2 Peter, 'To them that have obtained like precious faith with us;' 2 John, 'To the Elect lady;' Jude, 'To them that are sanctified by God the Father, and preserved in Jesus Christ, and called.'

There are thus fifteen epistles, expressly directed to the members of the Invisible Church. Philemon and Hebrews, and 1 and 3 John, are evidently also so written, though not so expressly inscribed. That of James, and that to the Galatians, are as evidently to the Visible Church: the one being general, and the other to persons[1] 'removed from Him that called them.' Missing out, therefore, these two epistles, but including Christ's words to His disciples, we find in the Scriptural addresses to members of the Invisible Church, fourteen if not more, direct injunctions 'not to be deceived.' So much for the Infallibility of the Church.—*On the Old Road*, vol. ii., §§ 190, 191.

S. Matt. xxiv. 4.
S. Mark xiii. 5.
S. Luke xxi. 8.
1 Cor. iii. 18; vi. 9; xv. 33.
Eph. iv. 14; v. 6.
Col. ii. 8.
2 Thess. ii. 3.
Heb. iii. 13.

'In His own Image.'

For the directest manifestation of Deity to man is in His own image, that is, in man.

'In His own image. After His likeness.' *Ad imaginem et Similitudinem Suam.* I do not know what people in general understand by those

Gen. i. 26.

---
[1] Galatians i. 6.

words. I suppose they ought to be understood. The truth they contain seems to lie at the foundation of our knowledge both of God and man; yet do we not usually pass the sentence by, in dull reverence, attaching no definite sense to it at all? For all practical purpose, might it not as well be out of the text.

I have no time, nor much desire, to examine the vague expressions of belief with which the verse has been encumbered. Let us try to find its only possible plain significance.

It cannot be supposed that the bodily shape of man resembles or resembled, any bodily shape in Deity. The likeness must therefore be, or have been, in the soul. Had it wholly passed away, and the divine soul been altered into a soul brutal or diabolic, I suppose we should have been told of the change. But we are told nothing of the kind. The verse still stands as if for our use and trust. It was only death which was to be our punishment. Not *change*. So far as we live, the image is still there; defiled, if you will; broken, if you will; all but effaced, if you will, by death and the shadow of it. But not changed. We are not made now in any other image than God's. There are, indeed, the two states of this image—the earthly and heavenly, but both Adamite, both human, both the same likeness; only one defiled, and one pure. So that the soul of man is still a mirror, wherein may be seen, darkly, the image of the mind of God.

These may seem daring words. I am sorry that they do; but I am helpless to soften them. Discover any other meaning of the text if you are able;—but be sure that it *is* a meaning—a meaning in your head and heart;—not a subtle gloss, nor a shifting of one verbal expression into another, both idealess. I repeat that, to me, the verse has, and can have, no other signification than this—that the soul of man is a mirror of the mind of God. A mirror, dark, distorted, broken, use what blameful words you please of its state; yet in the main, a true mirror, out of which alone, and by which alone, we can know anything of God at all.

'How?' the reader, perhaps, answers indignantly. 'I know the nature of God by revelation, not by looking into myself.'

Revelation to what? To a nature incapable of receiving truth? That cannot be; for only to a nature capable of truth, desirous of it, distinguishing it, feeding upon it, revelation is possible. To a being undesirous of it, and hating it, revelation is impossible. There can be none to a brute, or fiend. In so far, therefore, as you love truth, and live therein, in so far revelation can exist for you;—and in so far, your mind is the image of God's.

But consider, farther, not only *to* what, but *by* what, is the revelation. By sight? or word? If by sight, then to eyes which see justly. Otherwise, no sight would be revelation. So far, then, as your sight is just, it is the image of God's sight.

If by words,—how do you know their meanings? Here is a short piece of precious word revelation, for instance. 'God is love.' [1 John iv. 8.]

Love! yes. But what is *that*? The revelation does not tell you that, I think. Look into the mirror, and you will see. Out of your own heart, you may know what love is. In no other possible way,—by no other help or sign. All the words and sounds ever uttered, all the revelations of cloud, or flame, or crystal, are utterly powerless. They cannot tell you, in the smallest point, what love means. Only the broken mirror can.

Here is more revelation. 'God is just!' Just! What is that? The revelation cannot help you to discover. You say it is dealing equitably or equally. [Deut. xxxii. 4.] But how do you discern the equality? Not by inequality of mind; not by a mind incapable of weighing, judging, or distributing. If the length seem unequal in the broken mirror, for you they are unequal; but if they seem equal, then the mirror is true. So far as you recognize equality, and your conscience tells you what is just, so far your mind is the image of God's; and so far as you do *not* discern this nature of justice or equality, the words 'God is just' bring no revelation to you.

'But His thoughts are not as our thoughts.' No; the sea is not as the standing pool by the wayside. Yet when the breeze crisps the pool, you may see the image of the breakers, and a likeness of the foam. Nay, in some sort, the same foam. If the sea is for ever invisible to you, something you may learn of it from the pool. Nothing, assuredly, any otherwise.

<small>Isaiah lv. 8.</small>

'But this poor miserable Me! Is *this*, then, all the book I have got to read about God in?' Yes, truly so. No other book, nor fragment of book, than that, will you ever find; no velvet-bound missal, nor frankincensed manuscript;—nothing hieroglyphic nor cuneiform; papyrus and pyramid are alike silent on this matter;—nothing in the clouds above, nor in the earth beneath. That flesh-bound volume is the only revelation that is, that was, or that can be. In that is the image of God painted; in that is the law of God written; in that is the promise of God revealed. Know thyself; for through thyself only thou canst know God.

<small>1 Cor. xiii. 12.</small> Through the glass, darkly. But, except through the glass, in nowise.

A tremulous crystal, waved as water, poured out upon the ground;—you may defile it, despise it, pollute it, at your pleasure and at your peril; for on the peace of those weak waves must all the heaven you shall ever gain be first seen; and through such purity as you can win for those dark waves, must all the light of the risen Sun of righteousness be bent down, by faint refraction. Cleanse them, and calm them, as you love your life.—*Modern Painters*, vol. v., part ix., ch. i., §§ 9–15.

<small>Mal. iv. 2.</small>

Invisible Church.

What are the distinctive characters of the Invisible

Church? That is to say, What is it which makes a person a member of this Church, and how is he to be known for such? Wide question—if we had to take cognizance of all that has been written respecting it, remarkable as it has been always for quantity rather than carefulness, and full of confusion between Visible and Invisible: even the Article of the Church of England being ambiguous in its first clause: 'The *Visible* Church is a congregation of Faithful men.' As if ever it had been possible, except for God, to see Faith, or to know a Faithful man by sight! And there is little else written on this question, without some such quick confusion of the Visible and Invisible Church;— needless and unaccountable confusion. For evidently, the Church which is composed of Faithful men is the one true, indivisible, and indiscernible Church, built on the foundation of Apostles and Prophets, Jesus Christ Himself being the chief corner-stone. It includes all who have ever fallen asleep in Christ, and all yet unborn, who are to be saved in Him: its Body is as yet imperfect; it will not be perfected till the last saved human spirit is gathered to its God. [Eph. ii. 20.]

A man becomes a member of this Church only by believing in Christ with all his heart; nor is he positively recognizable for a member of it, when he has become so, by any one but God, not even by himself. Nevertheless, there are certain signs by which Christ's sheep may be guessed at. Not by their being in any definite Fold—for many are lost sheep at times; but by their sheep-like behaviour; and a great many are indeed sheep which, on the far mountain side, in their peacefulness, we take for stones. To themselves, the best proof of their being Christ's sheep is to find themselves on Christ's shoulders; and, between them, there are certain sympathies (expressed in the Apostles' Creed by the term 'communion of Saints'), by which they may in a sort recognize each other, and so become verily visible to each other for mutual comfort.—*On the Old Road,* vol. ii., § 188.

Irreverence.

We treat God with irreverence by banishing Him from our thoughts, not by referring to His will on slight occasions. His is not the finite authority or intelligence which cannot be troubled with small things. There is nothing so small but that we may honour God by asking His guidance of it, or insult Him by taking it into our own hands; and what is true of the Deity is equally true of His Revelation. We use it most reverently when most habitually: our insolence is in ever acting without reference to it, our true honouring of it is in its universal application. . . . We have them not often enough on our lips, nor deeply enough in our memories, nor loyally enough in our lives. The snow, the vapour, and the stormy wind fulfil His word. Are our acts and thoughts lighter and wilder than these—that we should forget it?—*Seven Lamps of Architecture*, Introductory, pp. 9, 10.

<small>Psalm cxlviii. 8.</small>

Israel.

When Israel *was* a child, God loved him and called his son out of Egypt. He preparatorily sent him *into* Egypt. And the first deliverer of Israel had to know the wisdom of Egypt before the wisdom of Arabia; and for the last deliverer of Israel, the dawn of infant thought, and the first vision of the earth He came to save, was under the palms of Nile.—*Fors Clavigera*, Letter LXIV.

<small>Hosea xi. 1.</small>

Jacob's Ladder.

I have seen, over the doors of many churches, the legend actually carved, '*This* is the house of God, and this is the gate of heaven.' Now, note where that legend comes from, and of what place it was first spoken. A boy leaves his father's house to go on a long journey on foot, to visit his uncle: he has to cross a wild hill-desert; just as if one of your own boys had to cross the wolds to visit an uncle at Carlisle.

<small>Gen. xxviii. 17.</small>

The second or third day your boy finds himself somewhere between Hawes and Brough, in the midst of the moors, at sunset. It is stony ground, and boggy; he cannot go one foot farther that night. Down he lies, to sleep, on Wharnside, where best he may, gathering a few of the stones together to put under his head;—so wild the place is, he cannot get anything but stones. And there, lying under the broad night, he has a dream; and he sees a ladder set up on the earth, and the top of it reaches to heaven, and the angels of God are seen ascending and descending upon it. And when he wakes out of his sleep, he says, 'How dreadful is this place; surely this is none other than the house of God, and this is the gate of heaven.' This PLACE, observe; not this church, not this city, not this stone, even, which he puts up for a memorial—the piece of flint on which his head was lain. But this *place;* this windy slope of Wharnside; this moorland hollow, torrent-bitten, snow-blighted! this *any* place where God lets down the ladder. And how are you to know where that will be? or how are you to determine where it may be, but by being ready for it always? Do you know where the lightning is to fall next? You *do* know that, partly; you can guide the lightning; but you cannot guide the going forth of the Spirit, which is as that lightning when it shines from the east to the west. Gen. xxviii. 17.

But the perpetual and insolent warping of that strong verse to serve a merely ecclesiastical purpose, is only one of the thousand instances in which we sink back into gross Judaism. We call our churches 'temples.' Now, you know perfectly well they are *not* temples. They have never had, never can have, anything whatever to do with temples. They are 'synagogues'—'gathering places'—where you gather yourselves together as an assembly; and by not calling them so, you again miss the force of another mighty text—'Thou, when thou prayest, shalt not be as the S. Matt. xviii. 20.
S. Matt. vi. 5, 6.

hypocrites are; for they love to pray standing in the *churches'* [we should translate it], 'that they may be seen of men. But thou, when thou prayest, enter into thy closet, and when thou hast shut thy door, pray to thy Father,'—which is, not in chancel or in aisle, but 'in secret.'

Now, you feel, as I say this to you—I know you feel—as if I were trying to take away the honour of your churches. Not so; I am trying to prove to you the honour of your houses and your hills; not that the Church is not sacred—but that the whole Earth is. I would have you feel what careless, what constant, what infectious sin there is in all modes of thought, whereby, in calling your churches only 'holy,' you call your hearths and homes 'profane'; and have separated yourselves from the heathen by casting all your household gods to the ground, instead of recognizing, in the places of their many and feeble Lares, the presence of your One and Mighty Lord and Lar.—*Crown of Wild Olive*, §§ 62-4.

Job.

Do you remember the questioning to Job? ... Look on to the thirty-eighth chapter, and read down to the question concerning this April time:—'Hath the rain a Father—and who hath begotten the drops of dew,—the hoary Frost of Heaven—who hath gendered it?'

<small>Job xxxviii. 28.</small>

That rain and frost of heaven; and the earth which they loose and bind; these, and the labour of your hands to divide them, and subdue, are your wealth, for ever—unincreasable. The fruit of Earth, and its waters, and its light—such as the strength of the pure rock can grow — such as the unthwarted sun in his season brings—these are your inheritance. You can diminish it, but cannot increase: that your barns should be filled with plenty—your presses burst with new wine,—is your blessing; and every year

<small>Prov. iii. 10.</small>

—when it is full—it must be new; and every year, no more.—*Fors Clavigera*, Letter XVI.

Joshua, the Soldier of Christ. (*Botticelli.*)

He had seen it, and often; and between noble persons;—knew the temper in which the noblest knights went out to it;—knew the strength, the patience, the glory, and the grief of it. He would fain see his Florence in peace; and yet he knows that the wisest of her citizens are her bravest soldiers. So he seeks for the ideal of a soldier, and for the greatest glory of war, that in the presence of these he may speak reverently, what he must speak. He does not go to Greece for his hero. He is not sure that even her patriotic wars were always right. But, by his religious faith, he cannot doubt the nobleness of the soldier who put the children of Israel in possession of their promised land, and to whom the sign of the consent of heaven was given by its pausing light in the valley of Ajalon. Must then setting sun [Joshua x. 12.] and risen moon stay, he thinks, only to look upon slaughter? May no soldier of Christ bid them stay otherwise than so? He draws Joshua, but quitting his hold of the sword: its hilt rests on his bent knee; and he kneels before the sun, not commands it; and this is his prayer:—

'Oh, King of kings, and Lord of lords, who alone rulest always in eternity, and who correctest all our wanderings,—Giver of melody to the choir of the angels, listen Thou a little to our bitter grief, and come and rule us, oh Thou highest King, with Thy love which is so sweet!'—*Ariadne Florentina*, § 202.

You have all been greatly questioning, of late, whether the sun, which you find to be now going out, ever stood still. Did you in any lagging minute, on those scientific occasions, chance to reflect what he was bid stand still *for?* or if not—will you please look [Psalm xix. 4, 5.] —and what also, going forth again as a strong man to run his course, he saw, rejoicing?

'Then Joshua passed from Makkedah unto Libnah —and fought against Libnah. And the Lord delivered it and the king thereof into the hand of Israel, and he smote it with the edge of the sword, and all the souls that were therein.' And from Lachish to Eglon, and from Eglon to Kirjath-Arba, and Sarah's grave in the Amorites' land, 'and Joshua smote all the country of the hills and of the south—and of the vale and of the springs, and all their kings: he left none remaining, but utterly destroyed all that breathed—as the Lord God of Israel commanded.' Thus 'it is written': though you perhaps do not so often hear *these* texts preached from, as certain others about taking away the sins of the world.—*On the Old Road*, vol. ii., §§ 57, 58.

<small>Joshua x. 29.</small>
<small>Joshua x. 40.</small>
<small>S. John i. 29.</small>

Jotham.

As I re-read the chapter of Judges,—now, except in my memory, unread, as it chances, for many a year,— the sadness of that story of Gideon fastens on me, and silences me. *This* the end of his angel visions, and dream-led victories, the slaughter of all his sons but this youngest,[1]—and he never again heard of in Israel!

You Scottish children of the Rock, taught through all your once pastoral and noble lives by many a sweet miracle of dew on fleece and ground,—once servants of mighty kings, and keepers of sacred covenant; have you indeed dealt truly with your warrior kings, and prophet saints, or are these ruins of their homes, and shrines, dark with the fire that fell from the curse of Jerubbael?—*Proserpina*, ch. vii., § 14.

<small>Judges vi. 37.</small>
<small>Judges ix. 20, 57.</small>

Judas Iscariot.

We do great injustice to Iscariot, in thinking him wicked above all common wickedness. He was only a

---

[1] 'Jotham, sum perfectio eorum,' or 'Consummatio eorum.' (Interpretation of name in Vulgate Index.)

common money-lover, and, like all money-lovers, did not understand Christ;—could not make out the worth of Him, or meaning of Him. He never thought He would be killed. He was horror-struck when he found that Christ would be killed; threw his money away instantly, and hanged himself. How many of our present money-seekers, think you, would have the grace to hang themselves, whoever was killed? But Judas was a common, selfish, muddle-headed, pilfering fellow; his hand always in the bag of the poor, not caring for them. Helpless to understand Christ, he yet believed in Him, much more than most of us do; had seen Him do miracles, thought He was quite strong enough to shift for Himself, and he, Judas, might as well make his own little bye-perquisites out of the affair. Christ would come out of it well enough, and he have his thirty pieces. Now, that is the money-seeker's idea, all over the world. He doesn't hate Christ, but can't understand Him— doesn't care for Him—sees no good in that benevolent business; makes his own little job out of it at all events, come what will. And thus, out of every mass of men, you have a certain number of bagmen—'your fee-first' men, whose main object is to make money. And they do make it—make it in all sorts of unfair ways, chiefly by the weight and force of money itself, or what is called the power of capital; that is to say, the power which money, once obtained, has over the labour of the poor, so that the capitalist can take all its produce to himself, except the labourer's food. That is the modern Judas' way of 'carrying the bag,' and 'bearing what is put therein.'—*Crown of Wild Olive*, § 33.

Justice.

It is the law of heaven that you shall not be able to judge what is wise or easy, unless you are first resolved to judge what is just, and to do it. That is the one thing constantly reiterated by our Master —the order of all others that is given oftenest—'Do

Gen. xviii. 19.

justice and judgment.' That's your Bible order; that's the 'Service of God,'—not praying nor psalm-singing. You are told, indeed, to sing psalms when you are merry, Prov. and to pray when you need anything; and, xxi. 3. by the perverseness of the evil Spirit in us, we get to think that praying and psalm-singing 'are service.' . . . The one Divine work—the **one** ordered sacrifice—is to do justice; and it is the last we are ever inclined to do. Anything rather than that! As much charity as you choose, but no justice. 'Nay,' you will say, 'charity is greater than justice.' Yes, it is greater; it is the summit of justice—it is the temple of which justice is the foundation. But you can't have the top without the bottom; you cannot build upon charity. You must build upon justice, for this main reason, that you have not, **at first,** charity **to** build with. It is the last reward of good work. Do justice **to** your brother (you can do that whether you love him or not), and you will come to love him. But do injustice to him, because you don't love him; and you will come to hate him.—*Crown of Wild Olive,* § 39.

Kingdom, The.

In what respect the kingdoms of the world, and the glory of *them,* differ from the Kingdom, the Power, and the Glory, which are God's for ever, is seldom, as far as I have heard, intelligibly explained from the pulpit; and still less the irreconcilable hostility between **the** two royalties and realms asserted in its sternness of decision.

Whether it be, indeed, Utopian **to** believe that the **kingdom we are** taught **to pray for** *may* come—verily come—**for the** asking, **it is surely not for man** to judge; but it is at least at his choice to resolve that he will no longer render obedience, nor ascribe glory and power, S. Matt. to the Devil. If he cannot find strength in xvi. 23. himself to advance towards Heaven, he may at least say to the power of Hell, 'Get thee behind me;' and staying himself on the testimony of Him who saith, 'Surely I come quickly,' ratify his happy prayer with the faithful 'Amen, even so, come, Lord Jesus.'— *On the Old Road*, vol. ii., § 246.

<small>Rev. xxii. 20.</small>

Knowledge.

Therefore, with respect to knowledge, we are to reason and act exactly as with respect to food. We no more live to know than we live to eat. We live to contemplate, enjoy, act, adore: and we may know all that is to be known in this world, and what Satan knows in the other, without being able to do any of these. We are to ask, therefore, first, is the knowledge we would have fit food for us, good and simple, not artificial and decorated? and secondly, how much of it will enable us best for our work; and will leave our hearts light, and our eyes clear? For no more than that is to be eaten without the old Eve-sin.

Observe, also, the difference between tasting knowledge and hoarding it. In this respect it is also like food; since, in some measure, the knowledge of all men is laid up in granaries, for future use; much of it is at any given moment dormant, not fed upon or enjoyed, but in store. And by all it is to be remembered that knowledge in this form may be kept without air till it rots, or in such unthreshed disorder that it is of no use; and that, however good or orderly, it is still only in being tasted that it becomes of use; and that men may easily starve in their own granaries, men of science, perhaps, most of all, for they are likely to seek accumulation of their store, rather than nourishment from it. Yet let it not be thought that I would undervalue them. The good and great among them are like Joseph, of whom all nations sought to buy corn; or like the sower going forth to sow beside all waters, sending forth thither the feet of the ox and the ass: only let us remember that this is not all men's

<small>Gen. xli. 57.</small>

<small>Isaiah xxxii. 20.</small>

work. We are not intended to be all keepers of granaries, nor all to be measured by the filling of the storehouse; but many, nay, most of us, are to receive day by day our daily bread, and shall be as well nourished and as fit for our labour, and often, also, fit for nobler and more divine labour, in feeding from the barrel of meal that does not waste and from the cruse of oil that does not fail, than if our barns were filled with plenty, and our presses bursting out with new wine.

<small>1 Kings xvii. 16.
Prov. iii. 10.</small>

It is for each man to find his own measure in this matter; in great part, also, for others to find it for him, while he is yet a youth.—*Stones of Venice*, vol. iii., ch. ii., §§ XXVI.–XXVIII.

Language of the Bible.

The language of the Bible is specifically distinguished from all other early literature, by its delight in natural imagery; and that the dealings of God with His people are calculated peculiarly to awaken this sensibility within them. Out of the monotonous valley of Egypt they are instantly taken into the midst of the mightiest mountain scenery in the peninsula of Arabia; and that scenery is associated in their minds with the immediate manifestation and presence of the Divine Power; so that mountains for ever afterwards become invested with a peculiar sacredness in their minds: while their descendants being placed in what was then one of the loveliest districts upon the earth, full of glorious vegetation, bounded on one side by the sea, on the north by 'that goodly mountain' Lebanon, on the south and east by deserts, whose barrenness enhanced by their contrast the sense of the perfection of beauty in their own land, they became, by these means, and by the touch of God's own hand upon their hearts, sensible to the appeal of natural scenery in a way in which no other people were at the time. And their literature is full of expressions, not only testifying a vivid sense of the

<small>Deut. iii. 25.</small>

power of nature over man, but showing that *sympathy with natural things themselves*, as if they had human souls, which is the especial characteristic of true love of the works of God. Consider such expressions as that tender and glorious verse in Isaiah, speaking of the cedars on the mountains as rejoicing over the fall of the king of Assyria: 'Yea, the fir trees rejoice at thee, and the cedars of Lebanon, saying, Since *thou* art gone down to the grave, no feller is come up against us.' See what sympathy there is here, as if with the very hearts of the trees themselves. So also in the words of Christ, in His personification of the lilies: 'They toil not, neither do they spin.' Consider such expressions as, 'The sea saw that, and fled. Jordan was driven back. The mountains skipped like rams; and the little hills like lambs.' Try to find anything in profane writing like this; and note farther that the whole book of Job appears to have been chiefly written and placed in the inspired volume in order to show the value of natural history, and its power on the human heart. I cannot pass by it without pointing out the evidences of the beauty of the country that Job inhabited. Observe, first, it was an arable country. 'The oxen were ploughing and the asses feeding beside them.' It was a pastoral country: his substance, besides camels and asses, was 7000 sheep. It was a mountain country, fed by streams descending from the high snows. 'My brethren have dealt deceitfully as a brook, and as the stream of brooks they pass away; which are blackish by reason of the ice, and wherein the snow is hid: What time they wax warm they vanish: when it is hot they are consumed out of their place.' Again: 'If I wash myself with snow water, and make my hands never so clean.' Again: 'Drought and heat consume the snow waters.' It was a rocky country, with forests and verdure rooted in the rocks. 'His branch shooteth forth in his

(Isaiah xiv. 8.)
(S. Matt. vi. 28.)
(Psalm cxiv. 3.)
(Job i. 14.)
(Job vi. 15-17.)
(Job ix. 30.)
(Job viii. 16, 17.)

garden; his roots are wrapped about the heap, and seeth the place of stones.' Again: 'Thou shalt be in league with the stones of the field.' It was a place visited, like the valleys of Switzerland, by convulsions and falls of mountains. 'Surely the mountain falling cometh to nought, and the rock is removed out of his place. The waters wear the stones; thou washest away the things which grow out of the dust of the earth.' 'He removeth the mountains and they know not: he overturneth them in his anger.' 'He putteth forth his hand upon the rock: he overturneth the mountains by the roots: he cutteth out rivers among the rocks.' . . . You see Job's country was one like your own, full of pleasant brooks and rivers, rushing among the rocks, and of all other sweet and noble elements of landscape. The magnificent allusions to natural scenery throughout the book are therefore calculated to touch the heart to the end of time.

Job v. 23.
Job xiv. 18.
Job v. 9.
Job xxviii. 9.

Then at the central point of Jewish prosperity, you have the first great naturalist the world ever saw, Solomon; not permitted, indeed, to anticipate, in writing, the discoveries of modern times, but so gifted as to show us that heavenly wisdom is manifested as much in the knowledge of the hyssop that springeth out of the wall as in political and philosophical speculation.

1 Kings iv. 33.

The books of the Old Testament, as distinguished from all other early writings, are thus prepared for an everlasting influence over humanity; and, finally, Christ Himself, setting the concluding example to the conduct and thoughts of men, spends nearly His whole life in the fields, the mountains, or the small country villages of Judea; and in the very closing scenes of His life, will not so much as sleep within the walls of Jerusalem, but rests at the little village of Bethphage, walking in the morning, and returning in the evening, through the peaceful avenues of the Mount

S. Matt. xxi. 1.

of Olives, to and from His work of teaching in the
temple.—*Lectures on Architecture and Painting*, §§ 79, 80.

Last Words of the Virgin.

'They have no wine.' 'Whatsoever He saith unto you,
do it.' These, the last recorded words of the S. John
Mother of Christ, and the only ones recorded ii. 3-5.
during the period of His ministry. . . . The first sentence of these two, contains the appeal of the workman's
wife, to her son, for the help of the poor of all the earth.

The second, the command of the Lord's Mother, to
the people of all the earth, that they should serve the
Lord. This day last year, I was walking with a dear
friend, and resting long, laid on the dry leaves in the
sunset, under the vineyard-trellises of the little range of
hills which, five miles west of Verona, look down on the
Lago di Garda at about the distance from its shore that
Cana is from the Lake of Galilee,—(the Madonna had
walked to the bridal some four miles and a half). It
was a Sunday evening, golden and calm; all the vine
leaves quiet; and the soft clouds held at pause in the
west, round the mountains that Virgil knew so well,
blue above the level reeds of Mincio. . . . If ever
peace and joy, and sweet life on earth might be possible
for men, it is so here, and in such places,—few, on the
wide earth, but many in the bosom of infinitely blessed,
infinitely desolate Italy. Its people were sitting at their
doors, quietly working—the women at least,—the old
men at rest behind them. A worthy and gentle race;
but utterly poor, utterly untaught the things that in *this*
world make for their peace. . . . There they sat—the
true race of Northern Italy, mere prey for the vulture,—
patient, silent, hopeless, careless: infinitude of accustomed and bewildered sorrow written in every line of
their faces, unnerving every motion of their hands,
slackening the spring in all their limbs. And their
blood has been poured out like water, age after age, and
risen round the wine-press, even to the horse-bridles.

And of the peace on earth, and the goodwill towards men, which He who trod the wine-press alone, and of the people there **was** none with Him—died to bring them, they have heard by the hearing of the ear,—their eyes have not seen. 'They have no wine.'

<small>Isaiah lxiii. 3.</small>

But He Himself has been always **with them,** though they saw Him not, and they have had the deepest of His blessings. 'Blessed *are* they that have not seen, and *yet* have believed.' And in the faith of these, and such as these,—in the voiceless religion and uncomplaining duty of the peasant races, throughout Europe,—is now that Church on earth, against which the gates of Hell shall not prevail. And on the part taken in ministry **to** them, or in oppressing them, depends now the judgment between the righteous and the wicked servant, which the Lord, who has so long delayed His coming, will assuredly now, at no far-off time, require.

<small>S. John xx. 29.</small>

<small>S. Matt. xvi. 18.</small>

'But and if that servant shall say in his heart, "My Lord delayeth His coming"'— Shall I go on writing? We have all read the passage so often that it falls on our thoughts unfelt, as if its words were dead leaves. We will **write** and read it more slowly to-day—so please you.

<small>S. Luke xii. 45.</small>

'Who then is a faithful and wise servant, whom his Lord hath made ruler over His household, to give them their meat in due season?'

<small>S. Matt. xxiv. 45.</small>

Over *His* household,—He probably having His eyes upon it, then, whether you have or not. But He has made you ruler over it, that you may give it meat, in due season. Meat—literally, first of all. And that seasonably, according to laws of duty, and not of chance. . . .

'Blessed *is* that servant whom his Lord, when He cometh, shall find so doing. Verily I say unto you, that He shall make him ruler over all His goods.'

<small>S. Matt. xxiv. 46.</small>

A vague hope, you think, to act upon? Well, if you only act on such hope, you will never either know, or get, what it means. No one but Christ can tell what *all* His goods are; and you have no business to mind, yet; for it is not the getting of these, but the doing His work, that you must care for yet awhile. . . . 'Let your loins be girded about, and your lights burning, and ye yourselves like unto men that wait for their Lord, *when He shall return* from the *wedding.*' Nor a hint of it merely, but you may even hear, at quiet times, some murmur and sylla- bling of its music in the distance—' The Spirit and the Bride, say, Come.'—*Fors Clavigera*, Letter LXXXIV.

<small>S. Luke xii. 35, 36.</small>

<small>Rev. xxii. 17.</small>

Law of the Spirit.

Law, so far as it can be reduced to form and system, and is not written upon the heart,—as it is, in a Divine loyalty, upon the hearts of the great hierarchies who serve and wait about the throne of the Eternal Lawgiver,—this lower and formally expressible law has, I say, two objects. It is either for the definition and restraint of sin, or the guidance of simplicity; it either explains, forbids, and punishes wickedness, or it guides the movements and actions both of lifeless things and of the more simple and untaught among responsible agents. And so long, therefore, as sin and foolishness are in the world, so long it will be necessary for men to submit themselves painfully to this lower law, in proportion to their need of being corrected, and to the degree of childishness or simplicity by which they approach more nearly to the condition of the unthinking and inanimate things which are governed by law altogether; yet yielding, in the manner of their submission to it, a singular lesson to the pride of man, —being obedient more perfectly in proportion to their greatness. But, so far as men become good and wise, and rise above the state of children, so far they become emancipated from this written law, and invested with the perfect freedom which consists in the fulness and joyfulness of compliance with a higher and unwritten law; a law so universal, so subtle, so glorious that nothing but the heart can keep it.

Now pride opposes itself to the observance of this Divine law in two opposite ways: either by brute resistance, which is the way of the rabble and its leaders, denying or defying law altogether; or by formal compliance, which is the way of the Pharisee, exalting himself while he pretends to obedience, and making void the infinite and spiritual commandment by the finite and lettered commandment. And it is easy to know which law we are obeying: for any law which we magnify and keep through pride, is always the law of the letter; but that which we love and keep through humility, is the law of the Spirit: and the letter killeth, but the Spirit giveth life.—*Stones of Venice*, vol. iii., ch. ii., §§ LXXXVII., LXXXVIII.

[2 Cor. iii. 6.]

Laymen.

Men not in office in the Church suppose themselves, on that ground, in a sort unholy; and that, therefore, they may sin with more excuse, and be idle or impious with less danger, than the Clergy: especially they consider themselves relieved from all ministerial function, and as permitted to devote their whole time and energy to the business of this world. No mistake can possibly be greater. Every member of the Church is equally bound to the service of the Head of the Church; and that service is pre-eminently the saving of souls. There is not a moment of a man's active life in which he may not be indirectly preaching; and throughout a great part of his life he ought to be *directly* preaching, and teaching both strangers and friends; his children, his servants, and all who in any way are put under him, being given to him as special objects of his ministration.
—*On the Old Road*, vol. ii., § 197.

Leaf.

In the leaf is the strength of the tree itself. Nay, rightly speaking, the leaves *are* the tree itself. Its trunk sustains; its fruit burdens and exhausts; but in the leaf it breathes and lives. And thus also, in the eastern symbolism, the fruit is the labour of men for others; but the leaf is their own life. 'He shall bring forth fruit in his time; and his own joy and strength shall be continual.'—*Proserpina*, ch. iii., § 2.

Lesson.

As we pass beneath the hills which have been shaken by earthquake and torn by convulsion, we find that periods of perfect repose succeed those of destruction. The pools of calm water lie clear beneath their fallen rocks, the water-lilies gleam, and the reeds whisper among their shadows; the village rises again over the forgotten graves, and its church-tower, white through the storm twilight, proclaims a renewed appeal to His protection in whose hand 'are all the corners of the earth, and the strength of the hills is His also.' [Psalm xcv. 4.] There is no loveliness of Alpine valley that does not teach the same lesson. It is just where 'the mountain falling cometh to nought, and the rock is removed out of his place,' [Job xiv. 18.] that, in process of years, the fairest meadows bloom between the fragments, the clearest rivulets murmur from their crevices among the flowers, and the clustered cottages, each sheltered beneath some strength of mossy stone, now to be removed no more, and with their pastured flocks around them, safe from the eagle's stoop and the wolf's ravin, have written upon their fronts, in simple words, the mountaineer's faith in the ancient promise—' Neither shalt thou be afraid of destruction when it cometh;' 'For thou shalt be in league with the Stones of the Field; and the beasts of the field shall be at peace with thee.' [Job v. 21-23.]—*Modern Painters*, vol. iv., ch. xviii., § 26.

Lessons from the Birds.

I believe verily for the first time, I have been able to put before you some means of guidance to understand the beauty of the bird which lives with you in your own houses, and which purifies for you, from its insect pestilence, the air that you breathe. Thus the sweet domestic thing has done, for men, at least these four thousand years. She has been their companion, not of the home merely, but of the hearth, and the threshold; companion only endeared by departure, and showing better her loving-kindness by her faithful return. Type sometimes of the stranger, she has softened us to hospitality; type always of the suppliant, she has enchanted us to mercy; and in her feeble presence, the cowardice, or the wrath, of sacrilege has changed into the fidelities of sanctuary. Herald of our summer, she glances through our days of gladness; numberer of our years, _{Psalm xc. 12.} she would teach us to apply our hearts to wisdom;—and yet, so little have we regarded her, that this very day, scarcely able to gather from all I can find told of her enough to explain so much as the unfolding of her wings, I can tell you nothing of her life—nothing of her journeying: I cannot learn how she builds, nor how she chooses the place of her wandering, nor how she traces the path of her return. Remaining thus blind and careless to the true ministries of the humble creature whom God has really sent to serve us, we in our pride, thinking ourselves surrounded by the pursuivants of the sky, can yet only invest them with majesty by giving them the calm of the bird's motion, and shade of the bird's plume:—and after all, it is well for us, if, when even for God's best mercies, and in _{Isaiah vi. 3.} His temples marble-built, we think that, 'with angels and archangels, and all the company _{Rev. iv. 8.} of Heaven, we laud and magnify His glorious name'—well for us, if our attempt be not only an insult, and His ears open rather to the inarticulate and unintended **praise, of** 'the Swallow, twittering from her straw-built shed.'—*Love's Meinie*, § 80.

Lessons from the Lips of a Heavenly King.

There is not any organic creature but, in its history and habits, will exemplify or illustrate to us some moral excellence or deficiency, or some point of God's providential government, which it is necessary for us to know. Thus the functions and the fates of animals are distributed to them, with a variety which exhibits to us the dignity and results of almost every passion and kind of conduct: some filthy and slothful, pining and unhappy; some rapacious, restless, and cruel; some ever earnest and laborious, and, I think, unhappy in their endless labour; creatures, like the bee, that heap up riches and cannot tell who shall gather them, [Psalm xxxix. 6.] and others employed, like angels, in endless offices of love and **praise.** Of which, when in right **condition of mind, we esteem those most beautiful, whose functions** are the most noble, whether as some, in mere energy, or as others, in moral honour: so that we look with hate on the foulness of the sloth, and the subtlety of the adder, and the rage of the hyæna; with the honour due to their earthly wisdom we invest the earnest ant and unwearied bee; but we look with full perception of sacred function to the tribes of burning plumage and choral voice. And so what lesson we might receive for our earthly conduct from the creeping and **laborious** things, was taught us by that earthly King who made silver to be in Jerusalem as stones (yet [2 Chron. i. 15.] thereafter was less rich towards God). But from the lips of a heavenly King, who had not where to lay His head, we were taught what lesson we [S. Matt. viii. 20.] have to learn from those higher creatures who sow not, nor reap, nor gather into barns, for [S. Matt. vi. 26.] their Heavenly Father feedeth them.—*Modern Painters*, vol. ii., sec. I., ch. xii., **§ 8.**

Liberty.

Now the fulfilment of all human liberty is in the peaceful inheritance of the earth, with its 'herb yielding seed, and fruit tree yielding fruit' after his kind; the pasture, or arable, land, and the blossoming, or wooded and fruited, land uniting the final elements of life and peace, for body and soul. Therefore, we have the two great Hebrew forms of benediction, 'His eyes shall be red with wine, and his teeth white with milk,' and again, 'Butter and honey shall he eat, that he may know to refuse the evil and choose the good.' And as the work of war and sin has always been the devastation of this blossoming earth, whether by spoil or idleness, so the work of peace and virtue is also that of the first day of Paradise, to 'Dress it and to keep it.' And that will always be the song of perfectly accomplished Liberty.—*Time and Tide*, § 168.

Gen. I. 11.
Gen. xlix. 12.
Isaiah vii. 15.
Gen. ii. 15.

Life.

As the art of life is learned, it will be found at last that all lovely things are also necessary;—the wild flower by the wayside, as well as the tended corn; and the wild birds and creatures of the forest, as well as the tended cattle; because man doth not live by bread only, but also by the desert manna; by every wondrous word and unknowable work of God.—*Unto this Last*, § 82.

Deut. viii. 3.
S. Matt. iv. 4.
S. Luke iv. 4.

Life and Death of the Blossom.

Without entering at all into the history of its fruitage, the life and death of the blossom *itself* is always an eventful romance, which must be completely told, if well. The grouping given to the various states of form between bud and flower is always the most important part of the design of the plant; and in the modes of its death are some of the most touching lessons, or symbolisms, connected with its existence. The utter loss and far-scattered ruin of the cistus and wild rose,—the dishonoured and dark contortion of the convolvulus,—the pale wasting of the crimson heath of Apennine, are strangely opposed by the quiet closing of the brown bells of the ling, each making of themselves a little cross as they die; and so enduring into the days of winter.—*Proserpina*, ch. iv., § 7.

Light of the World.

I speak of the picture by Holman Hunt. . . . The legend beneath it is the beautiful verse,—'Behold, I stand at the door and knock. If any man hear my voice, and open the door, I will come in to him, and will sup with him, and he with me.' [Rev. iii. 20.] On the left-hand side of the picture is seen this door of the human soul. It is fast barred: its bars and nails are rusty; it is knitted and bound to its stanchions by creeping tendrils of ivy, showing that it has never been opened. A bat hovers about it; its threshold is overgrown with brambles, nettles, and fruitless corn,—the wild grass 'whereof the mower filleth not his hand, nor he that bindeth the sheaves his bosom.' [Psalm cxxix. 7.] Christ approaches it in the night time,—Christ, in His everlasting offices, of prophet, priest, and king. He wears the white robe, representing the power of the Spirit upon Him; the jewelled robe and breastplate, representing the sacerdotal investiture; the rayed crown of gold, inwoven [Rev. xxii. 2.] with the crown of thorns; not dead thorns, but now bearing soft leaves, for the healing of the nations.

Now, when Christ enters any human heart, he bears with him a twofold light: first, the light of conscience, which displays past sin, and afterwards the light of peace, the hope of salvation. The lantern, carried in Christ's left hand, is this light of conscience.

Its fire is red and fierce; it falls only on the closed door, on the weeds which encumber it, and on an apple shaken from one of the trees of the orchard, thus marking that the entire awakening of the conscience is not merely to committed, but to hereditary guilt.

The light is suspended by a chain, wrapt about the wrist of the figure, showing that the light which reveals sin appears to the sinner also to chain the hand of Christ. The light which proceeds from the head of the figure, on the contrary, is that of the hope of salvation; it springs from the crown of thorns, and, though itself sad, subdued, and full of softness, is yet so powerful that it entirely melts into the glow of it the forms of the leaves and boughs, which it crosses, showing that every earthly object must be hidden by this light, where its sphere extends.—*Arrows of the Chace*, vol. i., pp. 98-101.

'Lilies of the Field.'

First, in their nobleness: the Lilies gave the lily of the Annunciation; the Asphodels, the flower of the Elysian fields; the Irids, the fleur-de-lys of chivalry; and the Amaryllids, Christ's lily of the field: while the rush, trodden always under foot, became the emblem of humility.—*Queen of the Air*, § 82.

<small>Matt. vi. 28.</small>

Lord's Prayer, The.

'Thy kingdom come.' I believe very few, even of the most earnest, using that petition, realize that it is the Father's—not the Son's—kingdom, that they pray may come,—although the whole prayer is foundational on that fact: '*For* Thine is the kingdom, the power, and the glory.'

And I fancy that the mind of the most faithful Christian is quite led away from its proper hope, by dwelling on the reign—or the coming again—of Christ; which, indeed, they are to look for, and *watch* for, but not to pray for.

Their prayer is to be for the greater kingdom to which He, risen and having all His enemies under His feet, is to surrender *His* 'that God may be All in All.'

And, though the greatest, it is that everlasting kingdom

which the poorest of us can advance. We cannot hasten Christ's coming. 'Of the day and the hour, knoweth none.'

But the kingdom of God is as a grain of mustard-seed:—we can sow of it; it is as a foam-globe of leaven:—we can mingle it; and its glory and its joy are that even the birds of the air can lodge in the branches thereof.—*On the Old Road*, vol. ii., § 233.

Lost Souls.

'Loss of life'! By the ship overwhelmed in the river, shattered on the sea; by the mine's blast, the earthquake's burial— you mourn for the multitude slain. You cheer the lifeboat's crew: you hear, with praise and joy, of the rescue of one still breathing body more at the pit's mouth:—and all the while, for one soul that is saved from the momentary passing away (according to your creed, to be with its God), the lost souls, yet locked in their polluted flesh, haunt, with worse than ghosts, the shadows of your churches, and the corners of your streets; and your weary children watch, with no memory of Jerusalem, [Psalm cxxxvii.] and no hope of return from *their* captivity, the weltering to the sea of your Waters of Babylon.—*Fors Clavigera*, Letter XCI.

Love and Fear.

Two great and principal passions are evidently appointed by the Deity to rule the life of man; namely, the love of God, and the fear of sin, and of its companion—Death. How many motives we have for Love, how much there is in the universe to kindle our admiration and to claim our gratitude. . . . Kindness is indeed everywhere and always visible; but not alone. Wrath and threatening are invariably mingled with the love; and in the utmost solitudes of nature, the existence of Hell seems to me as legibly declared by a thousand spiritual utterances, as that of Heaven. It is well for us to dwell with thankfulness on the unfolding of the flower, and the falling of the dew, and the sleep of the green fields in the sunshine; but the blasted trunk, the barren rock, the moaning of the bleak winds, the roar of the black, perilous, merciless whirlpools of the mountain streams, the solemn solitudes of moors and seas, the continual fading of all beauty into darkness, and of all strength into dust, have these no language for us? We may seek to escape their teaching by reasonings touching the good which is wrought out of all evil; but it is vain sophistry. The good succeeds to the evil as day succeeds the night, but so also the evil to the good. Gerizim and Ebal, birth and death, light and darkness, heaven and hell, divide the existence of man, and his Futurity.—*Stones of Venice*, vol. iii., ch. iii., §§ XLI., XLII.

<small>Deut. xi. 29; xxvii. 12, 13.
Joshua viii. 33.</small>

Love is stronger than Death; and through her, we have, first, Hope of life to come; then, surety of it; living by this surety, (the Just shall live by Faith,) Righteousness, and Strength to the end. Who bears on her scroll, 'The Lord shall break the teeth of the Lions.'—*St. Mark's Rest*, § 130.

<small>Rom. i. 17.
Gal. iii. 11.
Heb. x. 38.</small>

Luxury.

Consider whether, even supposing it guiltless, luxury would be desired by any of us, if we saw clearly at our sides the suffering which accompanies it in the world. Luxury is indeed possible in the future—innocent and exquisite; luxury for all, and by the help of all; but luxury at present can only be enjoyed by the ignorant; the cruelest man living could not sit at his feast, unless he sat blindfold. Raise the veil boldly; face the light; and if, as yet, the light of the eye can only be through tears, and the light of the body through sackcloth, go thou forth weeping, bearing precious seed, until the time come, and the kingdom, when Christ's gift of bread, and bequest of peace, shall be 'Unto this last as unto thee'; and when, for earth's severed

<small>S. Matt. xx. 14.</small>

multitudes of the wicked and the weary, there shall be holier reconciliation than that of the narrow home, and calm economy, where the wicked cease—not from trouble, but from troubling—and the weary are at rest.—*Unto this Last*, § 85. ^{Job iii. 17.}

Madonna, The, in the Church of Sts. Mary and Donato.

Far in the apse, is seen the sad Madonna standing in her folded robe, lifting her hands in vanity of blessing. There is little else to draw away our thoughts from the solitary image. . . . The figure wears a robe of blue, deeply fringed with gold, which seems to be gathered on the head and thrown back on the shoulders, crossing the breast, and falling in many folds to the ground. The under robe, shown beneath it where it opens at the breast, is of the same colour; the whole, except the deep gold fringe, being simply the dress of the women of the time. Round the dome there is a coloured mosaic border; and on the edge of its arch, legible by the whole congregation, this inscription:

'Quos Eva Contrivit, Pia Virgo Maria Redemit;
Hanc Cuncti Laudent, Qui Cristi Munere Gaudent.'[1]

The whole edifice is, therefore, simply a temple to the Virgin: to her is ascribed the fact of Redemption, and to her its praise.

'And is this,' it will be asked of me, 'the time, is this the worship, to which you would have us look back with reverence and regret?' Inasmuch as redemption is ascribed to the Virgin, No. Inasmuch as redemption is a thing desired, believed, rejoiced in, Yes,—and Yes a thousand times. As far as the Virgin is worshipped in place of God, No; but as far as there is the evidence of worship itself, and of the sense of a Divine presence, Yes. For there is a wider division of men than that into Christian and Pagan: before we ask what a man

[1] 'Whom Eve destroyed, the pious Virgin Mary redeemed;
All praise her, who rejoice in the Grace of Christ.'

worships, we have to ask whether he worships at all. Observe Christ's own words on this head: 'God is a spirit; and they that worship Him must worship Him in spirit, and in truth.' The worshipping in spirit comes first, and it does not necessarily imply the worshipping in truth. Therefore, there is first the broad division of men into Spirit worshippers and Flesh worshippers; and then, of the Spirit worshippers, the farther division into Christian and Pagan,—worshippers in Falsehood or in Truth. I therefore, for the moment, omit all inquiry how far the Mariolatry of the early Church did indeed eclipse Christ; or what measure of deeper reverence for the Son of God was still felt through all the grossest forms of Madonna worship. Let that worship be taken at its worst; let the goddess of this dome of Murano be looked upon as just in the same sense an idol as the Athene of the Acropolis, or the Syrian Queen of Heaven; and then, on this darkest assumption, balance well the difference between those who worship and those who worship not;—that difference which there is in the sight of God, in all ages, between the calculating, smiling, self-sustained, self-governed man, and the believing, weeping, wondering, struggling, Heaven-governed man; —between the men who say in their hearts 'There is no God,' and those who acknowledge a God at every step, 'if haply they might feel after Him and find Him.' For that is indeed the difference which we shall find, in the end, between the builders of this day, and the builders on that sand island long ago. They *did* honour something out of themselves; they did believe in spiritual presence judging, animating, redeeming them; they built to its honour and for its habitation; and were content to pass away in nameless multitudes, so only that the labour of their hands might fix in the sea-wilderness a throne for their guardian angel. In this was their strength, and there was indeed a Spirit walking with them on the waters, though they could not discern the form thereof, though the Master's voice came not to them, 'It is I.' What their error cost them, we shall see hereafter; for it remained when the majesty and the sincerity of their worship had departed, and remains to this day. Mariolatry is no special characteristic of the twelfth century; on the outside of that very tribune of San Donato, in its central recess, is an image of the Virgin which receives the reverence once paid to the blue vision upon the inner dome. With rouged cheeks and painted brows, the frightful doll stands in wretchedness of rags, blackened with the smoke of the votive lamps at its feet; and if we would know what has been lost or gained by Italy in the six hundred years that have worn the marbles of Murano, let us consider how far the priests who set up this to worship, the populace who have this to adore, may be nobler than the men who conceived that lonely figure standing on the golden field, or than those to whom it seemed to receive their prayer at evening, far away, where they only saw the blue clouds rising out of the burning sea.—*Stones of Venice*, vol. ii., ch. iii., §§ XXXIX., XL.

S. Mark vi. 48-50.
S. Matt. xiv. 27.

Madonna Worship.

To the common Protestant mind the dignities ascribed to the Madonna have been always a violent offence; they are one of the parts of the Catholic faith which are openest to reasonable dispute, and least comprehensible by the average realistic and materialist temper of the Reformation.

But after the most careful examination, neither as adversary nor as friend, of the influences of Catholicism for good and evil, I am persuaded that the worship of the Madonna has been one of its noblest and most vital graces, and has never been otherwise than productive of true holiness of life and purity of character. I do not enter into any question as to the truth or fallacy of the idea; I no more wish to defend the historical or theological position of the Madonna than that of St. Michael or St. Christopher; but I am certain that to the habit of reverent belief in, and contemplation of, the character ascribed to the heavenly hierarchies, we must ascribe the highest results yet achieved in human nature. . . . There has probably not been an innocent cottage home throughout the length and breadth of Europe during the whole period of vital Christianity, in which the imagined presence of the Madonna has not given sanctity to the humblest duties, and comfort to the sorest trials of the lives of women; and every brightest and loftiest achievement of the arts and strength of manhood has been the fulfilment of the assured prophecy of the poor Israelite maiden, 'He that is mighty hath magnified me, and Holy is His name.'—*Fors Clavigera*, Letter XLI.

<small>S. Luke i. 49.</small>

Magnitude.

In one sense, and that deep, there is no such thing as magnitude. The least thing is as the greatest, and one day as a thousand years, in the eyes of the Maker of great and small things. In another sense, and that close to us and necessary, there exist both magnitude and value. Though not a sparrow falls to the ground unnoted, there are yet creatures who are of more value than many; and the same Spirit which weighs the dust of the earth in a balance, counts the isles as a little thing.—*Modern Painters*, vol. v., pt. viii., ch. iii., § 1.

<small>Psalm xc. 4.
2 S. Peter iii. 8.
S. Matt. x. 29.
S. Luke xii. 6.
Isaiah xl. 15.</small>

Mammon.

'Mammon' is assigned for the direct adversary of the Master whom they are bound to serve. You cannot, by any artifice of reconciliation, be God's soldier, and his. Nor while the desire of gain is within your heart, can any true knowledge of the Kingdom of God come there. No one shall enter its stronghold, —no one receive its blessing, except, 'he that hath clean hands and a pure heart'; clean hands that have done no cruel deed,—pure heart, that knows no base desire. And, therefore, in the highest spiritual sense that can be given to words, be assured, not respecting the literal temple of stone and gold, but of the living temple of your body and soul, that no redemption, nor teaching, nor hallowing, will be anywise possible for it, until these two verses have been, for it also, fulfilled:— [Psalm xxiv. 4.]

'And He went into the temple, and began to cast out them that sold therein, and them that bought. And He taught daily in the temple.' [S. Luke xix. 45, 47.] —*Time and Tide*, § 180.

Manna.

The word 'bdellium' occurs only twice in the Old Testament: here, and in the book of Numbers, where you are told the manna was of the colour or look of bdellium. There, the Septuagint uses for it the word κρύσταλλος, crystal, or more properly anything congealed by cold; and in the other account of the manna, in Exodus, you are told that, after the dew round the camp was gone up, 'there lay a small round thing—as small as the hoar-frost upon the ground.' Until I heard from my friend Mr. Tyrrwhitt of the cold felt at night in camping on Sinai, I could not understand how deep the feeling of the Arab, no less than the Greek, must have been respecting the divine gift of the dew,—nor with what sense of thankfulness for miraculous blessing the question of Job would be uttered, 'The hoary frost of heaven, who hath gendered it?' Then compare the first words of the blessing of Isaac: 'God give thee of the dew of heaven, and of the fatness of earth;' and, again, the first words of the song of Moses: 'Give ear, oh ye [Gen. ii. 12. Numbers xi. 7. Exodus xvi. 14. Job xxxviii. 29. Gen. xxvii. 28. Deut. xxxii. 1, 2] heavens,—for my speech shall distil as the dew'; and you will see at once why this heavenly food was made to shine clear in the desert, like an enduring of its dew;—Divine remaining for continual need. Frozen, as the Alpine snow—pure for ever.—*Deucalion*, ch. vii., § 12.

Meekness.

My time fails me—my thoughts how much more—in trying to imagine what this sweet world will be, when the meek inherit it indeed, and the lowliness of *every* faithful handmaiden has been regarded of her Lord. For the day *will* come, the expectation of the poor shall not perish for ever. Not by might, nor by power, but by His Spirit—the meek shall He guide in judgment, and the meek shall He teach His way.—*Fors Clavigera*, Letter XCIII.

<small>S. Matt. v. 5.</small>
<small>S. Luke i. 48.</small>
<small>Psalm ix. 18.</small>
<small>Psalm xxv. 9.</small>

Ministering.

Having cultivated, in the time of your studentship, your powers truly to the utmost, then, in your manhood, be resolved they shall be spent in the true service of men—not in being ministered unto, but in ministering. Begin with the simplest of all ministries—breaking of bread to the poor. Think first of that, not of your own pride, learning, comfort, prospects in life: nay, not now, once come to manhood, may even the obedience to parents check your own conscience of what is your Master's work. 'Whoso loveth father and mother more than me is not worthy of me.' Take the perfectly simple words of the Judgment, 'Inasmuch as ye did it unto one of the least of these, ye did it unto me:' but you must *do* it, not preach it. And you must not be resolved that it shall be done only in a gentlemanly manner. Your pride must be laid down, as your avarice, and your fear. Whether as fishermen on the sea, ploughmen on the

<small>S. Matt. x. 37.</small>
<small>S. Matt. xxv. 40.</small>

earth, labourers at the forge, or merchants at the shop-counter, you must break and distribute bread to the poor, set down in companies—for that also is literally told you—upon the green grass, not crushed in heaps under the pavement of cities. Take Christ at His literal word, and, so sure as His word is true, He will be known of you in breaking of bread. Refuse that servant's duty because it is plain,—seek either to serve God, or know Him, in any other way: your service will become mockery of Him, and your knowledge darkness. Every day your virtues will be used by the evil spirits to conceal, or to make respectable, national crime; every day your felicities will become baits for the iniquity of others; your heroisms, wrecker's beacons, betraying them to destruction; and before your own deceived eyes and wandering hearts every false meteor of knowledge will flash, and every perishing pleasure glow, to lure you into the gulf of your grave.

S. Mark vi. 39.

But obey the word in its simplicity, in wholeness of purpose and with serenity of sacrifice, . . . and truly you shall receive sevenfold into your bosom in this present life, as in the world to come, life everlasting. All your knowledge will become to you clear and sure, all your footsteps safe; in the present brightness of domestic life you will foretaste the joy of Paradise, and to your children's children bequeath, not only noble fame, but endless virtue. 'He shall give his angels charge over you to keep you in all your ways; and the peace of God, which passeth all understanding, shall keep your hearts and minds through Christ Jesus.'—*On the Old Road*, vol. ii., §§ 296, 297.

Psalm xci. 11.

Phil. iv. 7.

Mirror.

Most men's minds are dim mirrors, in which all truth is seen, as St. Paul tells us, darkly: this is the fault most common and most fatal; dulness of the heart and mistiness of sight, increasing to utter hardness and blindness; Satan breathing upon the glass, so

1 Cor. xiii. 12.

Money.

For money is a **strange kind of seed**; scattered, it is poison; but **set, it is bread**: so that a man whom God has appointed **to be** a sower must bear as lightly as he may the burden of gold and of possessions, till he find the proper places to sow them in.—*Fors Clavigera*, Letter LXII.

Moses, Death of.

For forty years Moses had not been alone. The care and burden of all the people, the weight of their woe, and guilt, and death, had been upon him continually. The multitude had been laid upon him as if he had conceived them; their tears had been his meat, night and day, until he had felt as if God had withdrawn His favour from him, and he had prayed that he might be slain, and not see his wretchedness. _{Num. xi. 12, 15.} And now, at last, the **command** came, 'Get thee up into this mountain.' The weary hands _{Deut. xxxii. 49.} that had been so long stayed up against the enemies of Israel, might lean again upon the _{Exodus xvii. 12.} shepherd's staff, and fold themselves for the shepherd's prayer—for the shepherd's slumber. **Not** strange to his feet, though forty years unknown, the roughness of the bare mountain-path, as he climbed _{Deut. xxxii. 49.} from ledge to ledge of Abarim; not strange to his aged eyes the scattered clusters of the mountain herbage, **and** the broken shadows **of the** cliffs, indented far across the silence **of uninhabited** ravines; scenes such as those among which, with none, as now, beside him but God, he had led his flocks so often; and which he had left, how painfully! taking upon him the appointed power, to make of the fenced city a wilderness, and to fill the desert with songs of deliverance.

It was not to embitter the last hours of his life that God restored to him, for a day, the beloved solitudes he had lost; and breathed the peace of the perpetual hills around him, and cast the world in which he had laboured and sinned far beneath his feet, in that mist of dying blue;—all sin, all wandering, soon to be forgotten for ever; the Dead Sea—a type of God's anger understood by him, of all men, most clearly, who had seen the earth open her mouth, and the sea his depth, to overwhelm the companies of those who contended with his Master—laid waveless beneath him; and beyond it, the fair hills of Judah, and the soft plains and banks of Jordan, purple in the evening light as with the blood of redemption, and fading in their distant fulness into mysteries of promise and of love. There, with his unabated strength, his un- Deut. xxxiv. 7. dimmed glance, lying down upon the utmost rocks, with angels waiting near to contend for the spoils of his spirit, he put off his earthly armour. We do deep reverence to his companion prophet, for 2 Kings ii. 11. whom the chariot of fire came down from heaven; but was his death less noble, whom his Lord Himself buried in the vales of Moab, keeping, in the secrets of the eternal counsels, the knowledge of a sepulchre, from which he was to be called, S. Luke ix. 30, 31. in the fulness of time, to talk with that Lord, upon Hermon, of the death that He should accomplish at Jerusalem?—*Modern Painters*, vol. iv., ch. xx., § 47.

Mountains in the Bible.

Mark the significance of the earliest mention of mountains in the Mosaic books; at least, of those in which some Divine appointment or command is stated respecting them. They are first brought before us as refuges for God's people from the two judgments, of water and fire. The ark *rests* upon 'the moun- Gen. viii. 4. tains of Ararat;' and man, having passed through that great baptism unto death, kneels upon the earth first where it is nearest heaven, and mingles with the mountain clouds the smoke of his sacrifice of thanksgiving. Again: from the midst of the first judgment by fire, the command of the Deity to His servant is, 'Escape to the mountain'; and the morbid fear of the hills, which fills any human mind after long stay in places of luxury and sin, is strangely marked in Lot's complaining reply: 'I cannot escape to the mountain, lest some evil take me.' The third mention, in way of ordinance, is a far more solemn one: 'Abraham lifted up his eyes, and saw the place afar off.' 'The Place,' the Mountain of Myrrh, or of bitterness, chosen to fulfil to all the seed of Abraham, far off and near, the inner meaning of promise regarded in that vow: 'I will lift up mine eyes unto the hills, from whence cometh mine help.'

<small>Gen. xix. 17.</small>

<small>Gen. xix. 19.</small>

<small>Gen. xxii. 4.</small>

<small>Psalm cxxi. 1.</small>

And the fourth is the delivery of the law on Sinai. It seemed, then, to the monks, that the mountains were appointed by their Maker to be to man, refuges from Judgment, signs of Redemption, and altars of Sanctification and Obedience; and they saw them afterwards connected, in the manner the most touching and gracious, with the death, after his task had been accomplished, of the first anointed Priest; the death, in like manner, of the first inspired Lawgiver; and, lastly, with the assumption of his office by the Eternal Priest, Lawgiver, and Saviour. . . .

<small>Exodus xxxi. 18.</small>

If, in their remembrance of these things, and in their endeavour to follow in the footsteps of their Master, religious men of bygone days, closing themselves in the hill solitudes, forgot sometimes, and sometimes feared, the duties they owed to the active world, we may perhaps pardon them more easily than we ought to pardon ourselves, if we neither seek any influence for good nor submit to it unsought, in scenes to which thus all the men whose writings we receive as inspired, together with their Lord, retired whenever they had any task or trial laid upon them needing more than their usual strength of spirit. Nor, perhaps, should we have unprofitably entered into the mind of the earlier ages, if among our other thoughts, as we watch the chains of the snowy mountains rise on the horizon, we should sometimes admit the memory of the hour in which their Creator, among their solitudes, entered on His travail for the salvation of our race; and indulge the dream, that as the flaming and trembling mountains of the earth seem to be the monuments of the manifesting of His terror on Sinai,—these pure and white hills, near to the heaven, and sources of all good to the earth, are the appointed memorials of that Light of His Mercy, that fell, snow-like, on the Mount of Transfiguration.—*Modern Painters*, vol. iv., ch. xx., §§ 45, 49

S. Matt. xvii. 1, 2.

Music and Dancing.

The going forth of the women of Israel after Miriam with timbrels and with dances, was, as you doubtless remember, their expression of passionate triumph and thankfulness, after the full accomplishment of their deliverance from the Egyptians. That deliverance had been by the utter death of their enemies, and accompanied by stupendous miracle; no human creatures could in an hour of triumph be surrounded by circumstances more solemn. I am not going to try to excite your feelings about them. Consider only for yourself what that seeing of the Egyptians 'dead upon the sea-shore' meant to every soul that saw it. And then reflect that these intense emotions of mingled horror, triumph, and gratitude were expressed, in the visible presence of the Deity, by music and dancing. If you answer that you do not believe the Egyptians so perished, or that God ever appeared in a pillar of cloud, I reply, Be it so—believe or disbelieve, as you choose;—This is yet assuredly the fact, that the author of the poem or fable

Exodus xv. 20.

Exodus xiv. 30, 31.

Exodus xiii. 21.

of the Exodus supposed that, under such circumstances of Divine interposition as he had invented, the triumph of the Israelitish women would have been, and ought to have been, under the direction of a prophetess, expressed by music and dancing. Nor was it possible that he should think otherwise, at whatever period he wrote; both music and dancing being, among all great ancient nations, an appointed and very principal part of the worship of the gods. . . .

Returning to the Jewish history, you find soon afterwards this enthusiastic religious dance and song employed, in their more common and habitual manner, in the idolatries under Sinai; but beautifully again and tenderly, after the triumph of Jephthah, 'And behold his daughter came out to meet him with timbrels and with dances.' Again, still more notably, at the triumph of David with Saul, 'the women came out of all the cities of Israel, singing and dancing to meet King Saul with tabrets, with joy, and with instruments of music.' And you have this joyful song and dance of the virgins of Israel not only incidentally alluded to in the most solemn passages of Hebrew religious poetry (as in Psalm lxviii. 24, 25, and Psalm cxlix. 2, 3), but approved, and the restoration of it promised as a sign of God's perfect blessing, most earnestly by the saddest of the Hebrew prophets, and in one of the most beautiful of all his sayings.

<small>Exodus xxxii. 18, 19.</small>

<small>Judges xi. 34.</small>

<small>1 Sam. xviii. 6.</small>

'The Lord hath appeared of old unto me, saying, "Yea, I have loved thee with an everlasting love. Therefore, with loving-kindness have I drawn thee.— I will build thee, and thou shalt be built, O Virgin of Israel; thou shalt again be adorned with thy tabrets, and thou shalt go forth in dances with them that make merry"' (Jer. xxxi. 3, 4; and compare v. 13).

And finally, you have in two of quite the most important passages in the whole series of Scripture (one

in the Old Testament, one in the New), the rejoicing in
the repentance from, and remission of, sins, 2 Sam.
expressed by means of music and dancing, vi. 14.
namely, in the rapturous dancing of David S. Luke
before the returning ark; and in the joy of the xv. 25.
father's household at the repentance of the prodigal
son.—*Time and Tide*, §§ 41, 42, 43.

Mystery.

We need not wonder, **that mist and all its** phenomena
have been made delightful **to us,** since our happiness
as thinking beings must depend on our being content
to accept only partial knowledge, even in those matters
which chiefly concern us. If we insist upon perfect
intelligibility and complete declaration in every moral
subject, we shall instantly fall into misery of unbelief.
Our whole happiness and power of energetic action
depend upon our being able to breathe and live in
the cloud; content to see it opening here **and closing**
there; rejoicing to catch, through the thinnest **films**
of it, glimpses of stable and substantial things; but
yet perceiving **a nobleness** even in the concealment,
and rejoicing that the **kindly veil is** spread where the
untempered light might have scorched us, or the infinite
clearness wearied.

And I believe that the resentment of this interference
of the mist is one of the forms of proud error which
are too easily mistaken **for** virtues. To be content in
utter darkness and ignorance is indeed unmanly, and
therefore we think that to love light and seek knowledge must always be right. Yet (as in all matters
before observed), wherever *pride* has any share in the
work, even knowledge and light may be ill pursued.
Knowledge is good, and light is good, yet man perished
in seeking knowledge, and moths perish in seeking
light; and if we, who are crushed before the moth, will
not accept such mystery as is needful for us, we shall
perish in like manner. But accepted in humbleness,

it instantly becomes an element of pleasure; and I think that every rightly constituted mind ought to rejoice, not so much in knowing anything clearly, as in feeling that there is infinitely more which it cannot know. None but proud or weak men would mourn over this, for we may always know more if we choose, by working on; but the pleasure is, I think, to humble people, in knowing that the journey is endless, the treasure inexhaustible,—watching the cloud still march before them with its summitless pillar, and being sure that, to the end of time and to the length of eternity, the mysteries of its infinity will still open farther and farther, their dimness being the sign and necessary adjunct of their inexhaustibleness. I know there are an evil mystery and a deathful dimness,—the mystery of the great Babylon—the dimness of the sealed eye and soul; but do not let us confuse these with the glorious mystery of the things which the angels 'desire to look into,' or with the dimness which, even before the clear eye and open soul, still rests on sealed pages of the eternal volume.—*Modern Painters*, vol. iv., ch. v., §§ 3, 4.

[Rev. xvii. 5.]

[1 S. Peter i. 12.]

Mystery of Loss.

There is no subject of thought more melancholy, more wonderful, than the way in which God permits so often His best gifts to be trodden under foot of men, His richest treasures to be wasted by the moth, and the mightiest influences of His Spirit, given but once in the world's history, to be quenched and shortened by miseries of chance and guilt. I do not wonder at what men Suffer, but I wonder often at what they Lose. We may see how good rises out of pain and evil; but the dead, naked, eyeless loss, what good comes of that? The fruit struck to the earth before its ripeness; the glowing life and goodly purpose dissolved away in sudden death; the words, half spoken, choked upon the lips with clay for ever; or, stranger than all, the whole majesty of humanity raised to its fulness, and every gift and power necessary for a given purpose, at a given moment, centred in one man, and all this perfected blessing permitted to be refused, perverted, crushed, cast aside by those who need it most,—the city which is Not set on a hill, the candle that giveth light to None that are in the house;—these are the heaviest mysteries of this strange world, and, it seems to me, those which mark its curse the most.—*Stones of Venice*, vol. ii., ch. v., § XXXVI. [S. Matt. v. 14, 15.]

'Nations of the Earth.'

The power of every great people, as of every living tree, depends on its not effacing, but confirming and concluding, the labours of its ancestors. Looking back to the history of nations, we may date the beginning of their decline from the moment when they ceased to be reverent in heart, and accumulative in hand and brain; from the moment when the redundant fruit of age hid in them the hollowness of heart, whence the simplicities of custom and sinews of tradition had withered away. Had men but guarded the righteous laws, and protected the precious works of their fathers, with half the industry they have given to change and to ravage, they would not now have been seeking vainly, in millennial visions and mechanic servitudes, the accomplishment of the promise made to them so long ago: 'As the days of a tree are the days of My people, and Mine elect shall long enjoy the work of their hands; they shall not labour in vain, nor bring forth for trouble; for they are the seed of the blessed of the Lord, and their offspring with them.'— [Isaiah lxv. 22, 23.] *Modern Painters*, vol. v., Pt. vi., ch. viii., § 19.

Nebuchadnezzar Curse.

This Nebuchadnezzar curse, that sends men to grass like oxen, seems to follow but too closely on the excess or continuance of national power and peace. In the perplexities of nations, in their struggles for existence, in their infancy, their impotence, or even their disorganization, they have higher hopes and nobler passions. Out of the suffering comes the serious mind; out of the salvation, the grateful heart; out of endurance, fortitude; out of deliverance, faith: but when they have learned to live under providence of laws and with decency and justice of regard for each other, and when they have done away with violent and external sources of suffering, worse evils seem to arise out of their rest; evils that vex less and mortify more, that suck the blood though they do not shed it, and ossify the heart though they do not torture it. And deep though the causes of thankfulness must be to every people at peace with others and at unity in itself, there are causes of fear, also, a fear greater than of sword and sedition: that dependence on God may be forgotten, because the bread is given and the water sure; that gratitude to Him may cease, because His constancy of protection has taken the semblance of a natural law; that heavenly hope may grow faint amidst the full fruition of the world; that selfishness may take place of undemanded devotion, compassion be lost in vainglory, and love in dissimulation; that enervation may succeed to strength, apathy to patience, and the noise of jesting words and foulness of dark thoughts, to the earnest purity of the girded loins and the burning lamp.—*Modern Painters*, vol. ii., sec. i., ch. i., § 6.

Daniel iv. 25.

Rom. xii. 9.

S. Luke xii. 35.

Neglect.

You ought to be glad in thinking how much more beauty God has made, than human eyes can ever see;

but not glad in thinking how much more evil man has made, than his own soul can ever conceive,—much more, than his hands can ever heal. . . . The same law holds in our neglect of multiplied pain, as in our neglect of multiplied beauty.—*Ethics of the Dust*, p. 72.

Nobleness.

The finer the nature, the more flaws it will show through the clearness of it; and it is a law of this universe, that the best things shall be seldomest seen in their best form. The wild grass grows well and strongly, one year with another; but the wheat is, according to the greater nobleness of its nature, liable to the bitterer blight.—*Stones of Venice*, vol. ii., ch. vi., § xi.

Obedience.

One thing I solemnly desire to see all children taught —obedience; and one to all persons entering into life— the power of unselfish admiration. . . .

In what courtesy or in what affection are we even now carefully training ourselves;—above all, in what form of duty or reverence to those to whom we owe all our power of understanding even what duty or reverence means? I warned you . . . against the base curiosity of seeking for the origin of life in the dust; in earth instead of heaven: how much more must I warn you against forgetting the true origin of the life that is in your own souls, of that good which you have heard with your ears, and your fathers have told you. You buy the picture of the Virgin as furniture for your rooms; but you despise the religion, and you reject the memory, of those who have taught you to love the aspect of whatsoever things and creatures are good and pure: and too many of you, entering into life, are ready to think, to feel, to act, as the men bid you who are incapable of worship, as they are of creation;— [Psalm xliv. 1.]

whose power is only in destruction: whose gladness only in disdain; whose glorying is in their shame. You know well, I should think, by this time, that I am not one to seek to conceal from you any truth of nature, or superstitiously decorate for you any form of faith; but I trust deeply—(and I will strive, for my poor part, wholly, so to help you in steadfastness of heart)—that you, the children of the Christian chivalry which was led in England by the Lion-Heart, and in France by Roland, and in Spain by the Cid, may not stoop to become as these, whose thoughts are but to invent new foulness with which to blaspheme the story of Christ, and to destroy the noble works and laws that have been founded in His name.

Will you not rather go round about this England and tell the towers thereof, and mark well her bulwarks, and consider her palaces, that you may tell it to the generation following? Will you not rather honour with all your strength, with all your obedience, with all your holy love and never-ending worship, the princely sires, and pure maids, and nursing mothers, who have bequeathed and blest your life?—that so, for you also, and for your children, the days of strength, and the light of memory, may be long in this lovely land which the Lord your God has given you.—*The Eagle's Nest*, §§ 239-40.

[margin: Psalm xlviii. 12, 13.]

[margin: Exodus xx. 12.]

The first duty of a child is to obey its father and mother; as the first duty of a citizen is to obey the laws of his state. And this duty is so strict that I believe the only limits to it are those fixed by Isaac and Iphigenia. On the other hand, the father and mother have also a fixed duty to the child—not to provoke it to wrath. I have never heard this text explained to fathers and mothers from the pulpit, which is curious. For it appears to me that God will expect the parents to understand their duty to their children, better even than children can be expected to know their

[margin: Ephes. vi. 4.]

duty to their parents. But farther. A *child's* duty is to obey its parents. It is never said anywhere in the Bible, and never was yet said in any good or wise book, that a man's, or woman's is. *When*, precisely, a child becomes a man or a woman, it can no more be said, than when it should first stand on its legs. But a time assuredly comes when it should. In great states, children are always trying to remain children, and the parents wanting to make men and women of them. In vile states, the children are always wanting to be men and women, and the parents to keep them children. . . .

No point of duty has been more miserably warped and perverted by false priests, in all churches, than this duty of the young to choose whom they will serve. But the duty itself does not the less exist; and if there be any truth in Christianity at all, there will come, for all true disciples, a time when they have to take that saying to heart, 'He that loveth father or mother more than me, is not worthy of me.' S. Matt. x. 37.

'*Loveth*'—observe. There is no talk of disobeying fathers or mothers whom you do *not* love, or of running away from a home where you would rather not stay. But to leave the home which is your peace, and to be at enmity with those who are most dear to you,—this, if there be meaning in Christ's words, one day or other will be demanded of His true followers.

And there *is* meaning in Christ's words. Whatever misuse may have been made of them,—whatever false prophets—and Heaven knows there have been many—have called the young children to them, not to bless, but to curse, the assured fact remains, that if you will obey God, there will come a moment when the voice of man will be raised, with all its holiest natural authority, against you. The friend and the wise adviser—the brother and the sister—the father and the master—the entire voice of your prudent and keen-sighted acquaintance—the entire weight of the scornful stupidity of the vulgar world—for *once*, they will be against you, all at one. You have to obey God rather than man. The human race, with all its wisdom and love, all its indignation and folly, on one side,—God alone on the other. You have to choose.—*Mornings in Florence*, §§ 48–50.

Offices of the Clergy.

What should be the offices of the Clergy? That is to say, What are the possible spiritual necessities which at any time may arise in the Church, and by what means and men are they to be supplied?—evidently an infinite question. Different kinds of necessities must be met by different authorities, constituted as the necessities arise. Robinson Crusoe, in his island, wants no Bishop, and makes a thunderstorm do for an Evangelist. The University of Oxford would be ill off without its Bishop; but wants an Evangelist besides; and that forthwith. The authority which the Vaudois shepherds need is of Barnabas, the Son of Consolation; the authority which the city of London needs is of James, the Son of Thunder. Let us then alter the form of our question, and put it to the Bible thus: What are the necessities most likely to arise in the Church? and may they be best met by different men, or in great part by the same men acting in different capacities? and are the names attached to their offices of any consequence? Ah, the Bible answers now, and that loudly. The Church is built on the Foundation of the Apostles and Prophets, Jesus Christ Himself being the corner-stone. Well; we cannot have two foundations, so we can have no more Apostles nor Prophets:— then, as for the other needs of the Church in its edifying upon this foundation, there are all manner of things to be done daily;—rebukes to be given; comfort to be brought; Scripture to be explained;

[margin: Acts iv. 36.]
[margin: S. Mark iii. 17.]
[margin: Eph. ii. 20.]

warning to be enforced; threatenings to be executed; charities to be administered; and the men who do these things are called, and call themselves, with absolute indifference, Deacons, Bishops, Elders, Evangelists, according to what they are doing at the time of speaking. St. Paul almost always calls himself a deacon, St. Peter calls himself an elder, 1 Peter v. 1; and Timothy, generally understood to be addressed as a bishop, is called a deacon in 1 Tim. iv. 6—forbidden to rebuke an elder, in v. 1, and exhorted to do the work of an evangelist, in 2 Tim. iv. 5. But there is one thing which, as officers, or as separate from the rest of the flock, they *never* call themselves,—which it would have been impossible, as so separate, they ever *should* have called themselves; that is—*Priests*.

It would have been just as possible for the Clergy of the early Church to call themselves Levites, as to call themselves (ex-officio) Priests. The whole function of Priesthood was, on Christmas morning, at once and for ever gathered into His Person who was born at Bethlehem; and thenceforward, all who are united with Him, and who with Him make sacrifice of themselves; that is to say, all members of the Invisible Church become, at the instant of their conversion, Priests; and are so called in 1 Peter ii. 5 and Rev. i. 6 and xx. 6, where, observe, there is no possibility of limiting the expression to the Clergy; the conditions of Priesthood being simply having been loved by Christ, and washed in His blood.—*On the Old Road*, vol. ii., §§ 195-6.

Olive-tree.

What the elm and oak are to England, the olive is to Italy. . . . Its classical associations double its importance in Greece; and in the Holy Land the remembrances connected with it are of course more touching than can ever belong to any other tree of the field. . . . I do not want painters to tell me any scientific facts about olive-trees. But it had been well for them to have felt and seen the olive-tree; to have loved it for Christ's sake, partly also for the helmed Wisdom's sake which was to the heathen in some sort as that nobler Wisdom which stood at God's right hand, when He founded the earth and established the heavens. To have loved it, even to the hoary dimness of its delicate foliage, subdued and faint of hue, as if the ashes of the Gethsemane agony had been cast upon it for ever; and to have traced, line by line, the gnarled writhing of its intricate branches, and the pointed fretwork of its light and narrow leaves, inlaid on the blue field of the sky, and the small rosy-white stars of its spring blossoming, and the beads of sable fruit scattered by autumn along its topmost boughs—the right, in Israel, of the stranger, the fatherless, and the widow,—and, more than all, the softness of the mantle, silver grey, and tender like the down on a bird's breast, with which, far away, it veils the undulation of the mountains.—*Stones of Venice*, vol. iii., ch. iv., §§ XI., XII.

<small>S. Luke xxii. 39. 44.
Matt. xxvi. 36.</small>

Oppression of the Poor.

You cannot but have noticed how often in those parts of the Bible which are likely to be oftenest opened when people look for guidance, comfort, or help in the affairs of daily life,—namely, the Psalms and Proverbs, —mention is made of the guilt attaching to the *Oppression* of the poor. Observe: not the neglect of them, but the *Oppression* of them: the word is as frequent as it is strange. You can hardly open either of those books, but somewhere in their pages you will find a description of the wicked man's attempts against the poor: such as,—'He doth ravish the poor when he getteth him into his net.'

<small>Psalm x. 10.</small>

'He sitteth in the lurking places of the villages; his eyes are privily set against the poor.'

<small>Psalm x. 8.</small>

'In his pride he doth persecute the poor, and blesseth the covetous, whom God abhorreth.' *Psalm x. 2.*

'His mouth is full of deceit and fraud; in the secret places doth he murder the innocent. Have the workers of iniquity no knowledge, who eat up my people as they eat bread? They have drawn out the sword, and bent the bow, to cast down the poor and needy.' *Psalm x. 7, 8. Psalm xiv. 4. Psalm xxxvii. 14.*

'They are corrupt, and speak wickedly concerning oppression.' *Psalm lxxiii. 8.*

'Pride compasseth them about as a chain, and violence as a garment.' *Psalm lxxiii. 6.*

'Their poison is like the poison of a serpent. Ye weigh the violence of your hands in the earth.' *Psalm lviii. 4. Psalm lviii. 2.*

Yes: 'Ye weigh the violence of your hands':—weigh these words as well. The last things we ever usually think of weighing are Bible words. We like to dream and dispute over them; but to weigh them, and see what their true contents are—anything but that. Yet, weigh these; for I have purposely taken all these verses, perhaps more striking to you read in this connection than separately in their places, out of the Psalms, because, for all people belonging to the Established Church of this country, these Psalms are appointed lessons, portioned out to them by their clergy to be read once through every month. Presumably, therefore, whatever portions of Scripture we may pass by or forget, these, at all events, must be brought continually to our observance as useful for direction of daily life. Now, do we ever ask ourselves what the real meaning of these passages may be, and who these wicked people are, who are 'murdering the innocent'? You know it is rather singular language, this!—rather strong language, we might, perhaps, call it—hearing it for the first time. Murder! and murder of innocent people!—nay, even a sort of cannibalism. Eating people,—yes, and God's people, too—eating *My* people as if they *Psalm x. 8.*

were bread! swords drawn, bows bent, poison of serpents mixed! violence of hands weighed, measured, and trafficked with as so much coin!—where is all this going on? Do you suppose it was only going on in the time of David, and that nobody but Jews ever murder the poor? If so, it would surely be wiser not to mutter and mumble for our daily lessons what does not concern us; but if there be any chance that it may concern us, and if this description, in the Psalms, of human guilt is at all generally applicable, as the descriptions in the Psalms of human sorrow are, may it not be advisable to know wherein this guilt is being committed round about us, or by ourselves? and when we take the words of the Bible into our mouths in a congregational way, to be sure whether we mean merely to chant a piece of melodious poetry relating to other people—(we know not exactly to whom)—or to assert our belief in facts bearing somewhat stringently on ourselves and our daily business. And if you make up your minds to do this no longer, and take pains to examine into the matter, you will find that these strange words, occurring as they do, not in a few places only, but almost in every alternate psalm and every alternate chapter of proverb or prophecy, with tremendous reiteration, were not written for one nation or one time only, but for all nations and languages, for all places and all centuries; and it is as true of the wicked man now as ever it was of Nabal or Dives, that 'his eyes are set against the poor.'—*The Two Paths*, §§ 179, 180.

<small>Psalm xiv. 4.</small>

<small>1 Sam. xxv. 3.</small>

<small>S. Luke xvi. 19.</small>

<small>Psalm x. 8.</small>

'Our Father's Business.'

God is a kind Father. He sets us all in the places where He wishes us to be employed; and that employment is truly 'our Father's business.' He chooses work for every creature which will be delightful to them, if they do it simply and humbly. He gives us always strength enough, and sense enough,

<small>S. Luke ii. 49.</small>

for what He wants us to do; if we either tire ourselves or puzzle ourselves, it is our own fault. And we may always be sure, whatever we are doing, that we cannot be pleasing Him, if we are not happy ourselves.—*Ethics of the Dust*, pp. 125-6.

Parables.

Why prayer should be taught by the story of the unjust judge; use of present opportunity by that of the unjust steward; and use of the gifts of God by that of the hard man who reaped where he had not sown,—there is no human creature wise enough to know;—but there are the traps set; and every slack judge, cheating servant, and gnawing usurer may, if he will, approve himself in these.

'Thou knewest that I was a hard man.' Yes—and if God were also a hard God, and reaped where He had not sown—the conclusion would be true that earthly usury was right. But which of God's gifts to us are *not* His own? S. Matt. xxv. 26.
S. Luke xix. 22.

The meaning of the parable, heard with ears unbesotted, is this:—'*You*, among hard and unjust men, yet suffer their claim to the return of what they never gave; you suffer *them* to reap, where they have not strawed.—But to me, the Just Lord of your life—whose is the breath in your nostrils, whose the fire in your blood, who gave you light and thought, Gen. ii. 7. and the fruit of earth and the dew of heaven,—to me, of all this gift, will you return no fruit but only the dust of your bodies, and the wreck of your souls?'

Nevertheless, the Parables have still their living use, as well as their danger; but the Psalter has become practically dead; and the form of repeating it in the daily service only deadens the phrases of it by familiarity. —*Fors Clavigera*, Letter LIII.

Peace.

Who *giveth* peace? Many a peace we have made and named for ourselves, but the falsest is in that marvellous thought that we, of all generations of the earth, only know the right; and that to us at last,—to us alone,—all the scheme of God, about the salvation of men, has been shown. 'This is the light in which *we* are walking. **Those vain Greeks are gone down to their Persephone for ever** — Egypt and **Assyria,** Elam and her multitude,—uncircumcised, their graves are round about them—Pathros and careless Ethiopia—filled with the slain. Rome, with her thirsty sword, and poison wine, how did she walk in her darkness! **We** only have no idolatries—ours are the seeing eyes; **in our pure hands at last, the seven-sealed book is laid;** to our true tongues entrusted **the** preaching of a perfect gospel. Who shall come after us? **Is it not Peace?**

<small>2 Kings ix. 31.</small> The poor Jew, **Zimri, who slew** his master, there is no peace **for him**: but, for us? **tiara on head, may we not look out of the windows of heaven?**' Another kind of peace I look for than this.—*Modern Painters*, vol. v., Pt. ix., ch. xii., § 17.

Imagine the peace of heart which follows the casting out of the element of selfishness as the root of action; but it is peace, observe, only, **that is** promised to you, not at all necessarily, or at least primarily, *joy.*

<small>S. Matt. xi. 29.</small> You shall find rest unto your souls when first you take on you the yoke of Christ; but joy

<small>S. Matt. xxv. 21.</small> only when you have borne **it** as long **as He** wills, and are called to enter into **the joy of your** Lord. —*Fors Clavigera,* Letter LXXIX.

Peace and War.

Both peace and **war are noble** or ignoble according to their kind and occasion. No man has a profounder sense of the horror and guilt of ignoble war than I have: I have personally seen its effects, upon nations, of unmitigated **evil,** on soul and body, with perhaps as much pity, and **as much** bitterness of indignation, as any of those whom you will hear continually declaiming in the cause of peace. But peace may be sought in two ways. One way is as Gideon sought it, when he built his altar in Ophrah, naming it, 'God send peace,' yet sought this peace that he loved, as he was ordered to seek it, and the peace was sent, in God's way :—' the country was in quietness forty years in the days of Gideon.' And the other way of seeking peace is as Menahem sought it, when he gave the King of Assyria a thousand talents of silver, that 'his hand might be with him.' That is, you may either win your peace, or buy it :— win it, by resistance to evil; buy it, by compromise with evil. You may buy your peace, with silenced consciences ;—you may buy it, with broken vows,—buy it, with lying words,—buy it, with base connivances, —buy it, with the blood of the slain, and the cry of the captive, and the silence of lost souls—over hemispheres of the earth, while you sit smiling at your serene hearths, lisping comfortable prayers evening and morning, and counting your pretty Protestant beads (which are flat, and of gold, instead of round, and of ebony, as the monks' ones were), and so mutter continually to yourselves, 'Peace, Peace,' when there is No peace ; but only captivity and death, for you, as well as for those you leave unsaved ;—and yours darker than theirs.

Judges vi. 22, 23, 24.

Judges viii. 28.

2 Kings xv. 19.

Jer. viii. 11 ; vi. 14.

I cannot utter to you what I would in this matter ; we all see too dimly, as yet, what our great world duties are, to allow any of us to try to outline their enlarging shadows. . . . Reflect that their peace was not won for you by your own hands; but by theirs who long ago jeoparded their lives for you, their children ; and remember that neither this inherited peace, nor any other, can be kept, but through the same jeopardy. No peace was ever won from Fate by subterfuge or agreement ; no peace is ever in store for any of us, but that which we shall win by victory over shame or sin ;—victory over the sin that oppresses, as well as over that which corrupts. For many a year to come, the sword of every righteous nation must be whetted to save or to subdue; nor will it be by patience of other's suffering, but by the offering of your own, that you will ever draw nearer to the time when the great change shall pass upon the iron of the earth;— when men shall beat their swords into plough-shares, and their spears into pruning-hooks; neither shall they learn war any more. — *The Two Paths*, §§ 195–6.

<small>Isaiah ii. 4.</small>

Perfume.

The fact is, that of scents artificially prepared the extreme desire is intemperance; but of natural and God-given scents, which take their part in the harmony and pleasantness of creation, there can hardly be intemperance: not that there is any absolute difference between the two kinds, but that these are likely to be received with gratitude and joyfulness rather than those; so that we despise the seeking of essences and unguents, but not the sowing of violets along our garden banks. But all things may be elevated by affection, as the spikenard of Mary, and in the Song of Solomon the myrrh upon the handles of the lock, and the sense of Isaac of the field-fragrance upon his son. And the general law for all these pleasures is, that, when sought in the abstract and ardently, they are foul things; but when received with thankfulness and with reference to God's glory, they become Theoretic: and so we may find something divine in the sweetness of wild fruits, as well as in the pleasantness of the pure air, and the tenderness of its natural perfumes that come and go as they list.—*Modern Painters*, vol. ii., sec. i., ch. ii., § 7.

<small>S. Mark xiv. 3.
S. Luke vii. 37.
S. John xii. 3.
Cant. v. 5.
Gen. xxvii. 27.</small>

Physical Science.

Much as I reverence physical science as a means of mental education, I reverence it, at this moment, more

as the source of utmost human practical power, and the
means by which the far-distant races of the Psalm
world, who now sit in darkness and the shadow cvii. 10.
of death, are to be reached and regenerated. At home,
or far away, the call is equally instant:—here, for want
of more extended physical science, there is plague in our
streets, famine in our fields; the pest strikes root and
fruit over a hemisphere of the earth, we know not why;
the voices of our children fade away into silence of
venomous death, we know not why; the population of
this most civilised country resists every effort to lead it
into purity of habit and habitation,—to give it genuine-
ness of nourishment and wholesomeness of air,—as a
new interference with its liberty, and insists vociferously
on its right to helpless death. All this is terrible; but
it is more terrible yet that dim, phosphorescent, frightful
superstitions still hold their own over two-thirds of the
inhabited globe, and that all the phenomena of nature
which were intended by their Creator to enforce His
eternal laws of love and judgment, and which, rightly
understood, enforce them more strongly by their patient
beneficence and their salutary destructiveness, Judges
that the miraculous dew on Gideon's fleece, vi. 37, 38.
or the restrained lightnings of Horeb—that all these
legends of God's daily dealing with His creatures remain unread. . . .

How strange it seems that physical science should
ever have been thought adverse to religion! The pride
of physical science is, indeed, adverse, like every other
pride, both to religion and truth; but sincerity Isaiah
of science, so far from being hostile, is the path- lii. 7.
maker among the mountains for the feet of those who
publish peace.—*Arrows of the Chace*, vol. i., pp. 193-5.

Pity.

When any of you next go abroad, observe, and consider the meaning of, the sculptures and paintings, which
of every rank in art, and in every chapel and cathedral,

and by every mountain path, recall the hours, and represent the agonies, of the Passion of Christ: and try to form some estimate of the efforts that have been made by the four arts of eloquence, music, painting, and sculpture, since the twelfth century, to wring out of the hearts of women the last drops of pity that could be excited for this merely physical agony: for the art nearly always dwells on the physical wounds or exhaustion chiefly, and degrades, far more than it animates, the conception of pain.

Then try to conceive the quantity of time, and of excited and thrilling emotion, which have been wasted by the tender and delicate women of Christendom during these last six hundred years, in thus picturing to themselves, under the influence of such imagery, the bodily pain, long since passed, of One Person:—which, so far as they indeed conceived it to be sustained by a Divine Nature, could not for that reason have been less endurable than the agonies of any simple human death by torture: and then try to estimate what might have been the better result, for the righteousness and felicity of mankind, if these same women had been taught the deep meaning of the last words that were ever spoken by their Master to those who had ministered to Him of their substance: 'Daughters of Jerusalem, weep not for me, but weep for yourselves, and for your children.' If they had but been taught to measure with their pitiful thoughts the tortures of battle-fields— the slowly consuming plagues of death in the starving children, and wasted age, of the innumerable desolate those battles left;—nay, in our own life of peace, the agony of unnurtured, untaught, unhelped creatures, awaking at the grave's edge to know how they should have lived; and the worse pain of those whose existence, not the ceasing of it, is death; those to whom the cradle was a curse, and for whom the words they cannot hear, 'ashes to ashes,' are all that they have ever received of benediction. These,—you who would fain have wept

S. Luke xxiii. 28.

at His feet, or stood by His cross,—these you have always with you! Him, you have not always. —*Lectures on Art*, § 57. S. John xii. 8.

Poor, The.

The command to all of us is strict and straight, 'When thou seest the naked, that thou cover him, and that thou bring the poor that are cast out to *thy house.*' Not to the workhouse, observe, but to *thy* house: and I say it would be better a thousand-fold, that our doors should be beset by the poor day by day, than that it should be written of any one of us, ' They reap every one his corn in the field, and they gather the vintage of the wicked. They cause the naked to lodge without shelter, that they have no covering in the cold. They are wet with the showers of the mountains, and embrace the rock, for want of a shelter.'—*Lectures on Architecture and Painting*, § 25. Isaiah lviii. 7. Job xxiv. 6–8.

Poor of the Earth, The.

The poor we must have with us always, and sorrow is inseparable from any hour of life; but we may make their poverty such as shall inherit the earth, and the sorrow such as shall be hallowed by the hand of the Comforter with everlasting comfort. We *can*, if we will but shake off this lethargy and dreaming that is upon us, and take the pains to think and act like men, we can, I say, make kingdoms to be like well-governed households, in which, indeed, while no care or kindness can prevent occasional heart-burnings, nor any foresight or piety anticipate all the vicissitudes of fortune, or avert every stroke of calamity, yet the unity of their affection and fellowship remains unbroken, and their distress is neither embittered by division, prolonged by imprudence, nor darkened by dishonour. . . .

Now the cry for the education of the lower classes, which is heard every day more widely and loudly, is a wise and sacred cry, provided it be extended into one for the education of *all* classes, with definite respect to the work each man has to do, and the substance of which he is made. But it is a foolish and vain cry, if it be understood, as in the plurality of cases it is meant to be, for the expression of mere craving after knowledge, irrespective of the simple purposes of the life that now is, and blessings of that which is to come.

One great fallacy into which men are apt to fall when they are reasoning on this subject is: that light, as such, is always good; and darkness, as such, always evil. Far from it. Light untempered would be annihilation. It is good to them that sit in darkness and in the shadow of death; but, to those that faint in the wilderness, so also is the shadow of the great rock in a weary land. If the sunshine is good, so also the cloud of the latter rain. Light is only beautiful, only available for life, when it is tempered with shadow; pure light is fearful, and unendurable by humanity. And it is not less ridiculous to say that the light, as such, is good in itself, than to say that the darkness is good in itself. Both are rendered safe, healthy, and useful by the other; the night by the day, the day by the night; and we could just as easily live without the dawn as without the sunset, so long as we are human. Of the celestial city we are told there shall be 'no night there,' and then we shall know even as also we are known: but the night and the mystery have both their service here; and our business is not to strive to turn the night into day, but to be sure that we are as they that watch for the morning.—*Stones of Venice*, vol. iii., Appendix 7.

[margin: Psalm cvii. 10.]
[margin: Isaiah xxxii. 2.]
[margin: Rev. xxi. 25.]
[margin: Psalm cxxx. 6.]

Prayer.

All the true religions of the world are forms of the prayer 'Search me, and know my heart; prove me, and examine my thoughts; and see if there be any wicked way in me, and lead me in the way everlasting.'

[margin: Psalm cxxxix. 23, 24.]

And there are broadly speaking two ways in which the Father of men does this: the first, by making them eager to tell their faults to Him themselves, (Father, I have sinned against heaven and before Thee;) the second, by making them sure they cannot be hidden, if they would: 'If I make my bed in hell, behold Thou art there.' In neither case, do the men who love their Father fear that others should hear their confession, or witness His inquisition. But those who hate Him, and perceive that He is minded to make inquisition for blood, cry, even in this world, for the mountains to fall on them, and the hills to cover them. And in the actual practice of daily life you will find that wherever there is secrecy, there is either guilt or danger. It is not possible but that there should be things needing to be kept secret; but the dignity and safety of human life are in the precise measure of its frankness. . . . There is no fear for any child who is frank with its father and mother; none for men or women, who are frank with God. [S. Luke xv. 18. Psalm cxxxix. 8. Hosea x. 8. S. Luke xxiii. 30.]

I have told you that you can do nothing in policy without prayer. The day will be ill-spent, in which you have not been able, at least once, to say the Lord's Prayer with understanding: and if after it you accustom yourself to say, with the same intentness, that familiar one in your Church service, 'Almighty God, unto whom all hearts be open,' etc., you will not fear during the rest of the day, to answer any questions which it may conduce to your neighbour's good should be put to you.—*Fors Clavigera*, Letter LXXVII.

The whole confidence and glory of prayer is in its appeal to a Father who knows our necessities before we ask, who knows our thoughts before they rise in our hearts, and whose decrees, as unalterable in the eternal future as in the eternal past, yet in the close verity of visible fact, bend, like reeds, before the fore-ordained and faithful prayers of His children.—*On the Old Road*, vol. ii., § 286.

All that has ever been alleged against *forms* of worship, is justly said only of those which are compiled without sense, and employed without sincerity. The earlier services of the Catholic church teach men to think, as well as pray; nor did ever a soul in its immediate distress or desolation, find the forms of petition learnt in childhood, lifeless on the lips of age.—*Roadside Songs of Tuscany*, p. 142.

Preacher, The.

If once we begin to regard the preacher, whatever his faults, as a man sent with a message to us, which it is a matter of life or death whether we hear or refuse; if we look upon him as set in charge over many spirits in danger of ruin, and having allowed to him but an hour or two in the seven days to speak to them; if we make some endeavour to conceive how precious these hours ought to be to him, a small vantage on the side of God after his flock have been exposed for six days together to the full weight of the world's temptation, and he has been forced to watch the thorn and the thistle springing in their hearts, and to see what wheat had been scattered there snatched from the wayside by this wild bird and the other, and at last, when breathless and weary with the week's labour they give him this interval of imperfect and languid hearing, he has but thirty minutes to get at the separate hearts of a thousand men, to convince them of all their weaknesses, to shame them for all their sins, to warn them of all their dangers, to try

<small>Rev. iii. 20.</small> by this way and that to stir the hard fastenings of those doors where the Master Himself has stood and knocked yet none opened, and to call at the <small>Prov. i. 20, 24.</small> openings of those dark streets where Wisdom herself hath stretched forth her hands and no man regarded,—thirty minutes to raise the dead in,— let us but once understand and feel this, and we shall

look with changed eyes upon that frippery of gay furniture about the place from which the message of judgment must be delivered, which either breathes upon the dry bones that they may live, or, if ineffectual, remains recorded in condemnation, perhaps against the utterer and listener alike, but assuredly against one of them. We shall not so easily bear with the silk and gold upon the seat of judgment, nor with ornament of oratory in the mouth of the messenger; we shall wish that his words may be simple, even when they are sweetest, and the place from which he speaks like a marble rock in the desert, about which the people have gathered in their thirst.—*Stones of Venice*, vol. ii., ch. ii., § XIV. [Ezek. xxxvii. 5.]

Precious Stones.

Are we right in setting our hearts on these stones,—loving them, holding them precious?

Yes, assuredly; provided it is the stone we love, and the stone we think precious; and not ourselves we love, and ourselves we think precious. To worship a black stone, because it fell from heaven, may not be wholly wise, but it is half-way to being wise; half-way to worship of heaven itself. Or, to worship a white stone because it is dug with difficulty out of the earth, and to put it into a log of wood, and say the wood sees with it, may not be wholly wise; but it is half-way to being wise; half-way to believing that the God who makes earth so bright, may also brighten the eyes of the blind. It is no true folly to think that stones see, but it *is*, to think that eyes do not; it is no true folly to think that stones live, but it *is*, to think that souls die; it is no true folly to believe that, in the day of the making up of jewels, the palace walls shall be compact of life above their corner-stone, —but it *is*, to believe that in the day of dissolution the souls of the globe shall be shattered with its emerald; and no spirit survive, unterrified, above the ruin. [Mal. iii. 17.]

Yes, pretty ladies! love the stones, and take care of them; but love your own souls better, and take care <small>Mal. iii. 17.</small> of *them*, for the day when the Master shall make up His jewels. See that it be first the precious stones of the breastplate of justice you delight in, and are brave in; not first the stones, of your own diamond necklaces. . . . Get your breastplate of truth first, and every earthly stone will shine in it.

Alas! most of you know no more what justice means, than what jewels mean; but here is the pure practice of it to be begun, if you will, to-morrow.

For literal truth of your jewels themselves, absolutely search out and cast away all manner of false, or dyed, or altered stones. . . .

And lastly, as you are true in the choosing, be just in the sharing, of your jewels. They are but dross and dust, after all; and you, my sweet religious friends, who are so anxious to impart to the poor your pearls of great price, may surely also share with them your pearls of little price. Strangely (to my own mind at least), you are not so zealous in distributing your estimable rubies, as you are in communicating your *in*estimable wisdom. Of the grace of God, which you can give away in the quantity you think others are in need of, without losing any yourselves, I observe you to be affectionately lavish; but of the jewels of God, if any suggestions be made by charity touching the distri- <small>S. Matt. xxv. 9.</small> bution of *them*, you are apt, in your wisdom, to make answer like the wise virgins, 'Not so, lest there be not enough for us and you.'—*Deucalion*, ch. vii., § 41.

Pride.

Mortal Pride. For this we gather, for this we war, <small>James iii. 17.</small> for this we die—here and hereafter; while all the while the Wisdom which is from above stands vainly teaching us the way to Earthly Riches and to Heavenly Peace, 'What doth the Lord thy God require of thee, but to do justice, to love mercy, and to walk *humbly* with thy God?'—*On the Old Road*, vol. ii., § 181. ^{Micah vi. 8.}

Prodigal Son.

First, have you ever observed that all Christ's main teachings, by direct order, by earnest parable, and by His own permanent emotion, regard the use and misuse of *money?* We might have thought, if we had been asked what a divine teacher was most likely to teach, that he would have left inferior persons to give directions about money; and himself spoken only concerning faith and love, and the discipline of the passions, and the guilt of the crimes of soul against soul. But not so. He speaks in general terms of these. But He does not speak parables about them for all men's memory, nor permit Himself fierce indignation against them, in all men's sight. The Pharisees bring Him an adulteress. He writes her forgiveness on the dust of which He had formed her. Another despised of all for known sin, He recognised as a giver of unknown love. But he acknowledges no love in buyers and sellers in His house. One should have thought there were people in that house twenty times worse than they;—Caiaphas and his like—false priests, false prayer-makers, false leaders of the people—who needed putting to silence, or to flight, with darkest wrath. But the scourge is only against the *traffickers and thieves*. The two most intense of all the parables: the two which lead the rest in love and terror (this of the Prodigal, and of Dives), relate, both of them, to management of riches. The practical order given to the only seeker of advice, of whom it is recorded that Christ 'loved him,' is briefly about his property. 'Sell that thou hast.' And the arbitrament of the day of the Last Judgment is made to rest wholly, neither on belief in God, nor in any spiritual ^{S. Luke xv. 11-32; xvi. 19.} ^{S. Mark x. 21.} ^{S. Matt. xix. 21.} ^{S. Luke xviii. 22.}

virtue in man, nor on freedom from stress of stormy crime, but on this only, 'I was an hungred, and ye gave me drink; naked, and ye clothed me; sick, and ye came unto me.'

<small>S. Matt. xxv. 35, 36.</small>

. . . Then, secondly, I want you to note that when the prodigal comes to his senses, he complains of nobody but himself, and speaks of no unworthiness but his own. He says nothing against any of the women who tempted him—nothing against the citizen who left him to feed on husks—nothing of the false friends of whom 'no man gave unto him'—above all, nothing of the 'corruption of human nature,' or the corruption of things in general. He says that *he himself* is unworthy, as distinguished from honourable persons, and that *he himself* has sinned, as distinguished from righteous persons. And *that* is the hard lesson to learn, and the beginning of faithful lessons. All right and fruitful humility, and purging of heart, and seeing of God, is in that. It is easy to call yourself the chief of sinners, expecting every sinner round you to decline —or return—the compliment; but learn to measure the real degrees of your own relative baseness, and to be ashamed, not in heaven's sight, but in man's sight; and redemption is indeed begun. Observe the phrase, I have sinned '*against* heaven,' against the great law of that, and *before* thee, visibly degraded before my human sire and guide, unworthy any more of being esteemed of his blood, and desirous only of taking the place I deserve among his servants. Now I do not doubt but that I shall set many a reader's teeth on edge by what he will think my carnal and material rendering of this 'beautiful' parable. But I am just as ready to spiritualise it as he is, provided I am sure first that we understand it. If we want to understand the parable of the sower, we must first think of it as of literal husbandry; if we want to understand the parable of the prodigal, we must first understand it as of literal prodigality. And the

<small>S. Luke xv. 16.</small>

<small>S. Luke xv. 18.</small>

<small>S. Matt. xiii. 3.</small>

<small>S. Mark iv. 3.</small>

<small>S. Luke viii. 5.</small>

story has also for us a precious lesson in this literal sense of it, namely this, that all redemption must begin in subjection, and in the recovery of the sense of Fatherhood and authority, as all ruin and desolation begin in the loss of that sense. The lost son began by claiming his rights. He is found when he resigns them. He is lost by flying from his father, when his father's authority was only paternal. He is found by returning to his father, and desiring that his authority may be absolute, as over a hired stranger. And this is the practical lesson I want to leave with you.—*Time and Tide*, §§ 174-7.

Promise, The.

But surely the time is come when all these faithful armies should lift up the standard of their Lord,—not by might, nor by power, but by His spirit, bringing forth judgment unto victory. That they should no more be hidden, nor overcome of evil, but overcome evil with good. If the enemy cometh in like a flood, how much more may the rivers of Paradise? Are there not fountains of the great deep that open to bless, not destroy? _{Isaiah lix. 19.}

And the beginning of blessing, if you will think of it, is in that promise, 'Great shall be the peace of thy children.'—*Fors Clavigera*, Letter XCVI.

Promise of Old, The.

'The light shall be darkened in the heavens thereof, and the stars shall withdraw their shining.' All Greek, all Christian, all Jewish prophecy insists on the same truth through a thousand myths; but of all the chief, to former thought, was the fable of the Jewish warrior and prophet, for whom the sun hasted not to go down. . . . Whether you can affect the signs of the sky or not, you *can* the signs of the times. Whether you can bring the *sun* back or not, you can assuredly bring back your own

Isaiah v. 30.
Joel ii. 10.

cheerfulness, and your own honesty. You may not be able to say to the winds, 'Peace; be still,' but you can cease from the insolence of your own lips, and the troubling of your own passions. And all *that* it would be extremely well to do, even though the day *were* coming when the sun should be as darkness, and the moon as blood. But, the paths of rectitude and piety once regained, who shall say that the promise of old time would not be found to hold for us also?—'Bring ye all the tithes into my storehouse, and prove me now herewith, saith the Lord God, if I will not open you the windows of heaven, and pour you out a blessing, that there shall not be room enough to receive it.'—*The Storm-Cloud of the Nineteenth Century*, p. 62.

[margin: S. Mark iv. 39.]
[margin: Mal. iii. 10.]

Proverbs.

Read this first of Proverbs with me, please. The Proverbs of Solomon, the son of David, king of Israel.

'To *know* wisdom and instruction.'

(Not to opine them.)

'To *perceive* the words of understanding.'

(He that hath eyes, let him read—he that hath ears, hear, And for the Blind and the Deaf,—if patient and silent by the road-side,—there may also be some one to say, 'He is coming.')

'To receive the instruction of WISDOM, JUSTICE, and JUDGMENT, and EQUITY.'

Four things,—Oh friends, which you have not only to *perceive* but to *receive*. — *Fors Clavigera*, Letter LXXXVII.

Psalm of Life.

In the great Psalm of life, we are told that everything that a man doeth shall prosper, so only that he delight in the law of his God, that he hath not walked in the counsel of the wicked, nor sat

[margin: Psalm i. 1, 2.]

in the seat of the scornful. Is it among these leaves of the perpetual Spring,—helpful leaves for the healing of the nations,—that we mean to have our part and place, or rather among the ' brown skeletons of leaves that lag, the forest brook along'? For other leaves there are, and other streams that water them, —not water of life, but water of Acheron. Autumnal leaves there are that strew the brooks, in Vallombrosa. Remember you how the name of the place was changed: 'Once called "Sweet water" (Aqua bella), now, the Shadowy Vale.' Portion in one or other name we must choose, all of us,—with the living olive, by the living fountains of waters, or with the wild fig trees, whose leafage of human soul is strewed along the brooks of death, in the eternal Vallombrosa.—*Proserpina*, ch. iii., § 32.

<small>Rev. xxii. 2.</small>

Pure in Heart.

'Happy are the pure in heart, for they shall see God'; words always understood by me as having reference, like the other Beatitudes, to actual human life, according to the word of Job—'I have heard of Thee by the hearing of the ear, but now mine eye seeth Thee;' this revelation being given to Job entirely through the forms and life of the natural world, severally shown him by their unseen Creator. The same confession of faith, after the same instruction, is again uttered by Linnæus in the beginning of the 'Systema (properly Imperium) Naturæ': 'Deum sempiternum, immensum, omniscium, omnipotentem, expergefactus, transeuntem vidi, et obstupui.' 'As one awaked out of sleep, I saw the Lord passing by—eternal, infinite, omniscient, omnipotent, and I stood as in a trance.' He does not say 'all merciful'; the vision, to him, is as that of Eliphaz—'the hair of my flesh stood up'; yet note well, that the terror of Eliphaz, the self-abhorrence of Job, and the awe of Linnæus, are all entirely distinct from the spurious and prurient self-condemnation which

<small>S. Matt. v. 8.</small>
<small>Job xlii. 5.</small>
<small>Job iv. 15.</small>

is the watchword of modern Protestantism. The *perfect virtue* of Job, of Daniel, and of Noah, is directly, and at length, *asserted by the Deity Himself*, before these three men are taken for His best beloved friends; and the words 'Pure in heart' were never, in any place, used by me (and they are referred to again and again through the whole body of my works), or at any moment thought of, by me, as expressing states of religious belief or fantasy, such as modern theological writers suppose to be signified by the 'washing of sanctifica-tion,' or any other parallel phrase of doctrinal mystery; but only the definite human virtue possible to human effort, and *commanded* in the plain words, 'Cleanse your hands, ye sinners; and *purify your hearts, ye double-minded.*'—*Modern Painters*, vol. ii., Preface, §§ 4, 5.

<small>1 Cor. vi. 11.</small>

<small>S. James iv. 8.</small>

Purity.

And so in all cases I suppose that pureness is made to us desirable, because expressive of that constant presence and energizing of the Deity by which all things live and move, and have their being; and that foulness is painful as the accompaniment of disorder and decay, and always indicative of the withdrawal of Divine support. And the practical analogies of life, the invariable connection of outward foulness with mental sloth and degradation, as well as with bodily lethargy and disease, together with the contrary indications of freshness and purity belonging to every healthy and active organic frame (singularly seen in the effort of the young leaves when first their inward energy prevails over the earth, pierces its corruption, and shakes its dust away from their own white purity of life), all these circumstances strengthen the instinct by associations countless and irresistible. And then, finally, with the idea of purity comes that of spirituality; for the essential characteristic of matter is its inertia, whence, by adding to its purity of energy, we may in

<small>Acts xvii. 28.</small>

some measure spiritualize even matter itself. Thus in the Apocalyptic descriptions, it is the purity of every substance that fits it for its place in heaven; the river of the water of life, that proceeds out of the throne of the Lamb, is as clear as crystal, and the pavement of the city is pure gold 'like unto clear glass.'—*Modern Painters*, vol. ii., sec. i., ch. ix., § 8.

<small>Rev. xxii. 1.</small>
<small>Rev. xxi. 18-21.</small>

Put ye in the Sickle.

Death, not of myriads of poor bodies only, but of will and mercy, and conscience; death, not once inflicted on the flesh, but daily fastening on the spirit; death, not silent or patient, waiting his appointed hour, but voiceful, venomous; death with the taunting word, and burning grasp, and infixed sting.

'Put ye in the sickle, for the harvest is ripe.' The word is spoken in our ears continually to other reapers than the angels,—to the busy skeletons that never tire for stooping. When the measure of iniquity is full, and it seems that another day might bring repentance and redemption,—'Put ye in the sickle.' When the young life has been wasted all away, and the eyes are just opening upon the tracks of ruin, and faint resolution rising in the heart for nobler things, —'Put ye in the sickle.' When the roughest blows of fortune have been borne long and bravely, and the hand is just stretched to grasp its goal,—'Put ye in the sickle.' And when there are but a few in the midst of a nation to save it, or to teach, or to cherish; and all its life is bound up in those few golden ears,—'Put ye in the sickle, pale reapers, and pour hemlock for your feast of harvest home.'—*Modern Painters*, vol. v., Pt. ix., ch. ix., § 24.

<small>Joel iii. 13.</small>

Reformation.

The Church had become so mingled with the world that its witness could no longer be received; and the professing members of it, who were placed in circumstances such as to enable them to become aware of its corruptions, and whom their interest or their simplicity did not bribe or beguile into silence, gradually separated themselves into two vast multitudes of adverse energy, one tending to Reformation, and the other to Infidelity.

Of these, the last stood, as it were, apart, to watch the course of the struggle between Romanism and Protestantism; a struggle which, however necessary, was attended with infinite calamity to the Church. For, in the first place, the Protestant movement was, in reality, not *reformation* but *reanimation*. It poured new life into the Church, but it did not form or define her anew. In some sort it rather broke down her hedges, so that all they who passed by might pluck off her grapes. The reformers speedily found that the enemy was never far behind the sower of good seed: that an evil spirit might enter the ranks of reformation as well as those of resistance: and that though the deadly blight might be checked amidst the wheat, there was no hope of ever ridding the wheat itself from the tares. New temptations were invented by Satan wherewith to oppose the revived strength of Christianity: as the Romanist, confiding in his human teachers, had ceased to try whether they were teachers sent from God, so the Protestant, confiding in the teaching of the Spirit, believed every spirit, and did not try the spirits whether they were of God. And a thousand enthusiasms and heresies speedily obscured the faith and divided the force of the Reformation.

<small>Psalm lxxx. 12, Prayer-book.</small>

<small>S. Matt. xiii. 24, 25.</small>

<small>1 S. John iv. 1.</small>

But the main evils rose out of the antagonism of the two great parties; primarily, in the mere fact of the existence of an antagonism. To the eyes of the unbeliever the Church of Christ, for the first time since its foundation, bore the aspect of a house divided against itself. Not that many forms of schism had not before arisen in it; but either they had

<small>S. Matt. xii. 25.</small>

been obscure and silent, hidden among the shadows of the Alps and the marshes of the Rhine; or they had been outbreaks of visible and unmistakable error, cast off by the Church, rootless, and speedily withering away, while, with much that was erring and criminal, she still retained within her the pillar and ground of the truth. But here was at last a schism in which truth and authority were at issue. The body that was cast off withered away no longer. It stretched out its boughs to the sea and its branches to the river, and it was the ancient trunk that gave signs of decrepitude. On one side stood the reanimated faith, in its right hand the Book open, and its left hand lifted up to heaven, appealing for its proof to the Word of the Testimony and the power of the Holy Ghost. On the other stood, or seemed to stand, all beloved custom and believed tradition; all that for fifteen hundred years had been closest to the hearts of men, or most precious for their help. Long-trusted legend; long-reverenced power; long-practised discipline; faiths that had ruled the destiny, and sealed the departure, of souls that could not be told nor numbered for multitude; prayers that from the lips of the fathers to those of the children had distilled like sweet waterfalls, sounding through the silence of ages, breaking themselves into heavenly dew to return upon the pastures of the wilderness; hopes, that had set the face as a flint in the torture, and the sword as a flame in the battle, that had pointed the purposes and ministered the strength of life, brightened the last glances and shaped the last syllables of death; charities, that had bound together the brotherhoods of the mountain and the desert, and had woven chains of pitying or aspiring communion between this world and the unfathomable beneath and above; and more than these, the spirits of all the innumerable, undoubting dead, beckoning to the one way by which they had been content to follow the things that belonged unto their peace;—these all stood on the other side: and the

S. Luke xix. 42.

choice must have been a bitter one, even at the best; but it was rendered tenfold more bitter by the natural, but most sinful, animosity of the two divisions of the Church against each other.—*Stones of Venice*, vol. iii., ch. ii., §§ XCIII.–XCV.

Religion.

Religion is, of all subjects, that which will least endure a second place in the heart or thoughts, and a languid and occasional study of it was sure to lead to error or infidelity. On the other hand, what was heartily admired and unceasingly contemplated was soon brought nigh to being believed; and the systems of Pagan mythology began gradually to assume the places in the human mind from which the unwatched Christianity was wasting. Men did not indeed openly sacrifice to Jupiter, or build silver shrines for Diana, but the ideas of Paganism nevertheless became thoroughly vital and present with them at all times; and it did not matter in the least, as far as respected the power of true religion, whether the Pagan image was believed in or not, so long as it entirely occupied the thoughts. The scholar of the sixteenth century, if he saw the lightning shining from the east unto the west, thought forthwith of Jupiter, not of the coming of the Son of Man; if he saw the moon walking in brightness, he thought of Diana, not of the throne which was to be established for ever as a faithful witness in heaven; and though his heart was but secretly enticed, yet thus he denied the God that is above.—*Stones of Venice*, vol. iii., ch. ii., § CI.

<small>S. Matt. xxiv. 27.</small>
<small>Psalm lxxxix. 36, 37.</small>
<small>Job xxxi. 26, 28.</small>

The purest forms of our own religion have always consisted in sacrificing less things to win greater;— time, to win eternity,—the world, to win the skies. The order, 'Sell that thou hast,' is not given without the promise,—'thou shalt have treasure in heaven;' and well for the modern Christian if he

<small>S. Matt. xix. 21.</small>

accepts the alternative as his Master left it—and does not practically read the command and promise thus: 'Sell that thou hast in the best market, and thou shalt have treasure in eternity also.' But the poor Greeks of the great ages expected no reward from heaven but honour, and no reward from earth but rest;—though, when, on those conditions, they patiently, and proudly, fulfilled their task of the granted day, an unreasoning instinct of an immortal benediction broke from their lips in song: and they, even they, had sometimes a prophet to tell them of a land 'where there is sun alike by day, and alike by night—where they shall need no more to trouble the earth by strength of hands for daily bread—but the ocean breezes blow around the blessed islands, and golden flowers burn on their bright trees for evermore.'—*Queen of the Air*, ch. i., § 50.

Religion and Faith.

If, loving well the creatures that are like yourself, you feel that you would love still more dearly, creatures better than yourself—were they revealed to you;—if striving with all your might to mend what is evil, near you and around, you would fain look for a day when some Judge of all the Earth shall wholly do right, and the little hills rejoice on every side; [Psalm lxv. 12.] if, parting with the companions that have given you all the best joy you had on Earth, you desire ever to meet their eyes again and clasp their hands,—where eyes shall no more be dim, nor hands fail;—if, preparing yourselves to lie down beneath the grass in silence and loneliness, seeing no more beauty, and feeling no more gladness—you would care for the promise to you of a time when you should see God's light again, and know the things you have longed to know, and walk in the peace of everlasting Love—*then*, the Hope of these things to you is religion, the Substance of them in your life is Faith. And in the power of [Rev. xi. 15.] them, it is promised us, that the kingdoms of this world shall yet become the *kingdoms* of our Lord and of His Christ.—*Our Fathers Have Told Us*, ch. iv., § 60.

Religious Symbols.

The habit of employing some religious symbol, or writing some religious legend, over the door of the house, does not entirely disappear until far into the period of the Renaissance. The words, 'Peace be to this house,' occur on one side of a Veronese gateway, with the appropriate and veracious inscription S. P. Q. R., on a Roman standard, on the other; and 'Blessed is he that cometh in the name of the Lord,' is written on one of the doorways of a building added at the flank of the Casa Barbarigo, in the sixteenth or seventeenth century. It seems to be only modern Protestantism which is entirely ashamed of *all* symbols and words that appear in anywise like a confession of faith.

<small>1 Sam. xxv. 6.</small>
<small>S. Luke x. 5.</small>
<small>S. Matt. xxi. 9.</small>

This peculiar feeling is well worthy of attentive analysis. It indeed, in most cases, hardly deserves the name of a feeling; for the meaningless doorway is merely an ignorant copy of heathen models; but yet, if it were at this moment proposed to any of us, by our architects, to remove the grinning head of a satyr, or other classical or Palladian ornament, from the keystone of the door, and to substitute for it a cross, and an inscription testifying our faith, I believe that most persons would shrink from the proposal with an obscure and yet overwhelming sense that things would be sometimes done, and thought, within the house which would make the inscription on its gate a base hypocrisy. And if so, let us look to it, whether that strong reluctance to utter a definite religious profession, which so many of us feel, and which, not very carefully examining into its dim nature, we conclude to be modesty, or fear of hypocrisy, or other such form of amiableness, be not, in very deed, neither less nor more than Infidelity; whether Peter's 'I know not the man' be not the sum and

<small>S. Matt. xxvi. 72.</small>

substance of all these misgivings and hesitations; and whether the shamefacedness which we attribute to sincerity and reverence, be not such shame- S. Mark viii. 38. facedness as may at last put us among those of whom the Son of Man shall be ashamed.—*Stones of Venice*, vol. ii., ch. vii., §§ LVII.–LVIII.

Rest.

The desire of rest planted in the heart is no sensual nor unworthy one, but a longing for renovation and for escape from a state whose every phase is mere preparation for another equally transitory, to one in which permanence shall have become possible through perfection. Hence the great call of Christ to S. Matt. xi. 28. men, that call on which St. Augustine fixed as the essential expression of Christian hope, S. John xiv. 27. is accompanied by the promise of rest; and the death bequest of Christ to men is peace.—*Modern Painters*, vol. ii., sec. i., ch. vii., § 1.

Revelation.

Of no other sources than these visible ones, can we, by any effort in our present condition of existence, conceive. For what revelations have been made to humanity inspired, or caught up to heaven, of things to the heavenly region belonging, have been either by unspeakable words, or else by their very nature incommunicable, except in types and shadows; and ineffable by words belonging to earth, for, of things different from the visible, words appropriated to the visible can convey no image. How different Rev. xxi. 18. from earthly gold the clear pavement of the city might have seemed to the eyes of St. John, we of unreceived sight cannot know; neither of Rev. iv. 3, 6. that strange jasper and sardine can we conceive the likeness which He assumed that sat on the throne above the crystal sea; neither what seeming that was of slaying that the Root of David bore in the midst of the elders; neither what change it was upon the form of the fourth of them that walked in the furnace of Dura, that even the wrath of Idolatry knew for the likeness of the Son of God. The knowing that is here permitted to us is either of things outward only, as in those it is whose eyes Faith never opened, or else of that dark part that her glass shows feebly, of things supernatural, that gleaming of the Divine form among the mortal crowd, which all may catch if they will climb the sycamore and wait: nor how much of God's abiding at the house may be granted to those that so seek, and how much more may be opened to them in the breaking of bread, cannot be said; but of that only we can reason which is in a measure revealed to all, of that which is by constancy and purity of affection to be found in the things and the beings around us upon earth.—*Modern Painters*, vol ii., sec. i., ch. xv., § 1.

<small>Daniel iii. 25.</small>
<small>S. Luke xix. 4.</small>
<small>Acts ii. 42.</small>

Reverence.

We English have many false ideas about reverence; we should be shocked, for instance, to see a market-woman come into church with a basket of eggs on her arm: we think it more reverent to lock her out till Sunday; and to surround the church with respectability of iron railings. . . . I believe this to be *ir*reverence; and that it is more truly reverent, when the market-woman, hot and hurried, at six in the morning, her head much confused with calculations of the probable price of eggs, can nevertheless get within church porch, and church aisle, and church chancel, lay the basket down on the very steps of the altar, and receive thereat so much of help and hope as may serve her for the day's work.—*Modern Painters*, vol. iii., ch. x., § 22.

This is the thing which I KNOW—and which, if you labour faithfully, you shall know also,—that in Reverence is the chief joy and power of life;—Reverence, for what is pure and bright in your own youth; for what is true and tried in the age of others; for all that is gracious among the living,—great among the dead,—and marvellous, in the Powers that cannot die. —*Lectures on Art*, § 65.

Rod.

Virga—a 'rod';—the green rod, or springing bough of a tree, being the type of perfect human strength, both in the use of it in the Mosaic story, when it becomes a serpent, or strikes the rock; or when Aaron's bears its almonds; and in the metaphorical expressions, the 'Rod out of the stem of Jesse,' and the 'Man whose name is the Branch,' and so on. And the essential idea of real virtue is that of a vital human strength, which instinctively, constantly, and without motive, does what is right. You must train men to this by habit, as you would the branch of a tree; and give them instincts and manners (or morals) of purity, justice, kindness, and courage. Once rightly trained, they act as they should, irrespectively of all motive, of fear, or of reward.—*Ethics of the Dust*, p. 142.

[Exodus iv. 3; xvii. 5, 6. Num. xvii. 8. Isaiah xi. 1. Zech. vi. 12.]

Sacred Chord of Colour.

The ascertainment of the sanctity of colour is not left to human sagacity. It is distinctly stated in Scripture. . . . The sacred chord of colour (blue, purple, and scarlet, with white and gold) as appointed in the Tabernacle; this chord is the fixed base of all colouring with the workmen of every great age; the purple and scarlet will be found constantly employed by noble painters, in various unison, to the exclusion in general of pure crimson;—it is the harmony described by Herodotus as used in the battlements of Ecbatana, and the invariable base of all beautiful missal-painting; the mistake continually made by modern restorers, in supposing the purple to be a faded crimson,

[Exodus xxviii. 5.]

and substituting full crimson for it, being instantly fatal to the whole work, as, indeed, the slightest modification of any hue in a perfect colour-harmony must always be. In this chord the scarlet is the powerful colour, and is on the whole the most perfect representation of abstract colour which exists; blue being in a certain degree associated with shade, yellow with light, and scarlet, as absolute *colour*, standing alone. Accordingly, we find it used, together with cedar wood, hyssop, and running water, as an emblem of purification, in Leviticus xiv. 4, and other places, and so used not merely as representative of the colour of blood, since it was also to be dipped in the actual blood of a living bird. So that the cedar wood for its perfume, the hyssop for its searchingness, the water for its cleansing, and the scarlet for its kindling or enlightening, are all used as tokens of sanctification;[1] and it cannot be with any force alleged, in opposition to this definite appointment, that scarlet is used incidentally to illustrate the stain of sin,—' though thy sins be as scarlet,'—any more than it could be received as a diminution of the authority for using snow-whiteness as a type of purity, that Gehazi's leprosy is described as being 'white as snow.' An incidental image has no authoritative meaning, but a stated ceremonial appointment has; besides, we have the reversed image given distinctly in Prov. xxxi.: 'She is not afraid of the snow for her household, for all her household are clothed with *scarlet*.' And, again: 'Ye daughters of Israel, weep over Saul, who clothed you in scarlet, with other delights.' So, also, the arraying of the mystic Babylon in purple and scarlet may be interpreted exactly as we choose; either by those who think colour sensual, as an image of earthly pomp and guilt, or, by those who think it sacred, as an image of assumed or pretended sanctity. It is possible

_{Isaiah i. 18.}

_{2 Kings v. 27.}

_{2 Sam. i. 24.}

_{Rev. xviii. 16.}

_{Joshua i. 21.} [1] The redeemed Rahab bound for a sign a *scarlet* thread in the window. Compare Canticles iv. 3.

the two meanings may be blended, and the idea may be
that the purple and fine linen of Dives are worn S. Luke
in hypocritical semblance of the purple and fine xvi. 19.
linen of the high priest, being, nevertheless, themselves,
in all cases typical of all beauty and purity. . . . All
men, completely organized and justly tempered, enjoy
colour; it is meant for the perpetual comfort and delight
of the human heart; it is richly bestowed on the highest
works of creation, and the eminent sign and seal of perfection in them; being associated with *life* in the human
body, with *light* in the sky, with *purity* and hardness in
the earth,—death, night, and pollution of all kinds being
colourless.—*Modern Painters*, vol. iv., ch. iii., § 24.

Sacred Symbols.

Joseph's two dreams were evidently intended to be
signs of the steadfastness of the Divine purpose Gen.
towards him, by possessing the clearness of special xxxvii.
prophecy; yet were couched in such imagery, as 5, 9.
not to inform him prematurely of his destiny, and only
to be understood after their fulfilment. The sun, Gen.
and moon, and stars were at the period, and xxxvii. 9.
are indeed throughout the Bible, the symbols of high
authority. It was not revealed to Joseph that he should
be lord over all Egypt; but the representation Gen.
of his family by symbols of the most magnificent xli. 41.
dominion, and yet as subject to him, must have been
afterwards felt by him as a distinctly prophetic indication of his own supreme power. It was not revealed to
him that the occasion of his brethren's special Gen.
humiliation before him should be their coming xlii. 5, 6.
to buy corn; but when the event took place, must he
not have felt that there was prophetic purpose in the
form of the sheaves of wheat which first imaged Gen.
forth their subjection to him? And these two xxxvii. 7.
images of the sun doing obeisance, and the sheaves
bowing down,—narrowed and imperfect intimations of
great truth which yet could not be otherwise conveyed.

... Even if the symbolic vision itself be not terrible, the sense of what may be veiled behind it becomes all the more awful in proportion to the insignificance or strangeness of the sign itself; and, I believe, this thrill of mingled doubt, fear and curiosity lies at the very root of the delight which mankind take in symbolism. It was not an accidental necessity for the conveyance of truth by pictures instead of words, which led to its universal adoption wherever art was on the advance; but the Divine fear which necessarily follows on the understanding that a thing is other and greater than it seems; and which, it appears probable, has been rendered peculiarly attractive to the human heart, because God would have us **understand that this** is true not of **invented symbols merely, but of all** things amidst which we live; that there is a deeper meaning within them than eye hath seen, or ear hath heard; and that the whole visible creation is a mere perishable symbol of things eternal and true. It cannot but have been sometimes a subject of wonder with thoughtful men, how fondly, age after age, the Church has cherished the belief that the four living creatures which surrounded the Apocalyptic throne were symbols of the four Evangelists, and rejoiced to use those forms in its picture-teaching; that a calf, a lion, an eagle, and a beast with a man's face, should in all ages have been preferred by the Christian world, as expressive of Evangelistic power and inspiration, to the majesty of human form; and that quaint grotesques, awkward and often ludicrous caricatures even of the animals represented, should have been regarded by all men, not only with contentment, but with awe, and have superseded all endeavours to represent the characters and persons of the Evangelistic writers themselves (except in a few instances, confined principally to works undertaken without a definite religious purpose);—this, I say, might appear more than strange to us, were it not that we ourselves share the awe, and are still satisfied with the

<small>1 Cor. ii. 9.</small>

<small>Rev. iv. 7.</small>

symbol, and that justly. For, whether we are conscious of it or not, there is in our hearts, as we gaze upon the brutal forms that have **so holy a signification, an acknowledgment that it was** not Matthew, nor Mark, nor Luke, nor John, in whom the Gospel of Christ was unsealed; but that the invisible things of Him from the beginning of the Creation are clearly seen, being understood by the things that are made; that the whole world, and all that is therein, be it **low or high, great** or small, is a continual Gospel; and that as the heathen, in their alienation from God, changed His **glory** into an image made like unto corruptible man, and to birds, and four-footed beasts, the Christian, in his approach to God, is to undo this work, and to change the corruptible things into the image of His glory; believing that there is nothing so base in creation, but that our faith may give it wings which shall raise us into companionship with heaven; and that, on the other hand, there is nothing so great or so **goodly in creation, but** that it is a mean symbol of the Gospel of **Christ,** and of the things He has prepared for them that love Him.—*Stones of Venice*, vol. iii., ch. iii., §§ LXII., LXIII.

<small>Romans i. 23.</small>

<small>1 Cor. ii. 9.</small>

Satan.

In fearful truth, the Presence and Power of him *is* here; in the world, with us, and within us, mock **as** you may; and the fight with him, for the time, sore, and widely unprosperous. Do not think I am speaking metaphorically or rhetorically, or with any other than literal **and** earnest meaning of words. Hear me, I pray **you,** therefore, for a little while, as earnestly as I speak.

Every faculty of man's soul, and every instinct of it by which he is meant to live, is exposed to its own special form of corruption: and whether within Man, or in the external world, there is a power or condition **of** temptation which is perpetually endeavouring to reduce every glory of his soul, and every power of his life, **to such** corruption as is possible to them. And the more beautiful they are, the more fearful is the death which is attached as a penalty to their degradation. . . .

Now observe—I leave you to call this deceiving spirit what you like—or to theorise about it as you like. All that I desire you to recognize is the fact of its being here, and the need of its being fought with. If you take the Bible's account of it, or Dante's or Milton's, you will receive the image of it as a mighty spiritual creature, commanding others, and resisted by others: if you take Æschylus's or Hesiod's account of it, you will hold it for a partly elementary and unconscious adversity of fate, and partly for a group of monstrous spiritual agencies connected with death, and begotten out of the dust; if you take a modern rationalist's you will accept it for a mere treachery and want of vitality in our own moral nature exposing it to loathsomeness or moral disease, as the body is capable of mortification or leprosy. I do not care what you call it,—whose history you believe of it,—nor what you yourself can imagine about it; the origin, or nature, or name may be as you will, but the deadly reality of the thing is with us, and warring against us, and on our true war with it depends whatever life we can win. Deadly reality, I say. The puff-adder or horned asp is not more real. Unbelievable,—*those*,—unless you had seen them; no fable could have been coined out of any human brain so dreadful, within its own poor material sphere, as that blue-lipped serpent—working its way sidelong in the sand. As real, but with sting of eternal death—this worm that dies not, and fire that is not quenched, within our souls or around them. Eternal death, I say—sure, that, whatever creed you hold;—if the old Scriptural one, Death of perpetual banishment from before God's face; if the modern rationalist one, Death Eternal for *us*, instant and unredeemable ending of lives wasted in misery.—*Time and Tide*, §§ 51–2; 58.

Isaiah lxvi. 24.
S. Mark ix. 44–48.

Schism and Heresy.

I believe that the root of almost every schism and heresy from which the Christian church has ever suffered, has been the effort of men to earn, rather than to receive, their salvation; and that the reason that preaching is so commonly ineffectual is, that it calls on men oftener to work for God, than to behold God working for them. If, for every rebuke that we utter of men's vices, we put forth a claim upon their hearts; if, for every assertion of God's demands from them, we could substitute a display of His kindness to them; if side by side, with every warning of death, we could exhibit proofs and promises of immortality; if, in fine, instead of assuming the being of an awful Deity, which men, though they cannot and dare not deny, are always unwilling, sometimes unable, to conceive, we were to show them a near, visible, inevitable, but all beneficent Deity, whose presence makes the earth itself a heaven, I think there would be fewer deaf children sitting in the market-place.— *Modern Painters*, vol. ii., sec. i., ch. xv., § 11.

Servant of Christ.

You are called simply to be the servant of Christ, and of other men for His sake; that is to say, to hold your life and all its faculties as a means of service to your fellows. All you have to do is to be sure it *is* the service you are doing them, and not the service you do yourself, which is uppermost in your minds.

Now you continually hear appeals to you made in a vague way, which you don't know how far you can follow. You shall not say that, to-day; I both can and will tell you what Christianity requires of you in simplest terms. Read your Bible as you would any other book—with strictest criticism, frankly determining what you think beautiful, and what you think false or foolish. But be sure that you try accurately to understand it, and transfer its teaching to modern need by putting other names for those which have become superseded by time. For instance, in such a passage as that which follows and supports the 'Lie not one to another' of Colossians iii.—'seeing that ye have put on the new man, which is renewed in knowledge after the spirit of Him that created him, where' (meaning in that great creation where) 'there is neither Greek nor Jew, circumcision nor uncircumcision, barbarian, Scythian, bond nor free.' In applying that verse to the conduct and speech of modern policy, it falls nearly dead, because we suffer ourselves to remain under a vague impression—vague, but practically paralysing,—that though it was very necessary to speak the truth in the countries of Scythians and Jews, there is no objection to any quantity of lying in managing the affairs of Christendom. But now merely substitute modern for ancient names, and see what a difference it will make in the force and appeal of the passage, 'Lie not one to another, brethren, seeing that ye have put off the old man, with his deeds, and have put on the new man, which is renewed to knowledge,' εἰς ἐπίγνωσιν, according to the knowledge of Him that created him, in that great creation where there is neither Englishman nor German, baptism nor want of baptism, Turk nor Russian, slave nor free, but Christ is all, and in all.—*On the Old Road*, vol. ii., §§ 292, 293.

<small>Col. iii. 11.</small>

<small>Col. iii. 9, 10.</small>

<small>Col. iii. 11.</small>

Service of Heaven.

Whatever may be the inability, in this present life, to mingle the full enjoyment of the Divine works with the full discharge of every practical duty, and confessedly in many cases this must be, let us not attribute the inconsistency to any indignity of the faculty of contemplation, but to the sin and the suffering of the fallen state, and the change of order from the keeping of the garden to the tilling of the ground. We cannot say how far it is right or agreeable with God's will, while men are

<small>Gen. ii. 15.</small>

<small>Gen. iii. 23.</small>

perishing round about us; while grief and pain, and wrath, and impiety, and death, and all the powers of the air, are working wildly and evermore, and the cry of blood going up to heaven, that any of us should take hand **from the plough**; but this we know, that there will come a time **when** the service of God shall be the beholding of Him; and though in these stormy seas where we are **now driven up** and down, His Spirit is dimly seen **on the face of** the [Gen. i. 2.] waters, and we are left to cast anchors **out of the stern**, and **wish for the day**, that day will **come**, when, with the **evangelists on the crystal** and stable sea, all the **creatures of God** shall be full of eyes within, [Rev. iv. 6, 8.] and there shall be 'no more curse, but His servants shall serve Him, and shall see His face.'—*Modern Painters*, vol. ii., sec. i., ch. xv., § 12. [Rev. xxii. 3, 4.]

Seven Churches, The.

And so, out of the true earthly kingdom, in fulness of time, shall come the heavenly kingdom, when the tabernacle of God shall be with men; no [Rev. xxi. 3.] **priest** needed **more** for **ministry, because** all the earth will be Temple; nor bread nor wine needed more for mortal food, or fading memory, but [Rev. xxii. 17-22.] the water of life given to him that is athirst, and the fruits of the trees of healing.

Into which kingdom that we may enter let us read now the last words of the King when He left us for His Bridal, in which is the direct and practical warning of which the parable **of the Servant was** the shadow. It was given, as you know, **to Seven** Churches, that **live no more**,—they having refused the word of His lips, and **been** consumed by the sword of His lips. Yet to all men the command remains—He that hath an [Rev. ii. 29.] ear, let him hear what the Spirit saith unto the Churches.

They lie along the hills, and **across** the plains, of Lydia, sweeping in one wide curve like a flight of birds or a swirl of cloud—(if you draw them by themselves on the map you will see)—all of them either in Lydia itself, or on the frontier of it: in nature Lydian all—richest in gold, delicatest in luxury, softest in music, tenderest in art, of the then world. They unite the capacities and felicities of the Asiatic and the Greek: had the last message of Christ been given to the Churches in Greece, it would have been to Europe in imperfect age; if to the Churches in Syria, to Asia in imperfect age:—written to Lydia, it is written to the world, and for ever.

It is written 'to the Angels of the Seven Churches.
<small>Rev. i. 20.</small> . . . These things saith He which hath the
<small>Rev. i. 16;</small> Seven Stars in His right hand, *and*' (that is to
<small>iii. 1.</small> say) 'the Seven Spirits of God.'

And the charge is from the Spirit of God to each of these seven angels, reigning over and in the hearts
<small>Rev. ii. 7.</small> of the whole body of the believers in every Church; followed always by the dateless adjuration, 'He that hath an ear, let him hear what the *Spirit* saith unto the Churches.'

<small>Rev. ii. 2, 9, 13, 19; iii. 1, 8, 15.</small> The address to each consists of four parts: . . . Observe, first, they all begin with the same words, 'I know thy *works*.'

Not even the maddest and blindest of Antinomian teachers could have eluded the weight of this fact, but that, in the following address to each Church, its 'work' is spoken of as the state of its heart. Of which the interpretation is nevertheless quite simple, that the thing looked at by God first, in every Christian man, is his work;—without that, there is no more talk or thought
<small>S. Luke xiii. 7.</small> of him. 'Cut him down—why cumbereth he the ground?' But the work being shown, has next to be tested. In what spirit was this done,—in faith and charity, or in disobedient pride? . . .

<small>S. Matt. xxv. 1. S. Matt. v. 14.</small> I. Ephesus.—The attribute is essentially the spiritual power of Christ, in His people,—the 'lamp' of the virgins, the 'light of the world' of the Sermon on the Mount.

The Declaration praises the intensity of this in the

Church, and—which is the notablest thing for *us* in the whole series of the charges—it asserts the burning of the Spirit of Christ in the Church to be especially shown because it 'cannot bear them which are evil.' This fierceness against sin, which we are so proud of being well quit of, is the very life of a Church;—the toleration of sin is the dying of its lamp. How indeed should it shine before men, if it mixed itself in the soot and fog of sin? . . . The promise is of fullest life in the midst of the Paradise and garden of God. Compare all the prophetic descriptions of living persons, or states, as the trees in the garden of God; and the blessing of the first Psalm. Rev. ii. 1.
Rev. ii. 7.

II. Smyrna.—The attribute is that of Christ's endurance of death. The declaration that the faithful Church is now dying, with Him, the noble death of the righteous, and shall live for evermore. The promise, that over those who so endure the slow pain of death in grief, for Christ's sake, the second death hath no power. Rev. ii. 11.

III. Pergamos.—The attribute is of Christ the Judge, visiting for sin; the declaration, that the Church has in it the sin of the Nicolaitanes, or of Balaam,—using its grace and inspiration to forward its worldly interest, and grieved at heart because it *has* the Holy Ghost;—the darkest of blasphemies. Against this, 'Behold, I come quickly, and will fight against thee with the sword of my mouth.' Rev. ii. 14-16.

The promise, that he who has kept his lips from blasphemy shall eat of the hidden manna: the word, not the sword, of the lips of Christ. 'How sweet is Thy word unto my lips.' Rev. ii. 17.
Psalm cxix. 103.

The metaphor of the stone, and the new name, I do not yet securely understand.

IV. Thyatira.—The attribute: 'That hath his eyes like a flame of fire,' (searching the heart,) 'his feet like fine brass,' (treading the earth, yet in Rev. ii. 18.

purity, the type of all Christian practical life, unsoiled, whatever it treads on); but remember, lest you should think this in any wise opposed to the sense of the charge to Ephesus that you may *tread* on foulness, yet remain undefiled; but not lie down in it and remain so.

<small>Rev. ii. 26, 27.</small> The praise is for charity and active labour,—and the labour more than the charity. . . .

<small>Rev. ii. 28.</small> The reward of resistance is, to rule the nations with a rod of iron—(true work, against painted clay); and I will give him the morning star, (light of heaven, and morning-time for labour).

<small>Rev. iii. 1.</small> V. Sardis.—The attribute: 'That hath the Seven Spirits of God, and the seven stars.'

Again, the Lord of Life itself—the Giver of the Holy <small>S. John xx. 22.</small> Ghost. (Having said thus, He breathed on them.) He questions not of the poison or misuse of <small>Rev. iii. 2.</small> life, but of its *existence*. Strengthen the things that are left—that are ready to *die*. The white <small>S. Mark ix. 3.</small> raiment is the transfiguration of the earthly frame by the inner life, even to the robe of it, 'so as no fuller on earth can white them.'

The judgment: I will come unto thee as a thief (in <small>Rev. iii. 3, 5.</small> thy darkness, to take away even that thou hast). The promise: I will not blot his name out of the Book of Life.

VI. Philadelphia.—The attribute: He that is holy <small>Rev. iii. 7.</small> (separate from sin)—He that is true (separate from falsehood)—that hath the key of David, (of the city of David which is Zion, renewed and pure; <small>Rev. xxii. 15.</small> *conf.* verse 12); that openeth, and no man shutteth, (by *me* if any man enter in); and shutteth, and no man openeth,—(for without, are fornicators, and whosoever loveth and maketh a lie).

The praise for faithfulness with a little strength, as of a soldier holding a little fortress in the midst of <small>Psalm xxiv. 7, 8.</small> assaulting armies. Therefore the blessing, after that captivity of the strait siege—the lifting up of the heads of the gates, and setting wide of the everlasting doors by the Lord, mighty in battle. The promise: Him that overcometh will I make, not merely safe within my fortress temple, but a pillar of it—built on its rock, and bearing its vaults for ever. *Rev. iii. 12.*

VII. Laodicea.—The attribute: The Faithful, witness—the Word—the Beginning of Creation. *Rev. iii. 14.*

The sin, chaos of heart,—useless disorder of half-shaped life. Darkness on the face of the deep, and rejoicing in darkness,—as in these days of ours to the uttermost. Chaos in all things—dross for gold—slime for mortar—nakedness for glory—pathless morass for path—and the proud blind for guides.

The command, to try the gold, and purge the raiment, and anoint the eyes,—this order given as to the almost helpless—as men waked in the night, not girding their loins for journey, but in vague wonder at uncertain noise, who may turn again to their slumber, or, in wistful listening, hear the voice calling—'Behold, I stand at the door!' It is the last of the temptations, bringing back the throne of Annihilation; and the victory over it is the final victory, giving rule, with the Son of God, over the recreate and never to be dissolved order of the perfect earth. *Rev. iii. 18.* *Rev. iii. 20.*

In which there shall be no more death, neither sorrow, nor crying, for the 'former things are passed away.' *Rev. xxi. 4.*

'Now, unto Him that is able to keep you from falling, and to present you, faultless, before the Presence of His glory with exceeding joy; *S. Jude i. 24.*

'To the only wise God our Saviour, be glory and majesty, dominion and power, both now and ever. Amen.'—*Fors Clavigera*, Letter LXXXIV.

Shepherd's Tower, The.

Forty years ago, there was assuredly no spot of ground, out of Palestine, in all the round world, on which, if you knew, even but a little, the true course of that world's history, you saw with so much joyful reverence the dawn of morning, as at the foot of the Tower of Giotto. For there the traditions of faith and hope, of both the Gentile and Jewish races, met for their beautiful labour. The Baptistery of Florence is the last building raised on the earth by the descendants of the workmen taught by Dædalus; and the Tower of Giotto is the loveliest of those raised on earth under the inspiration of the men who lifted up the tabernacle in the wilderness. Of living Greek work there is none after the Florentine Baptistery; of living Christian work, none so perfect as the Tower of Giotto. . . . Next to declaration of the facts of the Gospel, its purpose (often in actual work the eagerest,) was to show the *power* of the Gospel. History of Christ in due place; yes, history of all He did, and how He died: but then, and often, as I say, with more animated imagination, the showing of His risen presence in granting the harvests and guiding the labour of the year. All sun and rain, and length or decline of days received from His hand; all joy, and grief, and strength, or cessation of labour, indulged or endured, as in His sight and to His glory. And the familiar employments of the seasons, the homely toils of the peasant, the lowliest skills of the craftsman, are signed always on the stones of the Church, as the first and truest condition of sacrifice and offering.—*Mornings in Florence*, §§ 120-1.

Sight.

Sight is an absolutely spiritual phenomenon; accurately, and only, to be so defined; and the 'Let there be light,' is as much, when you understand it, the ordering of intelligence as the ordering of vision. It is the appointment of change of what had been else only a mechanical effluence from things unseen to things unseeing,—from stars that did not shine to earth that could not perceive;—the change,

Gen. i. 3.

I say, of that blind vibration into the glory of the sun and moon for human eyes; so rendering possible also the communication out of the unfathomable truth, of that portion of truth which is good for us, and animating to us, and is set to rule over the day and night of our joy and sorrow. . . .

Have you ever considered how much literal truth there is in the words—'The light of the body S. Matt. is the eye. If, therefore, thine eye be evil'— vi. 22, 23. and the rest? How *can* the eye be evil? How, if evil, can it fill the whole body with darkness?

What is the meaning of having one's body *full* of darkness? It cannot mean merely being blind. Blind, you may fall in a ditch if you move; but you may be well, if at rest. But to be evil-eyed, is not that worse than to have no eyes? and instead of being only in darkness, to have darkness in *us*, portable, perfect, and eternal? . . .

Literally, if the eye be pure, the body is pure; but, if the light of the body be but darkness, how great is that darkness! . . .

You will find that, according to the clearness of sight, is indeed the kindness of sight, and that at last the noble eyes of humanity look through humanity, from heart into heart, and with no mechanical vision. And the Light of the body is the eye—yes, and in happy life, the light of the heart also.—*The Eagle's Nest,* §§ 99, 106, 108, 110.

Sons of Noah.

Remember that the three sons of Noah are, respectively, Shem, the father of the Imaginative and Contemplative races.

Japheth, Practical and Constructive.

Ham, Carnal and Destructive.

The sons of Shem are the perceivers of Splendour;— they see what is best in visible things, and reach forward to the invisible.

The sons of Japheth are the perceivers of Justice

and Duty; and deal securely with all that is under their hand.

The sons of Ham are the perceivers of Evil or Nakedness; and are slaves therefore for ever — 'servants of servants': when in power, therefore, either helpless or tyrannous. It is best to remember among the nations descending from the three great sires, the Persians, as the sons of Shem; Greeks, as the sons of Japheth; Assyrians, as the sons of Ham. The Jewish captivity to the Assyrians then takes its perfect meaning.—*Fors Clavigera*, Letter LXII.

Spirit of Prophecy, The.

It is to be noted that it is neither by us ascertainable what moments of **pure feeling or** aspiration may occur to men of minds apparently cold and lost, nor by us to be pronounced through what instruments, and in what strangely occurrent voices, God may choose to communicate good to men. It seems to me that much of what is great, and to all men beneficial, has been wrought by those who neither intended nor knew the good they did; and that many mighty harmonies have been discoursed by instruments that had been dumb or discordant, but that God knew their stops. The Spirit of Prophecy consisted with the avarice of Balaam, and the disobedience of Saul. Could we spare from its page that parable, which he said, who **saw the vision of the Almighty,** falling into a trance, but **having his eyes open;** though we know that the sword of his punishment was then sharp in its sheath beneath him in the plains of Moab? or shall we not lament with David over the shield, cast away on the Gilboa mountains, of him to whom God gave *another heart* that day, when he turned his back to go from Samuel? It is not our part to look hardly, nor to look always, to the character or the deeds of men, but to accept from all of them, and to hold fast, that which we can prove good, and feel to be

<small>Num. xxiv. 4, 16.</small>

<small>2 Sam. i. 21.</small>

ordained for us. We know that whatever good there is in them is itself divine; and wherever we see the virtue of ardent labour and self-surrendering to a single purpose, wherever we find constant reference made to the written scripture of natural beauty, this at least we know is great and **good**; this we know is not granted by the counsel of God without purpose, nor maintained without result: their interpretation we may accept, into their labour we may enter, but they themselves must look to it, if what they do has no intent of good, nor any reference to the Giver of all gifts. Selfish in their industry, unchastened in their wills, ungrateful for the Spirit that is upon them, they may yet be helmed by that Spirit whithersoever the Governor listeth; James iii. 4. involuntary instruments they may become of others' good; unwillingly they may bless Israel, doubtingly discomfit Amalek; but short-coming there Exodus xvii. 8-13. will be of their glory, and sure, of their punishment.—*Modern Painters*, vol. ii., sec. i., ch. xv., § 8.

Spirit of Sacrifice.

Can the Deity be indeed honoured by the presentation to Him of any material objects of value, or by any direction of zeal or wisdom which is not immediately beneficial to men? For, observe, it is not now the question whether the fairness and majesty of a building may or may not answer any moral purpose; it is not the *result* of labour in any sort of which we are speaking, but the bare and mere costliness—the substance and labour and time themselves: are these, we ask, independently of their result, acceptable offerings to God, and considered by Him as doing Him honour? So long as we refer this question to the decision of feeling, or of conscience, or of reason merely, it will be contradictorily or imperfectly answered; it admits of entire answer only when we have met another and a far different question, whether the Bible be indeed one book or two, and whether the character of God revealed in the

Old Testament be other than His character revealed in the New.

Now, it is a most secure truth, that, although the particular ordinances divinely appointed for special purposes at any given period of man's history, may be by the same divine authority abrogated at another, it is impossible that any character of God, appealed to or described in any ordinance past or present, can ever be changed, or understood as changed, by the abrogation of that ordinance. God is one and the same, and is pleased or displeased by the same things for ever, although one part of His pleasure may be expressed at one time rather than another, and although the mode in which His pleasure is to be consulted may be by Him graciously modified to the circumstances of men. Thus, for instance, it was necessary that, in order to the understanding by man of the scheme of Redemption, that scheme should be foreshown from the beginning by the type of bloody sacrifice. But God had no more pleasure in such sacrifice in the time of Moses than He has now; He never accepted, as a propitiation for sin, any sacrifice but the single one in perspective: and that we may not entertain any shadow of doubt on this subject, the worthlessness of all other sacrifice than this is proclaimed at the very time when typical sacrifice was most imperatively demanded. God was a Spirit, and could be worshipped only in spirit and in truth, as singly and exclusively when every day brought its claim of typical and material service or offering, as now when He asks for none but that of the heart.

<small>S. John iv. 24.</small>

So, therefore, it is a most safe and sure principle that, if in the manner of performing any rite at any time, circumstances can be traced which we are either told or may legitimately conclude, *pleased* God at that time, those same circumstances will please Him at all times, in the performance of all rites or offices to which they may be attached in like manner; unless it has been afterwards revealed that, for some special purpose, it is now His will that such circumstances should be withdrawn. And this argument will have all the more force if it can be shown that such conditions **were not essential** to the completeness of the rite in its human uses and bearings, and only were added to it as being in *themselves* pleasing to God.

Now, was it necessary to the completeness, as a type, of the Levitical sacrifice, or to its utility as an explanation of divine purposes, that **it should cost anything** to the person in whose behalf it was offered ? On the contrary, the sacrifice **which it foreshowed, was** to be God's free gift ; **and the cost** of, or difficulty of obtaining, the sacrificial type, **could** only render that type in a measure obscure, and less expressive of the offering which God would in the end provide for all men. Yet this costliness was *generally* a condition of the acceptableness of the sacrifice. ' Neither will I offer unto the Lord my God of that which doth cost me nothing.' That costliness, therefore, must be an acceptable condition in all human offerings at all times ; for if it was pleasing to God once, it must please Him always, unless directly forbidden by Him afterwards, which it has never been. 2 Sam. xxiv. 24. Deut. xvi. 16, 17.

Again, was it necessary to the typical perfection of the Levitical offering, that it should be the best of the flock ? Doubtless, the spotlessness of the sacrifice renders it more expressive to the Christian mind ; but was it because so expressive that it was actually, and in so many words, demanded by God ? Not at all. It was **demanded** by Him expressly on the same grounds **on** which an earthly governor would demand it, as a testimony of respect. ' Offer it **now** unto thy governor.' And the less valuable offering was rejected, not because it did not image Christ, nor fulfil the purposes of sacrifice, but because it indicated a feeling that would grudge the best of its possessions to Him who gave them ; and because it was a bold dishonouring of God in the sight of man. Whence it **may** be infallibly Mal. i. 8.

concluded, that in whatever offerings we may now see reason to present unto God (I say not what these may be), a condition of their acceptableness will be now, as it was then, that they should be the best of their kind.

But farther, was it necessary to the carrying out of the Mosaical system, **that** there should be either art or splendour in the form or services of the tabernacle or temple? Was it necessary to the perfection of any one of their typical offices, that there should be that hanging of blue, and purple, and scarlet? **those** taches of brass and sockets of silver? that working in cedar and overlaying with gold? One thing at least is evident: there was a deep and awful danger in it; a danger that the God whom they so worshipped, might be associated in the minds of the serfs of Egypt with the gods to whom they had seen similar gifts offered and similar honours paid. The probability, in our times, of fellowship with the feelings of the idolatrous Romanist is absolutely as nothing, compared with the danger to the Israelite of a sympathy with the idolatrous Egyptian; no speculative, no unproved danger; but proved fatally by their fall during a month's abandonment to their own will; a fall into the most servile idolatry; yet marked by such offerings to their idol as their leader was, in the close sequel, instructed to bid them offer to God. This danger was imminent, perpetual, and of the most awful kind: it was the one against which God made provision, not only by commandments, by threatenings, by promises, the most urgent, repeated, and impressive; but by temporary ordinances of a severity so terrible as almost to dim for a time, in the eyes of His people, His attribute of mercy. The principal object of every instituted law of that Theocracy, of every judgment sent forth in its vindication, was to mark to the people His hatred of idolatry; a hatred written under their advancing steps, in the blood of the Canaanite, and more sternly still in the darkness of their own desolation, when the children and

Exod. xxvi. 31-36.

the sucklings swooned in the streets of Jerusalem, and the lion tracked his prey in the desert of Samaria. Yet, against this mortal danger, provision was not made in one way, (to man's thoughts the simplest, the most natural, the most effective,) by withdrawing from the worship of the Divine Being whatever could delight the sense, or shape the imagination, or limit the idea of Deity to place. This one way God refused, demanding for Himself such honours, and accepting for Himself such local dwelling, as had been paid and dedicated to idol gods by heathen worshippers. And for what reason? Was the glory of the tabernacle necessary to set forth or image His divine glory to the minds of His people? What! purple or scarlet necessary, to the people who had seen the great river of Egypt run scarlet to the sea, under His condemnation? What! golden lamp and cherub necessary, for those who had seen the fires of heaven falling like a mantle on Mount Sinai, and its golden courts open to receive their mortal lawgiver? What! silver clasp and fillet necessary, when they had seen the silver waves of the Red Sea clasp in their arched hollows the corpses of the horse and his rider? There was but one reason, and that an eternal one; that as the covenant that He made with men was accompanied with some external sign of its continuance, and of His remembrance of it, so the acceptance of that covenant might be marked and signified by men, in some external sign of their love and obedience, and surrender of themselves and theirs to His will; and that their gratitude to Him and continual remembrance of Him, might have at once their expression, and their enduring testimony, in the presentation to Him, not only of the firstlings of the herd and fold, not only of the fruits of the earth and the tithe of time, but of all treasures of wisdom and beauty; of the thought that invents and the hand that labours; of wealth of wood, and weight of stone; of the strength of iron, and the light of gold.

Lam. ii. 11.
2 Kings xvii. 25.

And let us not now lose sight of this broad and unabrogated principle—I might say, incapable of being abrogated, so long as men shall receive earthly gifts from God. Of all that they have, His tithe must be rendered to Him, or in so far and in so much He is forgotten: of the skill and of the treasure, of the strength and of the mind, of the time and of the toil, offering must be made reverently; and if there be any difference between the Levitical and the Christian offering, it is that the latter may be just so much the wider in its range as it is less typical in its meaning, as it is thankful instead of sacrificial. There can be no excuse accepted because the Deity does not now visibly dwell in His temple; if He is invisible it is only through our failing faith: nor any excuse because other calls are more immediate or more sacred; this ought to be done, and not the other left undone. Yet this objection, as frequent as feeble, must be more specifically answered.

It has been said—it ought always to be said, for it is true,—that a better and more honourable offering is made to our Master in ministry to the poor, in extending the knowledge of His name, in the practice of the virtues by which that name is hallowed, than in material presents to His temple. Assuredly it is so: woe to all who think that any other kind or manner of offering may in any wise take the place of these! Do the people need place to pray, and calls to hear His word? Then it is no time for smoothing pillars or carving pulpits; let us have enough first of walls and roofs. Do the people need teaching from house to house, and bread from day to day? Then they are deacons and ministers we want, not architects. I insist on this, I plead for this; but let us examine ourselves, and see if this be indeed the reason for our backwardness in the lesser work. The question is not between God's house and His poor: it is not between God's house and His gospel. It is between God's house and ours. Have we no tessellated colours on our floors? no frescoed fancies on our roofs? no niched statuary in our corridors? no gilded furniture in our chambers? no costly stones in our cabinets? Has even the tithe of these been offered? They are, or they ought to be, the signs that enough has been devoted to the great purposes of human stewardship, and that there remains to us what we can spend in luxury; but there is a greater and prouder luxury than this selfish one—that of bringing a portion of such things as these into sacred service, and presenting them for a memorial that our pleasure as well as our toil has been hallowed by the remembrance of Him who gave both the strength and the reward. And until this has been done, I do not see how such possessions can be retained in happiness. I do not understand the feeling which would arch our own gates and pave our own thresholds and leave the church with its narrow door and foot-worn sill; the feeling which enriches our own chambers with all manner of costliness, and endures the bare wall and mean compass of the temple.—*Seven Lamps of Architecture*, The Lamp of Sacrifice, §§ iii.–vii.

[Psalm lxxvi. 11.]
[Num. xxxi. 54.]

Strength of Character.

All strength of character begins in temperance, prudence, and lowliness of thought. Without these, nothing is possible, of noble humanity: on these follow—kindness, (simple, as opposed to malice,) and compassion, (sympathy, a much rarer quality than mere kindness); then, self-*restriction*, a quite different and higher condition than temperance,—the first being not painful when rightly practised, but the latter always so;—('I held my peace, even from good'— 'quanto quisque sibi plura negaverit, ab Dis plura feret'). Then come pity and long-suffering, which have to deal with the sin, and not merely with the sorrow, of those around us.—*St. Mark's Rest*, § 130.

[Psalm xxxix. 1.]

Superstition and Religion.

Superstition, in all times and among all nations, is the fear of a spirit whose passions are those of a man, whose acts are the acts of a man; who is present in some places, not in others; who makes some places holy and not others; who is kind to one person, unkind to another; who is pleased or angry according to the degree of attention you pay to him, or praise you refuse to him; who is hostile generally to human pleasure, but may be bribed by sacrifice of a part of that pleasure into permitting the rest. This, whatever form of faith it colours, is the essence of superstition. And religion is the belief in a Spirit whose mercies are over all His works—who is kind even to the unthankful and the evil; who is everywhere present, and therefore is in no place to be sought, and in no place to be evaded; to whom all creatures, times, and things are everlastingly holy, and who claims—not tithes of wealth, nor sevenths of days—but all the wealth that we have, and all the days that we live, and all the beings that we are, but who claims that totality because He delights only in the delight of His creatures; and because, therefore, the one duty that they owe to Him, and the only service they can render Him, is to be happy. A Spirit, therefore, whose eternal benevolence cannot be angered, cannot be appeased; whose laws are everlasting and inexorable, so that heaven and earth must indeed pass away if one jot of them failed: laws which attach to every wrong and error a measured, inevitable penalty; to every rightness and prudence, an assured reward; penalty, of which the remittance cannot be purchased; and reward, of which the promise cannot be broken. . . .

S. Luke vi. 35.

S. Matt. xxiv. 35.

Religion proselytes by love, superstition by war; religion teaches by example, superstition by persecution. Religion gave granite shrine to the Egyptian, golden temple to the Jew, sculptured corridor to the Greek, pillared aisle and frescoed wall to the Christian. Superstition made idols of the splendours by which

Religion had spoken : reverenced pictures and stones, instead of truths; letters and laws, instead of acts, and for ever, in various madness of fantastic desolation, kneels in the temple while it crucifies the Christ.—*On the Old Road*, vol. i., part i., §§ 283, 284.

Symbolism.

Symbolism is the setting forth of a great truth by an imperfect and inferior sign (as for instance, of the hope of the resurrection by the form of the phœnix); and it is almost always employed by men in their most serious moods of faith, rarely in recreation. Men who use symbolism forcibly are almost always true believers in what they symbolize. . . . Thus symbolism constituted the entire system of the Mosaic dispensation : it occurs in every word of Christ's teaching; it attaches perpetual mystery to the last and most solemn act of His life. . . . And as we watch, thenceforward, the history of the Church, we shall find the declension of its faith exactly marked by the abandonment of symbolism.[1]— *Stones of Venice*, vol. ii., ch. viii., § LV.

Symbolism of the Thorn and Thistle.

All these lower organisms suffer and perish, or are gladdened and flourish, under conditions which are in utter precision symbolical, and in utter fidelity representative, of the conditions which induce adversity and prosperity in the kingdoms of men : and the Eternal Demeter,—Mother, and Judge,—brings forth, as the herb yielding seed, so also the thorn and the thistle, not to herself, but *to thee*. (Gen. i. 11. Gen. iii. 18.)

You have read the words of the great Law often enough ;—have you ever thought enough of them to know the difference between these two appointed means of Distress? The first, the Thorn, is the type of

---

[1] The transformation of a symbol into a reality, observe, as in transubstantiation, is as much an abandonment of symbolism as the forgetfulness of symbolic meaning altogether.

distress *caused by crime*, changing the soft and breathing leaf into inflexible and wounding stubbornness. The second is the distress appointed to be the means and herald of good,—Thou shalt see the stubborn thistle bursting into glossy purple, which outreddens all voluptuous garden roses. . . .

How literally may we go back from the living soul symbolized, to the strangely accurate earthly symbol, in the prickly weed. For if, with its bravery of endurance, and carelessness in choice of home, we find also definite faculty and habit of migration, volant mechanism for choiceless journey, not divinely directed in pilgrimage to known shrines; but carried at the wind's will by a spirit which listeth *not*,—it will go hard but that the plant shall become, if not dreaded, at least despised; and, in its wandering and reckless splendour, disgrace the garden of the sluggard, and possess the inheritance of the prodigal: until even its own nature seems contrary to good, and the invocation of the just man be made to it as the executor of Judgment, 'Let thistles grow instead of wheat, and cockle instead of barley.' Yet to be despised—either for men or flowers—may be no ill-fortune; the real ill-fortune is only to be despicable.—*Proserpina*, ch. vii., §§ 7, 8, 10, 11.

<small>S. John iii. 8.</small>

<small>Job xxxi. 40.</small>

Tabernacle.

The Tabernacle of God is now with men;—*in* men, and women, and sucklings also; which temple ye are, ye and your Christian sisters; of whom the poorest, here in London, are a very undecorated shrine indeed. *They* are the Tabernacle, fair friends, which you have got leave, and charge, to adorn. Not, in anywise, those charming churches and altars which you wreathe with garlands for God's sake, and the eloquent clergyman's. You are quite wrong, and barbarous in language, when you call *them* 'Churches' at all. They are only Synagogues;—the very same of which Christ spoke, with

<small>Rev. xxi. 3.</small>

<small>1 Cor. iii. 16.</small>

<small>S. Matt. vi. 5.</small>

eternal meaning, as the places that hypocrites would love to be seen in. Here, in St. Giles's, and the East, sister to that in St. George's and the West, is the Church! raggedly enough curtained, surely! . . .

You are yourselves the Church, and see that you be finally adorned, as women professing godli- <small>1 Tim.</small> ness, with the precious stones of good works, <small>ii. 10.</small> which may be quite briefly defined, for the present, as decorating the entire Tabernacle; and clothing your poor sisters, with yourselves. Put roses also in *their* hair, put precious stones also on *their* breasts; see that they also are clothed in your purple and <small>2 Sam.</small> scarlet, with other delights; that they also <small>i. 24.</small> learn to read the gilded heraldry of the sky; and, upon the earth, be taught, not only the labours of it, but the loveliness. For them, also, let the hereditary jewel recall their father's pride, their mother's beauty; <small>Exod.</small> so shall your days and theirs, be long in the <small>xx. 12.</small> sweet and sacred land which the Lord your God has given you: so, truly, shall THE GOLD OF THAT <small>Gen.</small> LAND BE GOOD, AND THERE ALSO, THE CRYSTAL, <small>ii. 12.</small> AND THE ONYX STONE.—*Deucalion*, ch. vii., § 46.

'Thou God seest me.'

This Morning Service of all England begins with the assertion that the Scripture moveth us in sundry places to confess our sins before God. *Does* it so? Have your congregations ever been referred to those sundry places? Or do they take the assertion on trust, or remain under the impression that, unless with the advantage of their own candour, God must remain ill-informed on the subject of their sins?

'That we should not dissemble nor cloke them.' *Can* we then? Are these grown-up congregations of the en- lightened English Church in the nineteenth <small>Gen.</small> century still so young in their nurseries that the <small>xvi. 13.</small> 'Thou, God, seest me' is still not believed by them if they get under the bed?—*On the Old Road*, vol. ii., § 258.

Thou shalt love the Lord thy God.

Men are guilty or otherwise, not for what they do, but for what they desire, the command being not Thou shalt obey, but Thou shalt love, the Lord thy God; a vain command if men were not capable of governing and directing their affections.—*Modern Painters*, vol. ii., sec. i., ch. iii., § 2.

<small>S. Matt. xxii. 37.</small>

Thy Kingdom come.

If you do not wish for His kingdom, don't pray for it. But if you do, you must do more than pray for it; you must work for it. And, to work for it, you must know what it is; we have all prayed for it many a day without thinking. Observe, it is a kingdom that is to come to us; we are not to go to it. Also, it is not to be a kingdom of the dead, but of the living. Also, it is not to come all at once, but quietly; nobody knows how. 'The kingdom of God cometh not with observation.' Also, it is not to come outside of us, but in our hearts: 'the kingdom of God is within you.' And, being within us, it is not a thing to be seen, but to be felt; and though it brings all substance of good with it, it does not consist in that: 'the kingdom of God is not meat and drink, but righteousness, peace, and joy in the Holy Ghost joy, that is to say, in the holy, healthful, and helpful Spirit. Now, if we want to work for this kingdom, and to bring it, and enter into it, there's one curious condition to be first accepted. You must enter it as children, or not at all: 'Whosoever will not receive it as a little child shall not enter therein.' And again, 'Suffer little children to come unto me, and forbid them not, *for of such is the kingdom of heaven*.'—*The Crown of Wild Olive*, § 46.

<small>S. Luke xvii. 20.</small>
<small>S. Luke xvii. 21.</small>
<small>Rom. xiv. 17.</small>
<small>S. Luke xviii. 17.</small>
<small>S. Mark x. 14.</small>

'Thy kingdom come,' we are bid to ask then! But how shall it come? With power and great glory, it is written; and yet not with observation, it is also written. Strange kingdom!

<small>S. Matt. vi. 10.</small>
<small>S. Matt. xxiv. 30.</small>

Yet its strangeness is renewed to us with every dawn.

When the time comes for us to wake out of the world's sleep, why should it be otherwise than out of the dreams of the night? Singing of birds, first, broken and low, as, not to dying eyes, but eyes that wake to life, 'the casement slowly grows a glimmering square'; and then the gray, and then the rose of dawn; and last the light, whose going forth is to the ends of heaven. Psalm xix. 6.

This kingdom it is not in our power to bring; but it is, to receive. Nay, it is come already, in part; but not received, because men love chaos best; and the Night, with her daughters. That is still the only question for us, as in the old Elias days, 'If ye will receive it.' With pains it may be shut out still from many a dark place of cruelty; by sloth it may be still unseen for many a glorious hour. But the pain of shutting it out must grow greater and greater:— harder, every day, that struggle of man with man in the abyss, and shorter wages for the fiend's work. But it is still at our choice; the simoom-dragon may still be served if we will, in the fiery desert, or else God walking in the garden, at cool of day. Coolness now, not of Hesperus over Atlas, stooped endurer of toil; but of Heosphorus over Sion, the joy of the earth.¹ The choice is no vague nor doubtful one. High on the desert mountain, full descried, sits throned the tempter, with his old promise —the kingdoms of this world, and the glory of them. He still calls you to your labour, as Christ to your rest;—labour and sorrow, base desire, and cruel hope. So far as you desire to possess, rather than to give; so far as you look for power to command, instead of to bless; so far as your own prosperity seems

---

¹ This joy it is to receive and to give, because its officers (governors of its acts) are to be Peace, and its exactors (governors of its dealings) Righteousness.—Isa. lx. 17.

to you to issue out of contest or rivalry, of any kind, with other men, or other nations; so long as the hope before you is for supremacy instead of love; and your desire is to be greatest, instead of least;—first, instead of last;—so long you are serving the Lord of all that is last, and least; the last enemy that shall be destroyed—Death; and you shall have death's crown, with the worm coiled in it; and death's wages, with the worm feeding on them; kindred of the earth shall you yourself become; saying to the grave, 'Thou art my father;' and to the worm, 'Thou art my mother, and my sister.'

<small>1 Cor. xv. 26.</small>
<small>Job xvii. 14.</small>

I leave you to judge, and to choose, between this labour, and the bequeathed peace; these wages, and the gift of the Morning Star; this obedience, and the doing of the will which shall enable you to claim another kindred than of the earth, and to hear another voice than that of the grave, saying, 'My brother, and sister, and mother.'—*Modern Painters*, vol. v., pt. ix., ch. xii., § 20.

<small>Rev. ii. 28.</small>
<small>S. Matt. xii. 50.</small>

Torcello, Cathedral of.

It has evidently been built by men in flight and distress, who sought in the hurried erection of their island church such a shelter for their earnest and sorrowful worship as, on the one hand, could not attract the eyes of their enemies by its splendour, and yet, on the other, might not awaken too bitter feelings by its contrast with the churches which they had seen destroyed. There is visible everywhere a simple and tender effort to recover some of the form of the temples which they had loved, and to do honour to God by that which they were erecting, while distress and humiliation prevented the desire, and prudence precluded the admission, either of luxury of ornament or magnificence of plan. The exterior is absolutely devoid of decoration, with the exception only of the western entrance and the lateral door, of which the former has carved sideposts and architrave, and the latter, crosses of rich sculpture; while the massy stone shutters of the windows, turning on huge rings of stone, which answer the double purpose of stanchions and brackets, cause the whole building rather to resemble a refuge from Alpine storm than the cathedral of a populous city; and, internally, the two solemn mosaics of the eastern and western extremities,—one representing the Last Judgment, the other the Madonna, her tears falling as her hands are raised to bless,—and the noble range of pillars which enclose the space between, terminated by the high throne for the pastor and the semicircular raised seats for the superior clergy, are expressive at once of the deep sorrow and the sacred courage of men who had no home left them upon earth, but who looked for one to come, of men 'persecuted but not forsaken, cast down but not destroyed.' 2 Cor. iv. 9.

I am not aware of any other early church in Italy which has this peculiar expression in so marked a degree; and it is so consistent with all that Christian architecture ought to express in every age (for the actual condition of the exiles who built the cathedral of Torcello is exactly typical of the spiritual condition which every Christian ought to recognise in himself, a state of homelessness on earth, except so far as he can make the Most High his habitation). . . . It is remarkable when we compare the Cathedral of Torcello with any of the contemporary basilicas in South Italy or Lombardic churches in the North, . . . they are all like sepulchral caverns compared with Torcello, where the slightest details of the sculptures and mosaics are visible, even when twilight is deepening. And there is something especially touching in our finding the sunshine thus freely admitted into a church built by men in sorrow. They did not need the darkness; they could not perhaps bear it. There was fear and depression upon them enough, without a material gloom. They sought for comfort in their Psalm xci. 9.

religion, for tangible hopes and promises, not for threatenings or mysteries; and though the subjects chosen for the mosaics on the walls are of the most solemn character, there are no artificial shadows cast upon them, nor dark colours used in them: all is fair and bright, and intended evidently to be regarded in hopefulness, and not with terror. . . .

Most other early churches are covered with imagery sufficiently suggestive of the vivid interest of the builders in the history and occupations of the world. Symbols or representations of political events, portraits of living persons, and sculptures of satirical, grotesque, or trivial subjects are of constant occurrence, mingled with the more strictly appointed representations of scriptural or ecclesiastical history; but at Torcello even these usual, and one should have thought almost necessary, successions of Bible events do not appear. The mind of the worshipper was fixed entirely upon two great facts, to him the most precious of all facts,—the present mercy of Christ to His Church, and His future coming to judge the world. That Christ's mercy was, at this period, supposed chiefly to be attainable through the pleading of the Virgin, and that therefore beneath the figure of the Redeemer is seen that of the weeping Madonna in the act of intercession, may indeed be matter of sorrow to the Protestant beholder, but ought not to blind him to the earnestness and singleness of the faith with which these men sought their sea-solitudes; not in hope of founding new dynasties, or entering upon new epochs of prosperity, but only to humble themselves before God, and to pray that in His infinite mercy He would hasten the time when the sea should give up the dead which were in it, and Death and Hell give up the dead which were in them, and when they might enter into the better kingdom, 'where the wicked cease from troubling and the weary are at rest.'—*Stones of Venice*, vol. ii., ch. ii., §§ 3, 4, 8, 9.

[Rev. xx. 13.]

[Job iii. 17.]

Towers of the Bible.

I need not remind you of the effect upon the northern mind which has always been produced by the heaven-pointing spire, nor of the theory which has been founded upon it of the general meaning of Gothic architecture as expressive of religious aspiration. In a few minutes, you may ascertain the exact value of that theory, and the degree in which it is true.

The first tower of which we hear as built upon the earth, was certainly built in a species of aspiration; but I do not suppose that any one will think it was a religious one. 'Go to now. Let us build a tower whose top may reach unto heaven.' [Gen. xi. 4.] From that day to this, whenever men have become skilful architects at all, there has been a tendency in them to build high; not in any religious feeling, but in mere exuberance of spirit and power—as they dance or sing—with a certain mingling of vanity—like the feeling in which a child builds a tower of cards; and, in nobler instances, with also a strong sense of, and delight in the majesty, height, and strength of the building itself, such as we have in that of a lofty tree or a peaked mountain. Add to this instinct the frequent necessity of points of elevation for watch-towers, or of points of offence, as in towers built on the ramparts of cities, and, finally, the need of elevations for the transmission of sound, as in the Turkish minaret and Christian belfry, and you have, I think, a sufficient explanation of the tower-building of the world in general. Look through your Bibles only, and collect the various expressions with reference to tower-building there, and you will have a very complete idea of the spirit in which it is for the most part undertaken. You begin with that of Babel; then you remember Gideon beating down the tower of Penuel, in order more completely to humble the pride of the men of the city; [Judges viii. 17.] you remember the defence of the tower of Shechem against Abimelech, [Judges ix. 48-53.] and the death of Abimelech by the casting of a stone

from it by a woman's hand; you recollect the husbandman building a tower in his vineyard, and
the beautiful expressions in Solomon's song,—
'The tower of Lebanon, which looketh towards
Damascus;' 'I am a wall, and my breasts like
towers;'—you recollect the Psalmist's expressions of love and delight, 'Go ye round about
Jerusalem; tell the towers thereof: mark ye
well her bulwarks; consider her palaces, that
ye may tell it to the generation following.' You see in
all these cases how completely the tower is a subject of
human pride, or delight, or defence, not in any wise associated with religious sentiment; the towers of Jerusalem
being named in the same sentence, not with her temple,
but with her bulwarks and palaces. And thus, when the
tower is in reality connected with a place of worship,
it was generally done to add to its magnificence, but not
to add to its religious expression.—*Lectures on Architecture and Painting*, § 19.

<small>S. Matt. xxi. 33;
S. Mark xii. 1.
Cant. vii. 4
Cant. viii. 10.
Psalm xlviii. 12, 13.</small>

Transfiguration, The.

We are all of us too much in the habit of passing it
by, as a thing mystical and inconceivable, taking place
in the life of Christ for some purpose not by us to be
understood, or, at the best, merely as a manifestation of
His divinity by brightness of heavenly light, and the
ministering of the spirits of the dead, intended to
strengthen the faith of His three chosen apostles. And
in this, as in many other events recorded by the Evangelists, we lose half the meaning, and evade the practical
power upon ourselves, by never accepting in its fulness
the idea that our Lord was 'perfect man,'
'tempted in all things like as we are.' Our
preachers are continually trying in all manner of subtle
ways, to explain the union of the Divinity with the
Manhood, an explanation which certainly involves first
their being able to describe the nature of Deity itself, or,
in plain words, to comprehend God. They never can

<small>Heb. iv. 15.</small>

explain, in any one particular, the union of the natures; they only succeed in weakening the faith of their hearers as to the entireness of either. The thing they have to do is precisely the contrary of this—to insist upon the *entireness* of both. We never think of Christ enough as God, never enough as Man; the instinctive habit of our minds being always to miss of the Divinity, and the reasoning and enforced habit to miss of the Humanity. We are afraid to harbour in our own hearts, or to utter in the hearing of others, any thought of our Lord, as hungering, tired, sorrowful, having a human soul, a human will, and affected by events of human life as a finite creature is; and yet one half of the efficiency of His atonement, and the whole of the efficiency of His example, depend on His having been this to the full.

Consider, therefore, the Transfiguration as it relates to the human feelings of our Lord. It was the first definite preparation for His death. He had foretold it to His disciples six days before; [S. Matt. xvii. 1.] then takes with Him the three chosen ones [S. Mark ix. 2.] into 'an high mountain apart.' From an exceeding high mountain, at the first taking on [S. Matt. iv. 8.] Him the ministry of life, He had beheld, and rejected the kingdoms of the earth, and their [S. Luke ix. 28–32.] glory; now, on a high mountain, He takes upon Him the ministry of death. Peter and they that were with him, as in Gethsemane, were heavy with sleep. Christ's work had to be done alone.

The tradition is, that the Mount of Transfiguration was the summit of Tabor; but Tabor is neither a high mountain, nor was it in any sense a mountain '*apart*'; being in those years both inhabited and fortified. All the immediately preceding ministries of Christ had been at Cesarea Philippi. There is no mention of travel southward in the six days that intervened between the warning given to His disciples, and the going up into the hill. What other hill could it be than the southward slope of that goodly mountain, Hermon, which is indeed the centre of all the Promised Land, from the entering in of Hamath unto the **river of** Egypt; the mount of fruitfulness, from which the springs of Jordan descended to the valleys of Israel? Along its mighty forest avenues, until the grass grew fair with the mountain lilies, His feet dashed in the dew of Hermon, He must have gone to **pray His** first recorded prayer about death; and from the steep of it, before He knelt, could **see to** the south all the dwelling-place of the people that <small>S. Matt. iv. 16.</small> had sat in darkness, and seen the great light, the land of Zabulon and of Naphtali, Galilee of the nations;—could see, even with His human sight, the gleam of that lake by Capernaum and Chorazin, and many a place loved by **Him, and** vainly ministered to, whose house was now **left unto** them desolate; and, chief **of all,** far in the **utmost blue, the hills** above Nazareth, sloping **down to His old home**: hills on which yet the stones lay loose, that had been taken **up to cast** at Him, when He left them for ever.

'And as He prayed, two men stood by Him.' Among <small>S. Luke ix. 29, 30.</small> the many ways in which we miss the help and hold of Scripture, none is more subtle than **our** habit of supposing that, **even as** man, Christ was **free** from the Fear of Death. How could He then have **been** tempted as we are? since among all the trials of the earth, none spring from **the** dust more terrible than that Fear. It had to be borne by Him, indeed, in a unity, which we can never comprehend, with the foreknowledge of victory,—as His sorrow for Lazarus, with the consciousness of the power to restore him; but it *had* to be borne, and that in its **full** earthly terror; and the presence of it is surely marked for us enough by the rising of those two at <small>S. Matt. iv. 11.</small> His side. When, in the desert, He was girding Himself for the work of life, angels of life came <small>S. Matt. xvii. 3.</small> and ministered unto Him; now, in the fair world, when He is girding Himself for the work of death, the ministrants come to Him from the grave.

But from the grave conquered. One, from that tomb under Abarim, which his own hand had sealed so long ago; the other, from the rest into which he had entered, without seeing corruption. There stood by Him Moses and Elias, and spake of His decease. *Num.* xxvii. 12, 13. *2 Kings* ii. 11. *S. Luke* ix. 30, 31.

Then, when the prayer is ended, the task accepted, first, since the star paused over Him at Bethlehem, the full glory falls upon Him from heaven, and the testimony is borne to His everlasting Sonship and power. 'Hear ye him.'—*Modern Painters*, vol. iv., ch. xx., §§ 47–49. *S. Matt.* xvii. 5.

Do but try to believe that Moses and Elias are really there talking with Christ. Moses in the loveliest heart and midst of the land which once it had been denied him to behold,—Elijah treading the earth again, from which he had been swept to heaven in fire; both now with a mightier message than ever they had given in life,—mightier, in closing their own mission,— mightier, in speaking to Christ 'of His decease, which He should accomplish at Jerusalem.'—*Modern Painters*, vol. iii., ch. iv., § 17, NOTE [2]. *S. Luke* ix. 31.

Tree-legend.

'And Christopher said, How can I preach, for I have no learning? how can I persuade them? and the child told him to plant in the earth the dry fir tree that he carried in his hand; and when he did so it became green and was covered with fresh leaves. And the child said, 'When you speak and they will not believe, plant your staff in the ground and it will grow green before their eyes, because with that staff in your hand you carried the Lord!' . . . It is, I suppose, only by the coincidence of thought which runs through all great legend and literature that the putting forth of blossom by the rod of Aaron, and of leaf by the staff of St. Christopher, teach the life and beneficence of the Sceptres of the just—as the for ever leafless sceptre of

Achilles, and the spear whose image was the pine, hewn for ships of battle from the Norwegian hills, show in their own death the power of the Kings of Death.—*Roadside Songs of Tuscany*, pp. 307, 308, 311, 312.

Tree Symbolism.

'He shall be like a tree planted by the river side, that bears its fruit in its season. His leaf also shall not wither; and you will see that whatever he does will prosper.'

<small>Psalm l. 3.</small>

I call it a curious statement, because the conduct to which this prosperity is promised is not that which the English, as a nation, at present think conducive to prosperity: but whether the statement be true or not, it will be easy for you to recollect the two eastern figures under which the happiness of the man is represented,— that he is like a tree bearing fruit 'in its season'; (not so hastily as that the frost pinch it, nor so late that no sun ripens it;) and that 'his leaf shall not fade.' I should like you to recollect this phrase in the Vulgate—'folium ejus non defluet'—shall not fall *away*,—that is to say, shall not fall so as to leave any visible bareness in winter time, but only that others may come up in its place, and the tree be always green. . . . Notice next the word 'folium.' In Greek, φυλλον, 'phyllon.'

<small>Ezekiel xlvii. 12.</small>

'The thing that is born,' or 'put forth.' 'When the branch is tender, and putteth forth her leaves, ye know that summer is nigh.' . . . Wherever men are noble, they love bright colour; and wherever they can live healthily, bright colour is given them—in sky, sea, flowers, and living creatures. . . . There are, of course, exceptions to all such widely founded laws; there are poisonous berries of scarlet, and pestilent skies that are fair. But . . . lovely flowers, and green trees growing in the open air, are the proper guides of men to the places which their Maker intended them to inhabit; while the flowerless

<small>S. Matt. xxiv. 32.</small>
<small>S. Mark xiii. 28.</small>

and treeless deserts—of reed, or sand, or rock,—are meant to be either heroically invaded and redeemed, or surrendered to the wild creatures which are appointed for them; happy and wonderful in their wild abodes.—*Proserpina*, ch. iii., §§ 1, 3; iv., § 22.

True Science.

All true science begins in the love, not the dissection, of your fellow-creatures; and it ends in the love, not the analysis, of God. Your alphabet of science is in the nearest knowledge, as your alphabet of science is in the nearest duty. 'Behold, it is nigh thee, even at the doors.' The Spirit of God is around you in the air that you breathe,—His glory in the light that you see; and in the fruitfulness of the earth, and the joy of its creatures, He has written for you, day by day, His revelation, as He has granted you, day by day, your daily bread.—*Deucalion*, ch. xii., § 40. [S. Mark xiii. 29.]

Truth in Art.

Wheresoever the search after truth begins, there life begins; wheresoever that search ceases, there life ceases. As long as a school of art holds any chain of natural facts, trying to discover more of them and express them better daily, it may play hither and thither as it likes on this side of the chain or that; it may design grotesques and conventionalisms, build the simplest buildings, serve the most practical utilities, yet all it does will be gloriously designed and gloriously done; but let it once quit hold of the chain of natural fact, cease to pursue that as the clue to its work; let it propose to itself any other end than preaching this living word, and think first of showing its own skill or its own fancy, and from that hour its fall is precipitate—its destruction sure; nothing that it does or designs will ever have life or loveliness in it more; its hour has come, and there is no work, nor device, nor knowledge, nor wisdom in the grave whither it goeth.—*The Two Paths*, § 23. [Eccl. ix. 10.]

Truth in Daily Life.

We may at least labour for a system of greater honesty and kindness in the minor commerce of our daily life.— . . . Every person who tries to buy an article for less than its proper value, or who tries to sell it at more than its proper value—every consumer who keeps a tradesman waiting for his money and every tradesman who bribes a consumer to extravagance by credit, is helping forward, according to his own measure of power, a system of baseless and dishonourable commerce, and forcing his country down into poverty and shame. And people of moderate means and average powers of mind would do far more real good by merely carrying out stern principles of justice and honesty. . . . There are three weighty matters of the law—justice, mercy, and truth; and of these the Teacher puts truth last, because that cannot be known but by a course of acts of justice and love. But men put, in all their efforts, truth first, because they mean by it their own opinions; and thus, while the world has many people who would suffer martyrdom in the cause of what they call truth, it has few, who will suffer even a little inconvenience, in that of justice and mercy.—*A Joy for Ever*, § 152.

Truth, Early education of.

This is especially to be insisted on in the early education of young people. It should be pointed out to them with continual earnestness that the essence of lying is in deception, not in words; a lie may be told by silence, by equivocation, by the accent on a syllable, by a glance of the eye attaching a peculiar significance to a sentence; and all these kinds of lies are worse and baser by many degrees than a lie plainly worded; so that no form of blinded conscience is so far sunk as that which comforts itself for having deceived, because the deception was by gesture or silence, instead of utterance.—*Modern Painters*, vol. v., pt. ix., ch. vii., § 14.

Truth spoken of in the Bible.

There is nothing more certain nor clear throughout the Bible: the Apostles themselves appeal constantly to their flocks, and actually *claim* judgment from them, as deserving it, and having a right to it, rather than discouraging it. But, first notice the way in which the discovery of truth is spoken of in the Old Testament: 'Evil men understand not judgment; but they that seek the Lord understand all things,' Proverbs xxviii. 5. God overthroweth, not merely the transgressor or the wicked, but even 'the words of the transgressor,' Proverbs xxii. 12, and 'the counsel of the wicked,' Job v. 13; xxi. 16; observe again, in Proverbs xxiv. 14, 'My son, eat thou honey, because it is good—so shall the knowledge of wisdom be unto thy soul: when thou hast *found it*, there shall be a reward'; and again, 'What man is he that feareth the Lord? him shall He teach in the way that He shall choose.' [Psalm xxv. 12.] —*On the Old Road*, vol. ii., § 203.

Types.

I trust that some day the language of Types will be more read and understood by us than it has been for centuries; and when this language, a better one than either Greek or Latin, is again recognized amongst us, we shall find, or remember, that as the other visible elements of the universe—its air, its water, and its flame—set forth, in their pure energies, the life-giving, purifying, and sanctifying influences of the Deity upon His creatures, so the earth, in its purity, sets forth His eternity and His TRUTH. . . . The earth which, like our own bodies, though dust in its degradation, is full of splendour when God's hand gathers its atoms; and which was for ever sanctified by Him, as the symbol no less of His love than of His truth, when He bade the High Priest bear the names of the Children of Israel on the clear stones of the Breastplate of Judgment. [Exod. xxviii. 15-21.] —*Stones of Venice*, vol. iii., ch. i., § XLVII.

Unity.

It is the great principle of Brotherhood, not by equality, nor by likeness, but by giving and receiving; the souls that are unlike, and the nations that are unlike, and the natures that are unlike, being bound into one noble whole by each receiving something from and of the others' gifts and the others' glory. . . . Whatever has been made by the Deity externally delightful to the human sense of beauty, there is some type of God's nature or of God's laws; nor are any of His laws, in one sense, greater than the appointment that the most lovely and perfect unity shall be obtained by the taking of one nature into another. . . . And it is just because it is so vast and so awful a law, that it has rule over the smallest things; and there is not a vein of colour on the slightest leaf which the spring winds are at this moment unfolding in the fields around us, but it is an illustration of an ordainment to which the earth and its creatures owe their continuance and their Redemption.—*Stones of Venice*, vol. iii., ch. i., § XXVI.

Unity is often understood in the sense of oneness or singleness, instead of universality; whereas the only unity which by any means can become grateful or an object of hope to men, and whose types therefore in material things can be beautiful, is that on which turned the last words and prayer of Christ before His crossing of the Kedron brook, 'Neither pray I for these alone, but for them also which shall believe on Me through their word; that they all may be one, as Thou, Father, art in Me, and I in Thee.'—*Modern Painters*, vol. ii., sec. i., ch. vi., § 1.

[S. John xvii. 20, 21.]

Usury.

For those of us who are Christians, our own way is plain. We can with perfect ease ascertain what usury is, and in what express terms forbidden. 'And if thy brother be poor, and powerless with his hands, at thy side, thou shalt take his part upon thee,

[Lev. xxv. 35-38.]

to help him, as thy proselyte and thy neighbour; and thy brother shall live with thee. Thou shalt take no usury of him, nor anything over and above, and thou shalt fear thy God. I am the Lord, and thy brother shall live with thee. Thou shalt not give him thy money, for usury; and thou shalt not give him thy food for increase.'

There is the simple law for all of us;—one of those which Christ assuredly came not to destroy, but to fulfil: and there is no national prosperity to be had but in obedience to it.—*Fors Clavigera*, Letter LXVIII. ^{S. Matt. v. 17.}

Vainglory.

Throughout the whole of Scripture history, nothing is more remarkable than the close connection of punishment with the sin of vainglory. Every other sin is occasionally permitted to remain, for lengthened periods, without definite chastisement; but the forgetfulness of God, and the claim of honour by man, as belonging to himself, are visited at once, whether in Hezekiah, Nebuchadnezzar, or Herod, with the most tremendous punishment.—*Stones of Venice*, vol. iii., ch. iii., § XVIII.

Venice, Fall of.

Need we go farther to learn the reason of the fall of Venice? She was already likened in her thoughts, and was therefore to be likened in her ruin, to the Virgin of Babylon. The Pride of State and the Pride of Knowledge were no new passions: the sentence against them had gone forth from everlasting. 'Thou saidst, I shall be a lady for ever, so that thou didst not lay these things to thine heart. . . . *Thy wisdom and thy knowledge, it hath perverted thee;* and thou hast said in thine heart, I am, and none else beside me. Therefore shall evil come upon thee; . . . thy merchants from thy youth, they shall wander every one to his quarter; none shall save thee.' ^{Isaiah xlvii. 7, 10.} ^{Isaiah xlvii. 11, 15.}

Thenceforward, year after year, **the** nation drank with deeper thirst from the fountains of forbidden pleasure, and dug for springs, hitherto unknown, in the dark places of the earth. In the ingenuity of indulgence, in the varieties of vanity, Venice surpassed the cities of **Christendom, as of** old she had surpassed them in fortitude and devotion; **and** as once the powers of Europe stood before her judgment-seat, to receive the decisions of her justice, so now the youth of Europe assembled in the halls of her luxury, to learn from her the arts of delight.

It is as needless as it is **painful** to trace the steps of her final **ruin.** That ancient curse was upon her, the curse of the Cities of the Plain, '**Pride, fulness of** bread, and abundance of idleness.' Ezek. xvi. 49.

By the inner burning of her own passions, as fatal as the fiery rain of Gomorrah, she was consumed from her place among the nations; and her ashes are choking the channels of the dead, salt sea.—*Stones of Venice*, vol. iii., ch. ii., § LXXXV.; iii., § LXXVI. Gen. xix. 24.

Virtues.

What is meant, in the Bible, by Righteousness, and Faith; or in heathen literature by Righteousness, Honour, and Piety? All these virtues imply **radically the** conception,—they lead ultimately to the revelation,—of personal and governing Deity: but they begin, practically, and themselves consist to the end, in truthful knowledge of *human power* and *human worth;* in respect for the **natural claims** and feelings of others; and in the precision and thoroughness of our obedience to the primary **laws of** probity and truth,—'A just ephah, and a just hin;' 'Let your yea be yea, and your nay, nay; for whatsoever is more than these cometh of evil.'—*Modern Painters*, vol. ii., Preface, § 6. Lev. xix. 36. S. Matt. v. 37.

Wealth.

Wealth ill used was as the net of the spider, entangling and destroying: but wealth well used is as the net of the sacred fisher who gathers souls of men out of the deep. A time will come—I do not think even now it is far from us—when this golden net of the world's wealth will be spread abroad as the flaming meshes of morning cloud are over the sky; bearing with them the joy of light and the dew of the morning, as well as the summons to honourable and peaceful toil. What less can we hope from your wealth than this, rich men of England, when once you feel fully how, by the strength of your possessions—not, observe, by the exhaustion, but by the administration of them and the power,—you can direct the acts—command the energies—inform the ignorance—prolong the existence, of the whole human race; and how, even of worldly wisdom, which man employs faithfully, it is true, not only that her ways are pleasantness, but that her paths are peace; and that, for all the children of men, as well as for those to whom she is given, Length of days is in her right hand, as in her left hand Riches and Honour?— *A Joy for Ever*, § 120. [Prov. iii. 17.] [Prov. iii. 16.]

Wild Flowers—the Thyme and the Daisy.

The one, scented as with incense—medicinal—and in all gentle and humble ways, useful. The other, scentless—helpless for ministry to the body; infinitely dear as the bringer of light, ruby, white and gold; the three colours of the Day, with no hue of shade in it. . . . Now in these two families you have typically Use opposed to Beauty in *wildness;* it is their wildness which is their virtue;—that the thyme is sweet where it is unthought of, and the daisies red, where the foot despises them: while, in other orders, wildness is their crime,—' Wherefore, when I looked that it should bring forth grapes, brought it [Isaiah v. 4.]

forth wild grapes?' But in all of them you must distinguish between the pure wildness of flowers and their distress. It may not be our duty to tame them; but it must be, to relieve.—*Proserpina*, ch. vii., §§ 1, 3.

Will of the Father, The.

Listen at least to the words of your children—let us in the lips of babes and sucklings find our strength; and see that we do not make them mock instead of pray, when we teach them, night and morning, to ask for what we believe never can be granted;—that the will of the Father,—which is, that His creatures may be righteous and happy,—should be done, *on earth*, as it is in Heaven.—*The Crown of Wild Olive*, § 160.

<small>S. Matt. vi. 10.</small>

Wisdom.

Wisdom stands calling at the corners of the streets, and the blessing of Heaven waits ready to rain down upon us, deeper than the rivers and broader than the dew, if only we will obey the first plain principles of humanity, and the first plain precepts of the skies: 'Execute true judgment, and show mercy and compassion, every man to his brother; and let none of you imagine evil against his brother in your heart.'—*A Joy for Ever*, § 112.

<small>Zech. vii. 9, 10.</small>

By only looking into your own hearts you may know what a *Man* is,—and know that his only true happiness is to live in Hope of something to be won by him, in Reverence of something to be worshipped by him, and in Love of something to be cherished by him, and cherished—for ever.

Having these instincts, his only rational conclusion is that the objects which can fulfil them may be by his effort gained, and by his faith discerned; and his only earthly wisdom is to accept the united testimony of the men who have sought these things in the way they were commanded. Of whom no single one has ever said that his obedience or his faith had been vain, or found himself cast out from the choir of the living souls, whether here, or departed, for whom the song was written :—

God be merciful unto us, and bless us, and cause His face to shine upon us ; Psalm lxvii.

That Thy way may be known upon earth, Thy saving health among all nations.

Oh let the nations rejoice and sing for joy, for Thou shalt judge the people righteously and govern the nations upon earth.

Then shall the earth yield her increase, and God, even our own God, shall bless us.

God shall bless us, and all the ends of the earth shall fear Him.—*The Storm-Cloud of the Nineteenth Century*, pp. 140-42.

Word of God, The.

By that Word, or Voice, or Breath, or Spirit, the heavens and earth, and all the host of them, were made; and in it they exist. It is your life; and speaks to you always, so long as you live nobly ;—dies out of you as you refuse to obey it ; leaves you to hear, and be slain by, the word of an evil spirit, instead of it. S. John i. 1.

It may come to you in books,—come to you in clouds,—come to you in the voices of men,—come to you in the stillness of deserts. You must be strong in evil, if you have quenched it wholly ; very desolate in this Christian land, if you have never heard it at all.— *Fors Clavigera*, Letter **XXXVI**.

Work.

It may be proved, with much certainty, that God intends no man to live in this world without working : but it seems to me no less evident that He intends every man to be happy in his work. Gen. iii. 19.

It is written, 'in the sweat of thy brow,' but it was

never written, 'in the breaking of thine heart,' thou shalt eat bread: and I find that, as on the one hand, infinite misery is caused by idle people, who both fail in doing what was appointed for them to do, and set in motion various springs of mischief in matters in which they should have had no concern, so on the other hand, no small misery is caused by over-worked and unhappy people, in the dark views which they necessarily take up themselves, and force upon others, of work itself. Were it not so, I believe the fact of their being unhappy is in itself a violation of divine law, and a sign of some kind of folly or sin in their way of life. Now in order that people may be happy in their work, these three things are needed: They must be fit for it: They must not do too much of it: and they must have a sense of success in it—not a doubtful sense, such as needs some testimony of other people for its confirmation, but a sure sense, or rather knowledge, that so much work has been done well, and fruitfully done, whatever the world may say or think about it.—*On the Old Road*, vol. i., part i., § 166.

You cannot serve two masters:—you *must* serve one or other. If your work is first with you, and your fee second, work is your master, and the lord of work, who is God. But if your fee is first with you, and your work second, fee is your master, and the lord of fee, who is the Devil; and not only the Devil, but the lowest of devils— 'the least erected fiend that fell.' So there you have it in brief terms; Work first—you are God's servants; Fee first—you are the Fiend's

And it makes a difference, now and ever, believe me, whether you serve Him Who has on His vesture and thigh written, 'King of Kings,' and whose service is perfect freedom; or him on whose vesture and thigh the name is written 'Slave of Slaves,' and whose service is perfect slavery.—*The Crown of Wild Olive*, § 32.

Rev. xix. 16.

Work of the Divine Master.
Look at the crest of the Alp, from the far-away plains over which its light is cast, whence human souls have communion with it by their myriads. The child looks up to it in the dawn, and the husbandman in the burden and heat of the day, and the old man in the going down of the sun, and it is to them all as the celestial city on the world's horizon; dyed with the depth of heaven, and clothed with the calm of eternity. There was it set, for holy dominion, by Him who marked for the sun his journey, and bade the moon know her going down. It was built for its place in the far-off sky; approach it, and, as the sound of the voice of man dies away about its foundation, and the tide of human life, shallowed upon the vast aërial shore, is at last met by the Eternal 'Here shall thy waves be stayed,' the glory of its aspect fades into blanched fearfulness; its purple walls are rent into grisly rocks, its silver fretwork saddened into wasting snow: the storm-brands of ages are on its breast, the ashes of its own ruin lie solemnly on its white raiment. Job xxxviii.11.
—*Stones of Venice*, vol. i., ch. xxi., § XVII.

I can hardly conceive any one standing face to face with one of these towers of central rock, and yet not also asking himself, Is this indeed the actual first work of the Divine Master on which I gaze? Was the great precipice shaped by His finger, as Adam was shaped out of the dust? Were its clefts and ledges carved upon it by its Creator, as the letters were on the Tables of the Law? The only answer is yet again,— 'Behold the cloud.' No eyes ever 'saw its substance, yet being imperfect'; its history is a monotone of endurance and destruction: all that we can certainly know of it, is that it was once greater than it is now, and it only gathers vastness, and still gathers, as it fades into the abyss of the unknown. Num. xvi. 41. Psalm cxxxix. 16.
—*Modern Painters*, vol. iv., ch. xiii., §§ 13, 14.

World, Fighting with the.

I do not, in the book we profess to live by, find anything very distinct about fighting with the world. I find something about fighting with the rulers of its darkness, and something also about overcoming it; but it does not follow that this conquest is to be by hostility, since evil may be overcome with good. But I find it written very distinctly that God loved the world, and that Christ is the light of it.

What the much-used words, therefore, mean, I cannot tell. But this, I believe, they *should* mean. That there is, indeed, one world which is full of care, and desire, and hatred: a world of war, of which Christ is not the light, which indeed is without light, and has never heard the great 'Let there be.' Which is, therefore, in truth, as yet no world; but chaos, on the face of which, moving, the Spirit of God yet causes men to hope that a world will come. The better one, they call it: perhaps they might, more wisely, call it the real one. Also, I hear them speak continually of going to it, rather than of its coming to them; which, again, is strange, for in that prayer which they had straight from the lips of the Light of the world, and which He apparently thought sufficient prayer for them, there is not anything about going to another world; only something of another government coming into this; or rather, not another, but the only government, —that government which will constitute it a world indeed. New heavens and new earth. Earth, no more without form and void, but sown with fruit of righteousness. Firmament, no more of passing cloud, but of cloud risen out of the crystal sea—cloud in which, as He was once received up, so He shall again come with power, and every eye shall see Him, and all kindreds of the earth shall wail because of Him.—*Modern Painters*, vol. v., pt. ix., ch. xii., §§ 18, 19.

[Gen. i. 3.]
[Gen. i. 2.]
[2 S. Peter iii. 13.]
[Gen. i. 2.]
[S. James iii. 18.]
[Rev. i. 7.]

Zedekiah.

An Eastern custom, as we know: grave in judgment; in the perfectness of it, joined with infliction of grievous Sight, before the infliction of grievous blindness; that so the last memory of this world's light might remain a grief. 'And they slew the sons of Zedekiah before his eyes; and put out the eyes of Zedekiah.' <small>2 Kings xxv. 7.</small>

Custom I know not how ancient. The sons of Eliab, when Judah was young in her Exodus, like Venice, appealed to it in their fury: 'Is it a small thing that thou hast brought us up out of a land that floweth with milk and honey, except thou make thyself altogether a Prince over us; wilt thou put out the eyes of these men?' <small>Num. xvi. 13, 14.</small>

The more wild Western races of Christianity, early Irish and the like,—Norman even, in the pirate times, —inflict the penalty with reckless scorn; but Venice deliberately, as was her constant way; such her practical law against leaders whom she had found spiritually blind: 'These, at least, shall guide no more.'—*St. Mark's Rest*, § 78.

SAINTS

SAINTS

Barbara, St.

St. Barbara, also an Egyptian, and St. Catherine's contemporary, though the most practical of the mythic saints, is also, after St. Sophia, the least corporeal: she vanishes far away into the 'Inclusa Danæ,' and her 'Turris ænea' becomes a myth of Christian safety, of which the Scriptural significance may be enough felt by merely looking out the texts under the word 'Tower,' in your concordance; and whose effectual power, in the fortitudes alike of matter and spirit, was in all probability made impressive enough to all Christendom, both by the fortifications and persecutions of Diocletian. . . .

As Gothic architecture becomes dominant, and at last beyond question the most wonderful of all temple-building, St. Barbara's Tower is, of course, its perfected symbol and utmost achievement; and whether in the coronets of countless battlements worn on the brows of the noblest cities, or in the Lombard bell-tower on the mountains, and the English spire on Sarum plain, the geometric majesty of the Egyptian maid became glorious in harmony of defence and sacred with precision of symbol.

As the buildings which showed her utmost skill were chiefly exposed to lightning, she is invoked in defence from it; and our petition in the Litany, against sudden death, was written originally to her.—*Pleasures of England*, Lecture IV., pp. 135-7.

Barnabas, St., and St. Mark.

'And so Barnabas took Mark, and sailed unto Cyprus.' If as the shores of Asia lessened upon his sight, the spirit of prophecy had entered into the heart of the weak disciple who had turned back when his hand was on the plough, and who had been judged, by the chiefest of Christ's captains, unworthy thenceforward to go forth with him to the work, how wonderful would he have thought it, that by the lion symbol in future ages he was to be represented among men! how woful, that the war-cry of his name should so often reanimate the rage of the soldier, on those very plains where he himself had failed in the courage of the Christian, and so often dye with fruitless blood that very Cypriot Sea, over whose waves, in repentance and shame, he was following the Son of Consolation!—*Stones of Venice*, vol. ii., ch. iv., § 1.

Acts xv. 39.
Acts xiii. 13.
Acts xv. 38, 39.
Acts iv. 36.

Benedict, St.

In that first year, 480, . . . there was born a boy of a senatorial house, who was brought up during childhood amidst all the pleasures, and shames, of the most godless city of the earth. . . . Such as it was, this strange boy, at fifteen years old, could no longer endure it; resolved to break with it and have done with it, left his father's house alone, and escaped to the hills beyond the Campagna. What search was made for him by his parents we know not. One person, however—his nurse —sought for him indefatigably; found him, was allowed to stay with him for a while, and take care of him. . . . Many a library shelf have I sifted, always in vain, to find out who gave him, or how he got, his name. He found his way to a hermit, who taught him the hope of a better life than that in Rome; and I suppose baptized him in such hope, and blessed him in the search for it. Thenceforth, for him also, the verse of the Virgin's song became true, 'All generations

S. Luke i. 48.

shall call me blessed.' Yet in a still higher sense, not merely happy, which is all that the Madonna claims to be called, but in the more solemn power of the S. Luke word in the Benedictus itself, 'Blessed be the i. 68. Lord God of Israel, for He has visited and redeemed His people.'

You will not, I think, find the working saints of whom this one is the Captain of the Host, lean much upon their miracles; and I suppose no modern philosophy could conceive the subsequent effect upon human imagination of the belief in that extremely tiny miracle with which St. Benedict's ministry traditionally begins: mending a corn-sieve. . . . Make what you will of it— break what you will of it, the absolute fact remains fast, that in all the choral services of the Church this legend holds the first place in the praise of St. Benedict. It is just as important in his life as the killing of the Nemean lion is in the life of Heracles. And when we come to reflect on the essential function of the Benedictine, I do not think there will remain any difficulty in seeing how this myth became the popular symbol of it. . . .

Finally, however, St. Benedict determines that Christian men ought not to be hermits, but actively helpful members of society: that they are to live by their own labour, and to feed other people by it to the best of their power. He is the apostle, first, of the peasant's agriculture, and secondly, of the squire's agricultural machines—for whatever good there is in them. The corn and the corn-sieve are alike sacred in his eyes. And once understanding that, and considering what part of the 'library' of his day, the Bible of St. Jerome's giving, would either touch himself most closely, or would be looked to by others as most descriptive of him, you will feel that the especially agricultural prophecy of Amos would become the guide of Benedictine expectation, and you may even, in thinking of him, Amos find a weight in the words of it yourselves, ix. 9. unperceived before. 'For lo, I will command, and I will sift the house of Israel among all nations, like as corn is sifted in a sieve, yet shall not the least grain fall upon the earth.'

'Behold, the days come, saith the Lord, that the ploughman shall overtake the reaper, and the treader of grapes, him that soweth seed, and the mountains shall drop sweet wine, and all the hills shall melt.

<small>Amos ix. 13, 14, 15.</small>

'And I will bring again the captivity of my people, and they shall build the waste cities and inhabit them,— they shall also make gardens, and eat the fruit of them, and I will plant them upon their land, and they shall no more be plucked up out of their land which I have given them, saith the Lord thy God.'

This is the efficient practical Benediction with which the active Saint begins the second æra of Christendom. —*Verona*, pp. 124–8.

Bernard, St.

He was the first of the noble Puritans, in the rejection of all that was unseemly, luxurious, or vain in the pretended service of God. He was the head and captain of the great race of northern farmers, who themselves preached, and to purpose, their more than one sermon a week, and stubbed Thornaby Waste as well. But all this he was because he loved God, and believed with all his heart and soul and strength. And whatever in the fullest glow of unsullied Christianity—whatever of comforting or purifying in the thoughts of a future state, we have associated most intimately with our social affections and earthly work, you will find to have been first rooted in the conviction and the benevolence of St. Bernard. . . . Looking from his native rock down the vast vale of the Saône, where, only fifteen miles to the south, the lines of poplar and aspen that soften the horizon, grow by the idle streams of what was once—Citeaux. Nothing is left of the abbey walls. . . . The first brothers who settled there, those from the abbey of Molesnes, had hard times for many a day. The marshes would not drain, the seeds would not grow; the monks themselves died one by one, of damp and fatigue. . . . At last Bernard heard of them—then a youth just back from Paris University. Gathered a few more fiery ones of his own sort, and plunged into the marsh to the rescue. The poor Abbot and his forlorn hope of friars went out to meet them, singing songs of deliverance. In less than twenty-five years there were more than sixty thousand Cistercian monks, at work on any bit of trenchable ground they were allowed to come at, between the bay of Genoa and the Baltic.

In 1090 he is born at La Fontaine, and whatever is loveliest in chivalry and ladyhood comes after that. . . . 'Let us eat and drink, for to-morrow we die:' the exact contradiction to St. Bernard's— 'Let us watch and pray, for to-morrow we live.'—*Verona*, pp. 138-43.   1 Cor. xv. 32.

Catherine, St.

Of St. Catherine of Egypt there are vestiges of personal tradition which may perhaps permit the supposition of her having really once existed, as a very lovely, witty, proud, and 'fanciful' girl. She afterwards becomes the Christian type of the Bride, in the 'Song of Solomon,' involved with an ideal of all that is purest in the life of a nun, and brightest in the death of a martyr. It is scarcely possible to overrate the influence of the conceptions formed of her, in ennobling the sentiments of Christian women of the higher orders.—*Pleasures of England*, Lecture IV., pp. 134-5.

Cecilia, St.

With much more clearness and historic comfort we may approach the shrine of St. Cecilia. . . .

The ruling conception of her is deepened gradually by the enlarged study of Religious music; and is at its best and highest in the thirteenth century, when she rather resists than complies with the already tempting and distracting powers of sound; **and we** are told that 'cantantibus organis, Cecilia virgo in corde suo soli Domino decantabat, dicens, "Fiat, Domine, cor meum et corpus meum immaculatum, ut non confundar."'

('While the instruments played, Cecilia the virgin sang in her heart only to the Lord, saying, "Oh Lord, be my heart and body made stainless, that I be not confounded."')

This sentence occurs in my great Service-book of the convent of Beau-pré, written in 1290, and it is illustrated with a miniature of Cecilia sitting silent at a banquet, where all manner of musicians are playing. I need not point out to you how the law, **not of** sacred music only, so called, but of *all* music, is determined by this sentence; which means in effect **that unless music exalt and purify, it is not under Cecilia's ordinance, and it is not, virtually, music at all.**

Unconfessed, she is of all the mythic saints for ever the greatest; and the child in its nurse's arms, and every tender and gentle spirit which resolves to purify in itself, —as the eye for seeing, so the ear for hearing,—may still, whether behind the Temple veil, or at the fireside, and by the wayside, hear Cecilia sing.—*Pleasures of England*, Lecture IV., pp. 138-40.

Firmin, St.

At the birth of Christ, all this hillside, and the brightly-watered plain below, with the corn-yellow champaign above, were inhabited by a Druid-taught race, **wild enough in** thoughts and ways, but under Roman government, **and gradually becoming** accustomed to **hear the names, and partly to** confess the power, of Roman gods. For three hundred years after the birth of Christ they heard the name of no other God.

Three hundred years! and neither apostles nor inheritors of apostleship had yet gone into all the world and preached the gospel to every creature. Here, on their peaty ground, the wild people, still trusting in Pomona for apples, in Silvanus for acorns, in Ceres for bread, and in Proserpina for rest, hoped but the season's blessing from the Gods of Harvest, and feared no eternal anger from the Queen of Death.

But at last, three hundred years being past and gone, in the year of Christ 301, there came to this hillside of Amiens, on the sixth day of the Ides of October, the Messenger of a new Life.

His name, Firminius (I suppose) in Latin, Firmin in French,—so to be remembered here in Picardy. Firmin, not Firminius; as Denis, not Dionysius; coming out of space—no one tells what part of space. But received by the pagan Amienois with surprised welcome, and seen of them—Forty days—many days, we may read—preaching acceptably, and binding with baptismal vows even persons in good society: and that in such numbers, that at last he is accused to the Roman governor, by the priests of Jupiter and Mercury, as one turning the world upside-down. And in the last day of the Forty—or of the indefinite many meant by Forty—he is beheaded. . . .

The old, old story, you say? Be it so; you will the more easily remember it. . . .

Following in the meantime the tale of St. Firmin as of old time known, his body was received, and buried, by a Roman senator, his disciple, (a kind of Joseph of Arimathea to St. Firmin,) in the Roman senator's own garden. Who also built a little oratory over his grave. The Roman senator's son built a church to replace the oratory, dedicated it to Our Lady of Martyrs, and established it as an episcopal seat—the first of the French nation's.—*Our Fathers Have Told Us*, pp. 6–8.

Genevieve, St.

Not for dark Rialto's dukedom, nor for fair France's

kingdom, only, are these two years (421 and 481) to be remembered above all others in the wild fifth century; but because they are also the birth-years of a great Lady, and greater Lord, of all future Christendom—St. Genevieve, and St. Benedict.

Genevieve, the 'white wave' (Laughing water)—the purest of all the maids that have been named from the sea-foam or the rivulet's ripple. . . .

White wave on the blue—whether of pure lake or sunny sea—(thenceforth the colours of France, blue field with white lilies), she is always the type of purity, in active brightness of the entire soul and life—(so distinguished from the quieter and restricted innocence of St. Agnes),—and all the traditions of sorrow in the trial or failure of noble womanhood are connected with her name. . . .

A shepherd maid she was—a tiny thing, barefooted, bareheaded—such as you may see running wild and innocent, less cared for now than their sheep, over many a hillside of France and Italy. Tiny enough; seven years old, all told, when first one hears of her. . . . The little thing keeps her flock, not even her own, nor her father's flock, like David; she is the hired servant of a richer farmer of Nanterre. . . . Seven years old she was, then, when on his way to *England* from Auxerre, St. Germain passed a night in her village, and among the children who brought him on his way in the morning in more kindly manner than Elisha's convoy, noticed this one—wider-eyed in reverence than the rest; drew her to him, questioned her, and was sweetly answered That she would fain be Christ's handmaid. And he hung round her neck a small copper coin, marked with the cross. Thenceforward Genevieve held herself 'as separated from the world.' . . . More than Nitocris was to Egypt, more than Semiramis to Nineveh, more than Zenobia to the city of palm trees—this seven-years-old shepherd maiden became to Paris and her France. You have not heard of her in that kind?—No: how should you?—for she did not lead armies, but stayed them, and all her power was in peace. . . . The first thing, then, you have to note of her, is that she is a pure native *Gaul*. She does not come as a missionary out of Hungary, or Illyria, or Egypt, or ineffable space; but grows at Nanterre, like a marguerite in the dew, the first 'Reine Blanche' of Gaul. . . . It is lovely to see how, even thus early, the Feudal chivalry depended for its life on the nobleness of its womanhood. There was no *vision* seen, or alleged, at Tolbiac. The King prayed simply to the God of Clotilde. . . .

But over Clovis, there was extended yet another influence—greater than his queen's. When his kingdom was first extended to the Loire, the shepherdess of Nanterre was already aged,—no torch-bearing maid of battle, like Clotilde, no knightly leader of deliverance like Jeanne, but grey in meekness of wisdom, and now 'filling more and more with crystal light.' Clovis's father had known her; he himself made her his friend, and when he left Paris on the campaign of Poitiers, vowed that if victorious, he would build a Christian Church on the hills of Seine. He returned in victory, and with St. Genevieve at his side, stood on the site of the ruined Roman Thermæ, just above the 'Isle' of Paris, to fulfil his vow: and to design the limits of the foundations of the first metropolitan church of Frankish Christendom. The King 'gave his battle-axe the swing,' and tossed it with his full force. Measuring with its flight also, the place of his own grave, and of Clotilde's and St. Genevieve's.

There they rested, and rest,—in soul,—together.— *Our Fathers Have Told Us*, pp. 43–47, 87, 88.

Geoffroy, St.

St. Geoffroy was born in the year of the battle of Hastings, at Molincourt in the Soissonais, and was Bishop of Amiens from 1104 to 1150. A man of entirely simple, pure, and right life: one of the severest of ascetics, but without gloom—always gentle and merciful. Many miracles are recorded of him, but all indicating a tenour of life which was chiefly miraculous by its justice and peace. Consecrated at Rheims, and attended by a train of other bishops and nobles to his diocese, he dismounts from his horse at St. Acheul, the place of St. Firmin's first tomb, and walks barefoot to his cathedral, along the causeway now so defaced: at another time he walks barefoot from Amiens to Picquigny to ask from the Vidame of Amiens the freedom of the Chatelain Adam. He maintained the privileges of the citizens, with the help of Louis le Gros, against the Count of Amiens, defeated him, and razed his castle; nevertheless, the people not enough obeying him in the order of their life, he blames his own weakness, rather than theirs, and retires to the Grande Chartreuse, holding himself unfit to be their bishop. The Carthusian superior questioning him on his reasons for retirement, and asking if he had ever sold the offices of the Church, the Bishop answered, 'My father, my hands are pure of simony, but I have a thousand times allowed myself to be seduced by praise.'—*Our Fathers Have Told Us*, pp. 198, 199.

George, St.

St. George's 'true' story, how far literally true is of no moment; it is enough for us that a young soldier, in early days of Christianity, put off his armour, and gave up his soul to his Captain, Christ: and that his death did so impress the hearts of all Christian men who heard of it, that gradually he became to them the leader of a sacred soldiership, which conquers more than its mortal enemies, and prevails against the poison, and the shadow, of Pride, and Death.—*Fors Clavigera*, Letter XXVI.

Jerome, St.

Thus much you should be clear in knowing about

him, as not in the least doubtful or mythical, but wholly true, and the beginning of facts quite limitlessly important to all modern Europe—namely, that he was born of good, or at least rich family, in Dalmatia, virtually midway between the east and the west; that he made the great Eastern book, the Bible, legible in the west; that he was the first great teacher of the nobleness of ascetic scholarship and courtesy, as opposed to ascetic savageness: the founder, properly, of the ordered cell and tended garden, where before was but the desert and the wild wood; and that he died in the monastery he had founded at Bethlehem.—*St. Mark's Rest*, § 178.

At earlier dates, the teaching of every master trained in the Eastern schools was necessarily grafted on the wisdom of the Greek mythology; and thus the story of the Nemean Lion, with the aid of Athena in its conquest, is the real root-stock of the legend of St. Jerome's companion, conquered by the healing gentleness of the Spirit of Life.

I call it a legend only. Whether Heracles ever slew, or St. Jerome ever cherished, the wild or wounded creature, is of no moment to us in learning what the Greeks meant by their vase-outlines of the great contest, or the Christian painters by their fond insistence on the constancy of the Lion-friend. Former tradition, in the story of Samson,—of the disobedient Prophet,—of David's first inspired victory, and finally of the miracle wrought in the defence of the most favoured and most faithful of the greater Prophets, runs always parallel in symbolism with the Dorian fable: but the legend of St. Jerome takes up the prophecy of the Millennium, and foretells, with the Cumæan Sibyl, and with Isaiah, a day when the Fear of Man shall be laid in benediction, not enmity, on inferior beings, —when they shall not hurt nor destroy in all the holy Mountain, and the Peace of the Earth shall be as far removed from its present sorrow, as the

Isaiah xi. 9.

present gloriously animate universe from the nascent desert, whose deeps were the place of dragons, and its mountains, domes of fire. Of that day knoweth no man; but the Kingdom of God is already come to those who have tamed in their own hearts what was rampant of the lower nature, and have learned to cherish what is lovely and human, in the wandering children of the clouds and fields.—*Our Fathers Have Told Us*, pp. 135, 136.

<small>S. Matt. xxiv. 36.</small>

Margaret, St., of Antioch.

St. Margaret of Antioch was a shepherdess; the St. Genevieve of the East; the type of feminine gentleness and simplicity. Traditions of the resurrection of Alcestis perhaps mingle in those of her contest with the dragon; but at all events, she differs from the other three great mythic saints, in expressing the soul's victory over temptation or affliction, by Christ's miraculous help, and without any special power of its own. She is the saint of the meek and of the poor; her virtue and her victory are those of all gracious and lowly womanhood; and her memory is consecrated among the gentle households of Europe; no other name, except those of Jeanne and Jeanie, seems so gifted with a baptismal fairy power of giving grace and peace.—*Pleasures of England*, Lecture IV., p. 137.

Martin, St.

Somewhere about this spot, or in the line between it and St. Acheul, stood the ancient Roman gate of The Twins, whereon were carved Romulus and Remus being suckled by the wolf; and out of which, one bitter winter's day, a hundred and seventy years ago when Clovis was baptized—had ridden a Roman soldier, wrapped in his horseman's cloak, on the causeway which was part of the great Roman road from Lyons to Boulogne.

And it is well worth your while also, some frosty

autumn or winter day when the east wind is high, to feel the sweep of it at this spot, remembering what chanced here, memorable to all men, and serviceable, in that winter of the year 332, when men were dying for cold in Amiens streets:—namely, that the Roman horseman, scarce gone out of the city gate, was met by a naked beggar, shivering with cold; and that, seeing no other way of shelter for him, he drew his sword, divided his own cloak in two and gave him half of it.

No ruinous gift, nor even enthusiastically generous: Sidney's cup of cold water needed more self-denial. . . But this Roman soldier was no Christian, and did his serene charity in simplicity, yet with prudence. Nevertheless, that same night, he beheld in a dream the Lord Jesus, who stood before him in the midst of angels, having on his shoulders the half of the cloak he had bestowed on the beggar.

And Jesus said to the angels that were around Him, 'Know ye who hath thus arrayed me? My servant Martin, though yet unbaptized, has done this.' And Martin after this vision hastened to receive baptism, being then in his twenty-third year. Whether these things ever were so, or how far so, credulous or incredulous reader, is no business whatever of yours or mine. What is, and shall be, everlastingly, so,—namely, the infallible truth of the lesson herein taught, and the actual effect of the life of St. Martin on the mind of Christendom,—is, very absolutely, the business of every rational being in any Christian realm.

You are to understand, then, first of all, that the especial character of St. Martin is a serene and meek charity to all creatures. He is not a preaching saint —still less a persecuting one: not even an anxious one. Of his prayers we hear little—of his wishes, nothing. What he does always, is merely the right thing at the right moment;—rightness and kindness being in his mind one. Converted and baptized— and conscious of having seen Christ—he nevertheless gives his officers no trouble whatever—does not try to make proselytes in his cohort. 'It is Christ's business, surely!—if He wants them, He may appear to them, as He has to me,' seems the feeling of his first baptized days. He remains seventeen years in the army on those tranquil terms. At the end of that time, thinking it might be well to take other service, he asks for his dismissal from the Emperor Julian,—who, accusing him of faintheartedness, Martin offers, unarmed, to lead his cohort into battle, bearing only the sign of the cross. Julian takes him at his word, —keeps him in ward till time of battle comes; but, the day before he counts on putting him to that war ordeal, the barbarian enemy sends embassy with irrefusable offers of submission and peace. The story is not often dwelt upon: how far literally true, again observe, does not in the least matter;—here *is* the lesson for ever given of the way in which a Christian soldier should meet his enemies. . . .

But true in some practical and effectual way the story *is*; for after a while, without any oratorizing, anathematizing, or any manner of disturbance, we find the Roman Knight made Bishop of Tours, and becoming an influence of unmixed good to all mankind, then, and afterwards. And virtually the same story is repeated of his bishop's robe as of his knight's cloak —not to be rejected because so probable an invention; for it is just as probable an act. . . .

Gentleness was his strength; and the issue of it is best to be estimated by comparing its scope with that of the work of St. Firmin. . . . St. Martin teazes nobody, spends not a breath in unpleasant exhortation, understands, by Christ's first lesson to himself, that undipped people may be as good as dipped if their hearts are clean; helps, forgives, and cheers, (companionable even to the loving-cup). . . . And somehow —the idols totter before him far and near—the Pagan gods fade, *his* Christ becomes all men's Christ—his name is named over new shrines innumerable in all lands; high on the Roman hills, lowly in English fields; —St. Augustine baptized his first English converts in St. Martin's church at Canterbury; and the Charing Cross station itself has not yet effaced wholly from London minds his memory or his name. . . .

As gathering years told upon him, he seems to have felt that he had carried weight of crozier long enough— that busy Tours must now find a busier Bishop—that, for himself, he might innocently henceforward take his pleasure and his rest where the vine grew and the lark sang. For his episcopal palace, he takes a little cave in the chalk cliffs of the up-country river: arranges all matters therein, for bed and board, at small cost. Night by night the stream murmurs to him, day by day the vine leaves give their shade; and, daily by the horizon's breadth so much nearer Heaven, the fore-running sun goes down for him beyond the glowing water;—there, where now the peasant woman trots homewards between her panniers, and the saw rests in the half-cleft wood, and the village spire rises grey against the farthest light.[1]

And be this much remembered by you, of the power over French souls, past and to come, of St. Martin of Tours. —*Our Fathers Have Told Us*, pp. 22–6; 28, 29; 31, 33.

Matthew, St.—*Carpaccio's Picture of.*

For, indeed, the Gospel which the publican wrote for us, with its perfect Sermon on the Mount, and mostly more harmonious and gentle fulness, in places where St. Luke is formal, St. John mysterious, and St. Mark brief,—this Gospel according to St. Matthew I should think, if we had to choose one out of all the books in the Bible for a prison or desert friend, would be the one we should keep.

And we do not enough think how much that leaving the receipt of custom meant, as a sign of the man's nature, who was to leave us such a not- able piece of literature. *S. Matt. ix. 9.*

---

[1] In Turner's Loire-side.

Yet, observe, Carpaccio **does** not mean to express the fact, or anything like the fact, of the literal calling of Matthew. What the actual character of the publicans of Jerusalem was at that time, in its general aspect, its admitted degradation, and yet power of believing, with the harlot, what the masters and the mothers in Israel could not believe, it is not his purpose to teach you. This call from receipt of custom, he takes for the symbol of the universal call to leave all that we have, and are S. Luke doing. 'Whosoever forsaketh not all that he xiv. 33. hath, cannot be my disciple.' For the other calls were easily obeyed in comparison of this. To leave one's often empty nets and nightly toil on sea, and become fishers of men, probably you might find pescatori enough on the Riva there, within a hundred paces of you, who would take the chance at once, if any gentle person offered it them. James and Jude—Christ's cousins—no thanks to them for following Him; their own home conceivably no richer than His. Thomas and Philip, I suppose, somewhat thoughtful persons on spiritual matters, questioning of them long since; going out to hear St. John preach, and to see whom he had seen. But *this* man, busy in the place of business—engaged in the interests of foreign governments—thinking no more of an Israelite Messiah but only of Egyptian finance, and the like—suddenly the Messiah, passing S. Matt. by, says 'Follow me!' and he rises up, gives ix. 9. Him his hand. 'Yea! to the death'; and absconds from his desk in that electric manner on the instant, leaving his cash-box unlocked, and his books for whoso list to balance! a very remarkable kind of person indeed, it seems to me.

Carpaccio takes him, as I said, for a type of such sacrifice at its best. . . .

For do not think Christ would have called a bad or S. Luke corrupt publican—much less that a bad or xix. 10. corrupt publican would have obeyed the call. . . . That which is *lost* He comes to save,—yes; but not that which is defiantly going the way He has forbidden. He showed you plainly enough what kind of publican He would call, having chosen two, both of the best: 'Behold, Lord, if I have taken anything from any man, I restore it fourfold!'—a beautiful manner of trade. Carpaccio knows well that there were no defalcations from Levi's chest—no oppressions in his tax-gathering. This whom he has painted is a true merchant of Venice, uprightest and gentlest of the merchant race; yet with a glorious pride in him. What merchant but one of Venice would have ventured to take Christ's hand, as his friend's—as one man takes another's? Not repentant, he, of anything he has done; not crushed or terrified by Christ's call; but rejoicing in it, as meaning Christ's praise and love. 'Come up higher then, for there are nobler treasures than these to count, and a nobler King than this to render account to. Thou hast been faithful over a few things; enter thou into the joy of thy Lord.' [S. Luke xix. 8. / S. Luke xix. 17. / S. Matt. xxv. 21, 23.]

A lovely picture, in every sense and power of painting; natural, and graceful, and quiet, and pathetic;—divinely religious, yet as decorative and dainty as a bank of violets in spring.—*St. Mark's Rest*, §§ 173-4-5.

Saints, Mythic.

The most mythic is of course St. Sophia; the shade of the Greek Athena passing into the 'Wisdom' of the Jewish Proverbs and Psalms, and the Apocryphal 'Wisdom of Solomon.' She always remains understood as a personification only; and has no direct influence on the mind of the unlearned multitude of Western Christendom, except as a god-mother,—in which kindly function she is more and more accepted as times go on.—*Pleasures of England*, Lecture IV., p. 134. [1 Kings iv. 29, 30.]

Sophia, Santa.

'Invocavi, et venit in me Spiritus Sapientiæ'—'I

prayed, and the Spirit of Wisdom came upon me.'
<small>Wisdom vii. 7.</small> The *personal* power of Wisdom: the 'σοφία' or Santa Sophia, to whom the first great Christian temple was dedicated. This higher wisdom, governing by her presence, all earthly conduct, and by her teaching, all earthly art.—*Mornings in Florence*, § 91.

Theodore, St.

St. Michael is the angel of war against the dragon of sin; but St. Theodore, who also is not merely a saint, but an angel, is the angel of noble fleshly life in man and animals, leading both against base and malignant life in men and animals. He is the Chevalier, or Cavalier of Venice,—her first of loving knights, in war against all baseness, all malignity; in the deepest sense, St. Theodore, literally 'God gift,' is Divine Life in nature; Divine Life in the flesh of the animal, and in the substance of the wood and of the stone, contending with poison and death in the animal,—with rottenness in the tree, and in the stone. He is first seen (I can find no account of his birth) in the form of a youth of extreme beauty; and his first contest is with a dragon very different from St. George; and it is fought in another manner.—*Fors Clavigera*, Letter LXXV.

He differs from St. George in contending with material evil, instead of with sinful passion: the crocodile on which he stands is the Dragon of Egypt; slime-begotten of old, worshipped in its malignant power, for a God. St. Theodore's martyrdom was for breaking such idols; and with beautiful instinct Venice took him in her earliest days for her protector and standard-bearer, representing the heavenly life of Christ in men, prevailing over chaos and the deep.

With far more than instinct,—with solemn recognition, and prayerful vow, she took him in the pride of her chivalry, in mid-thirteenth century, for the master of that chivalry in their gentleness of home ministries. The 'Mariegola' (Mother-Law) of the school of St.

Theodore, by kind fate yet preserved to us, contains the legend they believed, in its completeness, and their vow of service and companionship in all its terms.

Either of which, if you care to understand,—several other matters and writings must be understood first; and, among others, a pretty piece of our own much boasted,—how little obeyed,—Mother-Law, sung still by statute in our churches at least once in the month; the eighty-sixth Psalm. 'Her foundations are in the Holy Mountains.'—*St. Mark's Rest*, §§ 23-4.

Ursula, St.

Of that legend of St. Ursula, you remember, I doubt not, that the one great meaning is the victory of her faith over all fears of death. It is the laying down of all the joy, of all the hope, nay of all the Love, of this life, in the eager apprehension of the rejoicing and the love of Eternity. What truth there was in such faith I dare not say that I know; but what manner of human souls it made, you may for yourselves *see*. . . . This maid in her purity is no fable; this is a Venetian maid, as she was seen in the earthly dawn, and breathed on by the breeze of her native sea. And here she is in her womanhood, in her courage and perfect peace, waiting for her death. . . . St. Ursula kneels, as daily she knelt, before the altar, giving herself up to God for ever. . . .

Such creatures as these *have* lived—do live yet, thank God, in the faith of Christ.

You hear it openly said that this, their faith, was a foolish dream. Do you choose to find out whether it was or not? You may if you will, but you can find it out in one way only.—*On the Old Road*, vol. ii., §§ 290-1.

Zita, Santa.

In reading the legends of the saints, the reader who cares for the truth that remains in them must always observe first, whether the saint is only a symbolic one, like St. Sophia and St. Catherine; or a real one, like

St. Genevieve and St. Benedict. In the second place, if they are real people, he must observe whether the miracles are done *by* them, or *for* them. Legends of consciously active miracles are rare: the modesty of the great saints prevents them from attempting such, and all the loveliest and best witnessed stories are of miracles done for them or through their ministry, often without their knowledge,—like the shining of Moses' face, or the robing of St. Martin by the angels.

Now Santa Zita, 'St. Maid,' was a real, living, hard-worked maid-servant, in the town you still know as a great oil mart, in the thirteenth century. As real a person as your own kitchen-maid, and not a bit better, probably, than yours is, if she's a good one;—only, living in the most vital and powerful days of Christianity, she was made to feel and know many things which your kitchen-maid can never feel, nor even hear of; and therefore, having also extremely fine intellect as well as heart, she became a very notable creature indeed, and one of wide practical power throughout Europe; for though she lived and died a servant of all-work at a clothier's,—thirty years after her death, Dante acknowledges her the patron saint of her city: and she has ever since been the type of perfectness in servant life, to the Christian world.—*Roadside Songs of Tuscany*, pp. 17, 18.

APPENDICES

I. SUPPLEMENTARY REFERENCES

II. THE BOOKS OF THE BIBLE AS QUOTED OR REFERRED TO IN THIS VOLUME

APPENDICES

APPENDIX I

SUPPLEMENTARY REFERENCES

A

SUBJECT	WORK QUOTED	BIBLE REFERENCE
Abbot	VERONA, p. 131.	Rom. xii. 13. 1 Tim. iii. 2.
Abram's mountain home	FORS CLAVIGERA, Letter lxv.	Gen. xiii. 18. ,, xiv. 13. Joshua xv. 17, 18. ,, xiv. 15. Deut. xi. 10, 12, 17.
Advent, Second Sunday	,, ,, ,, xlviii.	Ephes. vi. 14-17. 1 S. John ii. 14. Psalm xcvi. 1, 10, 11, 13.
Ahab's sin	THE STONES OF VENICE, vol. ii., ch. viii., § 90	1 Kings xxi. 2-16. Col. iii. 5.
Alabaster	DEUCALION, ch. vii., § 15c.	S. Matt. ii. 11. S. Mark xiv. 3.
Apostolic words	MODERN PAINTERS, vol. ii., sec. i., ch. ii., § 8	Ephes. iv. 18, 19.
Arab's faith	OUR FATHERS HAVE TOLD US, pp. 101-102.	Gen. xvi. 7. ,, xii. 1.
Authority, Two great forms of	ARIADNE FLORENTINA, § 198.	S. James i. 17. Rev. xix. 16. S. Matt. vi. 10.
Avarice	FORS CLAVIGERA, Letter lxii.	Exod. xx. 17. S. Luke xii. 15. Gen. ii. 11, 12.

B

Barnabas' Confession of Faith	TIME AND TIDE, § 109	S. Mark iii. 17. Acts iv. 36, 37.
Bramble	MODERN PAINTERS, vol. v., pt. ix., ch. iii., §§ 13, 14.	S. Luke vi. 44.
Brotherly law	MODERN PAINTERS, vol. iii., ch. xviii., § 38	1 Cor. x. 24.

APPENDIX I

SUBJECT	WORK QUOTED	BIBLE REFERENCE
Buildings	Lectures on Architecture and Painting, § 28	Jer. i. 18. Ephes. ii. 20. S. Luke xiv. 28.
Burden of Tyre	S. Mark's Rest, § 40	Isa. xxiii. 2, 3.

C

SUBJECT	WORK QUOTED	BIBLE REFERENCE
Chief of Cities	Val D'Arno, §§ 31, 32	Isa. lx. 18.
Christians	Fors Clavigera, Letter lxxxii.	Psalm viii. 4. ,, xxxvi. 6. Eccles. vii. 12.
Christmas carols	,, ,, ,, xlviii.	Psalm xciv.
Church	On the Old Road, vol. ii., §§ 184-185	Eph. v. 25, 27, 32. Col. i. 18. 1 Cor. x. 32. ,, xv. 9. Gal. i. 13. 1 Tim. iii. 5. Acts vii. 38. ,, xiii. 1. 1 Cor. i. 2. ,, xvi. 19. Acts xix. 32, 41. S. Matt. xvi. 18. ,, xviii. 17.
Colour, Joy and Nobleness of	Laws of Fésole, Letter vii., § 11. Stones of Venice, vol. ii., ch. v., §§ 30, 31	Rev. xxi. 11. Lam. i. 12. Prov. xiv. 13.
Creed	The Crown of Wild Olive, §§ 13, 14	Eccles. ix. 10. S. John iv. 36, 37.
Crystal	Deucalion, ch. vii., § 13	Job xxviii. 16, 17. Ezek. i. 22. Rev. iv. 6. ,, xxii. 1. ,, xxi. 2.

D

SUBJECT	WORK QUOTED	BIBLE REFERENCE
Daily bread	Fors Clavigera, Letters lxxiv., lxxxvi.	Exod. xvi. 19. S. Matt. xx. 2. Acts ii. 46, 47.
Day is coming, The	,, ,, ,, lxxxii.	Isa. xxxiii. 14-17.
Dead, The	,, ,, ,, xlv.	Rev. xiv. 13.
Death	,, ,, ,, lxxii.	,, xx. 12. Exod. xv. 10. Rev. xiii. 9.
Desolate souls	,, ,, ,, lxvi.	Joshua x. 12, 13. Psalm cxlvii. 8.
Divine power	Storm-Cloud, p. 4	Acts xiv. 17.

APPENDIX I

SUBJECT	WORK QUOTED	BIBLE REFERENCE
Divinity in nature	S. Mark's Rest, § 66	2 S. Peter i. 4. 2 Cor. iii. 18. Amos v. 18.
Dress	{ Verona, p. 49 { Arrows of the Chace, { vol. ii., p. 227	2 Sam. i. 24. Lev. xiv. 4. Prov. xxxi. 21, 22. 2 Sam. i. 24. Psalm xlv. 13, 14. Prov. xxxi. 15. ,, xxii. 25.
Dry land	{ Modern Painters, vol. { iv., pt. v., ch. vii., § 1	Gen. i. 9. Exod. xiv. 22 Psalm xcv. 5.
Duty of loving God	Fors Clavigera, Letter xcvi.	1 Cor. iii. 11. S. Matt. vi. 5, 6. 2 Kings vi. 17. Rom. xii. 21. Isa. liv. 13. ,, lv. 12. ,, xxxv. 1.

E

Education	Time and Tide, § 92	1 Cor. xv. 36
Egyptian slavery	Fors Clavigera, Letter lxiv.	Acts viii. 36, 37. Psalm lxviii. 31. Isa. xlv. 13, 14. Gen. xlii. 1, 2, ,, l. 10, 11. Hosea xi. 1.
Entombment of Christ	{ Modern Painters, vol. { ii., sec. ii., ch. iii., § 16	Isa. liii. 9. S. Matt. viii. 20. S. Luke ix. 58.
Esdras	Fors Clavigera, Letter xlix.	2 Esdras xv. 16, 17.
Ezekiel's vision	{ Modern Painters, vol. { iii., ch. viii., § 21	Ezek. i. 19, 20.

F

Faith	{ Modern Painters, vol. { v., pt. viii., ch. i., § 17	Rev. xxii. 6.
Father	Fors Clavigera, Letter lxx.	Psalm lxxiii. 25.
Fold, One great	{ On the Old Road, vol. { ii., §§ 221, 222	S. Mark ix. 50. S. Matt. x. 34. S. John xiv. 27.
Freedom, Nation's	Val d'Arno, § 197	Psalm cxix.

G

Genesis, Book of	Fors Clavigera, Letter xli.	Psalm xxvii. 36. Gen. v. 24.
Give	,, ,, ,, lxi.	S. Matt. v. 42. S. Luke xiv. 33.

SUBJECT	WORK QUOTED	BIBLE REFERENCE
Gold and precious stones	DEUCALION, ch. vii., § 10 ch. vii., §§ 14-16	Gen. ii. 12. Exod. xxvii. 7. ,, xxxv. 27. Ezek. xxviii. 13. Exod. xxviii. 9, 10, 20.
Good for evil	ARROWS OF THE CHACE, vol. ii., p. 93	Exod. xxi. 24.
Grain of corn	PROSERPINA, ch. xiv., § 3	S. Luke ix. 62. S. Matt. xxiv. 41. S. Matt. vi. 30.

H

SUBJECT	WORK QUOTED	BIBLE REFERENCE
Heavenly host, The	FORS CLAVIGERA, Letter xii.	Gen. ii. 1. S. Luke ii. 13, 14.
Heavens	MODERN PAINTERS, vol. iv., ch. vi., § 6.	Psalm xviii. 9, 11. ,, civ. 3.
Helpful	MODERN PAINTERS, vol. v., pt. viii., ch. i., § 5, NOTE	S. James v. 4. Rom. xi. 16.
Heraldry of our Faith	DEUCALION, ch. vii., § 30	Gen. ix. 13, 16.
Heritage	FORS CLAVIGERA, Letter xlv.	Judges xvii. 1. Micah i. 1. ,, iii. 1-3.
Holy Field	VAL D'ARNO, § 27.	Gen. xxiii. 19, 20. ,, xlix. 31. S. Matt. xxvii. 7, 8.
House of God	ON THE OLD ROAD, vol. ii., § 185, NOTE.	1 Tim. iii. 15. 1 Cor. iii. 16, 17.
Humanity and Immortality	STONES OF VENICE, vol. i., ch. ii., § 10	Psalm xlix. 12, 20. S. Matt. x. 16. Prov. vi. 6. ,, xx. 12. S. John vi. 40, 44, 54.
Hypocrisy	ON THE OLD ROAD, vol. ii., § 231.	Jer. xxiii. 6. Exod. xx. 7. 1 Sam. xvi. 7.
Hyssop	MODERN PAINTERS, vol. v., pt. ix., ch. xi., § 8	Exod. xii. 22, 24. Psalm li. 7.

I

SUBJECT	WORK QUOTED	BIBLE REFERENCE
Idealism, Grotesque	MODERN PAINTERS, vol. iii., ch. viii., § 5	Jer. i. 13, 14.
Idolatry	MODERN PAINTERS, vol. iii., ch. v., § 13	Hosea iv. 12, 13, 19.

APPENDIX I

SUBJECT	WORK QUOTED	BIBLE REFERENCE
Infidelity	STONES OF VENICE, vol. iii., ch. ii., § 103	Job xxxviii. 11. Ezek. vii. 10, 11, 12.
Israelites, True	FORS CLAVIGERA, Letter xlix.	S. Luke xviii. 10–14.

J

Jeremiah, Promise of	TIME AND TIDE, § 45	Jer. xxxi. 4, 5.
Jewish altar	MODERN PAINTERS, vol. iii., ch. ix., § 6	Exod. xx. 25.
Jewish womanhood	MORNINGS IN FLORENCE, §§ 60, 61	Apocrypha, ch. viii. ix. x. xiii. xv. xvi.
Joab	FORS CLAVIGERA, Letter xl.	2 Sam. x. 12. 2 Chron. xix. 2.
Justice or righteousness	,, ,, ,, viii.	Isa. liv. 11, 14, 17.

K

Kingdoms, Christian and heathen	MORNINGS IN FLORENCE, § 63 *et seq.*	Isa. xliv. 24. ,, xiv. 13. 1 Esdras vi. 24. Ezra i. 3. 2 Esdras ii. 3.
Kinghood and priesthood	ROADSIDE SONGS OF TUSCANY, p. 109, NOTE	1 Sam. xv. 33. 2 Kings i. 10.
Knowledge	EAGLE'S NEST, § 80	Eccles. i. 18.

L

Law of the covenant	DEUCALION, ch. vii., § 32	Gen. ix. 8–13.
Liberty	VAL D'ARNO, § 197	Psalm cxix. 45.
Light	EAGLE'S NEST, §§ 115, 116	Mal. iv. 2. S. John i. 9.
Light and sound	STORM-CLOUD OF THE NINETEENTH CENTURY, pp. 34, 35	Psalm xciv. 9.
Lord of hosts	FORS CLAVIGERA, Letter xiv.	Isa. vi. 3.
Love	ON THE OLD ROAD, vol. i., pt. i., § 235	Heb. xiii. 8. Job xxxviii. 7. Jer. xxxi. 13. Isa. lxii. 5.

M

Man	MODERN PAINTERS, vol. v., pt. ix., ch. ii., § 1	S. Matt. v. 14.
Mental State	EAGLE'S NEST, §§ 68, 69	S. Mark v. 3–15.

APPENDIX I

SUBJECT	WORK QUOTED	BIBLE REFERENCE
Message, The	FORS CLAVIGERA, Letter lxxxi.	1 S. John iii. 11. „ „ ii. 1. „ „ iii. 8. „ „ iii. 7. „ „ iv. 2–20.
Miracles	„ „ „ lxxiv.	S. John ii. 7–10. Psalm civ. 15. S. Mark xiv. 12, 13. S. Matt. iii. 13. Heb. ix. 19. „ xii. 24. 1 Cor. x. 2.
Monastic life	OUR FATHERS HAVE TOLD US, p. 109	Gen. xxviii. 11. Exod. iii. 3. 1 Sam. xvii. 28. S. Luke i. 80.
Mosaic Law	FORS CLAVIGERA, Letter liii.	Heb. i. 3.
Mountain gloom	MODERN PAINTERS, vol. iv., ch. xix., § 33	Gen. iii. 8. Psalm cxxi. 4. Jer. iii. 6. Isa. ii. 2. Exod. xxiv. 1–10. Micah vi. 2. Hosea x. 8. Psalm lxxii. 3.
Mountains	MODERN PAINTERS, vol. iv., ch. vii., § 3 MODERN PAINTERS, vol. iv., ch. vii., § 10	Gen. iii. 19. Job xiv. 18, 19. Psalm xxxvi. 6.

N

National worship	BIBLIOTHECA PASTORUM, vol. i., Pref.	Ps. cxxxix. 8. S. Matt. xviii. 20.

O

Obedience	FORS CLAVIGERA, Letter liv.	Psalm xiv. 1. „ liii. 1.
Offering to God	ON THE OLD ROAD, vol. i., pt. ii., § 556	2 Sam. xxiv. 24. S. Matt. x. 6. S. Luke x. 35. Prov. xix. 17.
Order	MODERN PAINTERS, vol. v., pt. vi., ch. iii., § 14	Isa. lxi. 11.
Our Common Prayer	FORS CLAVIGERA, Letter xxx.	Rom. ii. 3–11.

P

Patience	ON THE OLD ROAD, vol. i., pt. ii., §§ 340–41	S. Mark iv. 28. Psalm lxv. 13.

APPENDIX I

SUBJECT	WORK QUOTED	BIBLE REFERENCE
Peace-makers	THE EAGLE'S NEST, §§ 204-205	S. Matt. v. 9.
Peace, Song of	FORS CLAVIGERA, Letter xii.	S. James v. 4. Isa. vi. 3.
Perfect work	STONES OF VENICE, vol. ii., ch. vi., § 40	Gen. i. 31.
Perfume	S. MARK'S REST, p. 86	Prov. vii. 5. Psalm xlv. 8.
Pharisee, The	SESAME AND LILIES, § 140	S. Luke xviii. 11.
Precious stones	DEUCALION, ch. vii., § 32, II.	Exod. xxiv. 9, 10, 11. Rev. iv. 3. ,, xxi. 21.
Precious Stones	*See* Gold.	
Priest and King	ROADSIDE SONGS OF TUSCANY, p. 108	Jude 1, 13.
Psalm Psalter	FORS CLAVIGERA, Letters	xxxvi. Psalm xiv. xxxvi. ,, xv. liii. ,, cxix. liii. ,, viii.

R

Rahab	S. MARK'S REST, § 26	Psalm lxxxvii.
Reed	MODERN PAINTERS, vol. iii., ch. xiv., § 53	S. Matt. xxvii. 29, 48.
Religious service	FORS CLAVIGERA, Letter lxxxii.	Psalm viii. 4. ,, xxxvi. 6. Eccles. vii. 12.
Renaissance builders	STONES OF VENICE, vol. iii., ch. ii., § 45	Psalm cxxiii. 4.
Rock	MODERN PAINTERS, vol. iv., ch. xviii., § 26 MODERN PAINTERS, vol. iv., ch. xii., § 23	Deut. xxi. 4. Amos vi. 12. Isa. lvii. 5, 6. Psalm cxiv. 5, 6.
Rose and Lily	OUR FATHERS HAVE TOLD US, ch. iv., § 32	Cant. ii. 1. S. John xv. 1.

S

Sabbath	FORS CLAVIGERA, Letter xl.	S. Matt. xii. 8. S. Mark ii. 27, 28.
Science	STONES OF VENICE, vol. iii., ch. ii., § 9 MODERN PAINTERS, vol. iii., ch. xvii., § 40	Psalm xix. 5, 6. Job xl. 18, ,, xli. 18, 22. S. Matt. vi. 28.
Sermon on the Mount	MODERN PAINTERS, vol. iii., App. ii.	S. Matt. v. 29, 30. ,, vii. 5.
Sight	MODERN PAINTERS, vol. ii., sec. i., ch. i., § 5.	S. Matt. vi. 25. Joshua ix. 21. Eccles. iii. 11.

APPENDIX I

SUBJECT	WORK QUOTED	BIBLE REFERENCE
Sin	MODERN PAINTERS, vol. v., pt. ix., ch. xii., §§ 2, 3	S. Matt. vii. 1. Gen. xviii. 19. Prov. iii. 3.
Solomon's song	MODERN PAINTERS, vol. ii., sec. ii., ch. iii., § 8	Cant. vi. 10.
Son of Man	ON THE OLD ROAD, vol. ii., § 232. MODERN PAINTERS, vol. iv., ch. vi., § 5, NOTE	S. John xiv. 9. S. 1 Cor. i. 24. S. Matt. xxvi. 39. ,, xxiv. 30. Exod. xiii. 21. ,, xvi. 10. ,, xix. 9. ,, xxiv. 16. ,, xxxiv. 5. Levit. xvi. 2. Num. x. 34. Judges v. 4. 1 Kings viii. 10. Ezek. i. 4. Dan. vii. 13. 1 Thess. iv. 17. Rev. i. 7.
Sophia	THE EAGLE'S NEST, §§ 29, 30	1 Cor. viii. 1.
Soul and body	STONES OF VENICE, vol. iii., ch. iv., §§ 7, 8	S. Luke xiv. 23. Rom. xii. 15.
Spiritual change	ARROWS OF THE CHACE, vol. i., p. 241	Acts xvii. 28.
Sun	DEUCALION, ch. vii., § 32, I.	Psalm xix. 5. Prov. iv. 18. S. Matt. v. 16.
Syria	OUR FATHER'S HAVE TOLD US, ch. iii., § 14	Deut. xxvi. 5.

T

Teaching of Heaven	FORS CLAVIGERA, Letter xlii.	S. Luke vii. 47. Psalm l. 18
Terror	MODERN PAINTERS, vol. i., pt. i., sec. ii., ch. iii., § 2	S. Luke xxiii. 30. Hosea x. 8. Job xix. 26.
Theft, Sin of	TIME AND TIDE, § 85	S. Matt. xxvii. 38. S. Mark xv. 27, 28. S. John xviii. 40.
Theoretic faculty, The	MODERN PAINTERS, vol. ii., sec. i., ch. xi., § 4	Psalm lxv. 11.
Theory, Ancient	THE EAGLE'S NEST, § 121	Job xix. 26. S. Matt. v. 8.
Thirst after God	FORS CLAVIGERA, Letter liii.	Psalm xlii. 2. ,, lxiii. 1. ,, cxliii. 6. ,, lxvii. 2.

SUBJECT	WORK QUOTED	BIBLE REFERENCE
Trespasses	On the Old Road, vol. ii., § 241	2 Sam. xii. 13. S. Matt. xxv. 42.
Trust	Modern Painters, vol. v., pt. viii., ch. i., § 17 and Note	Rev. xix. 11. ,, xxii. 6. 1 Tim. i. 15.

U

Usurer, Parable of the	Fors Clavigera, Letter lxviii.	S. Matt. vi. 20. S. Luke xii. 33. S. Mark x. 23.

V

Vanity	Stones of Venice, vol. ii., ch. viii., § 92	Job xv. 31. Eccles. i. 2. Psalm xciv. 11. 1 Cor. iii. 20.

W

Wages of Sin	Verona, ch. iii., §§ 8, 9	S. Mark ix. 43, 44. Isa. lxvi. 24. Rom. vi. 23.
Wandering Israel	Fors Clavigera, Letter lxxvi.	S. James i. 1. Micah vi. 8. Exod. xv. 2.
Wisdom	The Eagle's Nest, § 19	Prov. iii. 15. ,, viii. 30, 31.
Words and actions	On the Old Road, vol. ii., § 201, Note	1 Tim. vi. 4–20. 2 ,, ii. 14, 19–22, 23. Titus i. 10, 14, 16. Titus iii. 8, 9. ,, i. 4–7.
Work of the hand	Crown of Wild Olive, § 36	Gen. iii. 19. Rev. xiv. 13.

Z

Zaccheus' portion	Time and Tide, § 109	S. Luke xix. 18.

APPENDIX II

THE BOOKS OF THE BIBLE
AS QUOTED OR REFERRED TO IN THIS VOLUME

GENESIS — PAGES OF THIS VOLUME

CHAP.	
I	3, 4, 12, 49, 50, 59, 103, 112, 125, 148, 211, 216, 227, 252. (Appendix I.) 281, 285.
II	22, 87, 88, 89, 148, 157, 177, 210, 229. (Appendix I.) 282.
III	40, 87, 88, 210, 227, 231, 249. (Appendix I.) 284, 287.
V	(Appendix I.) 282.
VIII	65, 113, 161.
IX	85. (Appendix I.) 282.
XI	235.
XII	(Appendix I.) 279.
XIII	(Appendix I.) 279.
XIV	8. (Appendix I.) 279.
XV	3, 8.
XVI	229. (Appendix I.) 279.
XVIII	24, 135. (Appendix I.) 286.
XIX	162, 246.
XXII	91, 162.
XXIII	8.
XXVII	157, 180.
XXVIII	130, 131. (Appendix I.) 284.
XXIX	91.
XXXVII	115, 205.
XLI	137, 205.
XLII	205. (Appendix I.) 281.
XLIX	148.

APPENDIX II

EXODUS   PAGES OF THIS VOLUME

CHAP.		
	II	92.
	III	114, 124. (Appendix I.) 284.
	IV	203.
	XII	(Appendix I.) 282.
	XIII	50, 66, 124, 163. (Appendix I.) 286.
	XIV	84, 163. (Appendix I.) 281.
	XV	163. (Appendix I.) 280.
	XVI	157. (Appendix I.) 280, 286.
	XVII	160, 203, 219.
	XIX	50. (Appendix I.) 286.
	XX	170, 229. (Appendix I.) 282, 283.
	XXI	(Appendix I.) 282.
	XXIV	(Appendix I.) 284, 285, 286.
	XXVI	222.
	XXVIII	203, 243.
	XXX	48.
	XXXI	162.
	XXXII	164.
	XXXIII	9, 108.
	XXXIV	(Appendix I.) 286.
	XXXV	108.
	XXXVI	115.

LEVITICUS

	V	53.
	XIV	204. (Appendix I.) 281.
	XVI	50, 53. (Appendix I.) 286.
	XIX	246.
	XXV	244.
	XXVI	53.

NUMBERS

	V	53.
	X	(Appendix I.) 286.
	XI	157, 160.
	XVI	48, 251, 253.
	XVII	203.

T

NUMBERS (contd.)   **PAGES OF THIS VOLUME**

CHAP.	
XX	2, 214.
XXIV	96, 218.
XXVII	239.
XXXI	225.
XXXIII	66.

DEUTERONOMY

III	138.
VIII	148.
XI	98, 152. (Appendix I.) 279.
XIV	28.
XVI	221.
XXI	(Appendix I.) 285.
XXVI	(Appendix I.) 286.
XXVII	152.
XXXII	61, 127, 157, 160.
XXXIII	114.
XXXIV	114, 161.

JOSHUA

II	32, 204.
VII	54.
VIII	152.
IX	93.
X	133, 134. (Appendix I.) 280.
XXIV	29.

JUDGES

III	8.
VI	134, 179, 181.
VIII	179, 235.
IX	134, 235.
XI	114, 164.

1 SAMUEL

XIV	109.
XV	(Appendix I.) 283.

APPENDIX II

1 SAMUEL *(contd.)*   PAGES OF THIS VOLUME
CHAP. XVII | 90. (Appendix I.) 284.
    XVIII | 164.
    XXV | 176, 200.

2 SAMUEL

    I | 96, 204, 218, 229. (Appendix I.) 281.
    V | 69.
    VI | 165.
    X | (Appendix I.) 283.
    XII | 58, 86. (Appendix I.) 287.
    XIII | 115.
    XIX | 91.
    XXII | 84.
    XXIV | 8, 221. (Appendix I.) 284.

1 KINGS

    II | 48.
    IV | 140, 273.
    VI | 63.
    VIII | 52.
    XVII | 71, 114, 138.
    XIX | 124.
    XXI | (Appendix I.) 279.

2 KINGS

    I | 72. (Appendix I.) 283.
    II | 161, 239.
    V | 122, 204.
    IX | 60, 178.
    XII | 48.
    XV | 179.
    XVII | 223.
    XXV | 253.

1 CHRONICLES

    XI | 92.

2 CHRONICLES   PAGES OF THIS VOLUME

CHAP.
	I	147.
	V	50.
	VI	52.
	XIX	(Appendix I.) 283.

EZRA

I	(Appendix I.) 283.
X	54.

JOB

I	139.
III	153, 234.
IV	193.
V	140, 145, 243.
VI	139.
VIII	71, 139.
IX	139.
XIV	140, 145. (Appendix I.) 284.
XVII	232.
XIX	(Appendix I.) 286.
XXI	243.
XXIV	183.
XXVI	46.
XXVII	121
XXVIII	43, 140. (Appendix I.) 280.
XXXI	198, 228.
XXXVI	10, 108.
XXXVII	106.
XXXVIII	132, 157, 251.
XL	52, 121.
XLII	193.

PSALMS

I, VIII, XII, XIV, XV, XIX, XXIII, XXIV	18.
I	90, 192, 213, 240.

APPENDIX II

PSALMS (contd.)	PAGES OF THIS VOLUME
IV	61.
VIII	46, 75, 108. (Appendix I.) 285.
IX	158.
X	80, 174, 175.
XIV	175, 176. (Appendix I.) 285.
XV	(Appendix I.) 285.
XVIII	51. (Appendix I.) 282.
XIX	63, 80, 85, 101, 106, 133, 231. (Appendix I.) 286.
XXIII	12.
XXIV	157, 214.
XXV	12, 158, 243.
XXVII	84. (Appendix I.) 281.
XXIX	11.
XXXII	53.
XXXIV	101.
XXXVI	51. (Appendix I.) 284, 285.
XXXXVII	120, 175.
XXXIX	147, 225.
XLI	29.
XLII	12. (Appendix I.) 286.
XLIV	169.
XLV	24. (Appendix I.) 281, 285.
XLVIII	170, 231, 236.
XLIX	(Appendix I.) 282.
L	(Appendix I.) 286.
LI	(Appendix I.) 282
LIII	57, 154.
LV	65.
LVIII	175.
LXIII	(Appendix I.) 286.
LXV	87, 199. (Appendix I.) 284.
LXVII	249. (Appendix I.) 286.
LXVIII	51, 65, 85.
LXXII	(Appendix I.) 284.
LXXIII	175. (Appendix I.) 281.
LXXIV	66.
LXXVI	225.

PSALMS (contd.)	PAGES OF THIS VOLUME
LXXVII	51.
LXXX	196.
LXXXVI	275.
LXXXVII	(Appendix I.) 285.
LXXXIX	198.
XC	51, 146, 156.
XCI	159, 233.
XCIV	(Appendix I.) 280, 283.
XCV	45, 59, 145. (Appendix I.) 281.
XCVI	(Appendix I.) 279.
XCVII	51.
CIV	(Appendix I.) 282, 284.
CVII	181, 184.
CXIV	139. (Appendix I.) 285.
CXIX	24, 63, 72, 84, 213. (Appendix I.) 281, 283, 285.
CXXI	162. (Appendix I.) 284.
CXXIII	(Appendix I.) 285.
CXXIX	149.
CXXX	184.
CXXXVII	151.
CXXXIX	184, 185, 251.
CXLI	72.
CXLIII	(Appendix I.) 286.
CXLV	101.
CXLVII	103. (Appendix I.) 280.
CXLVIII	130.

PROVERBS

I	186, 192.
II	43.
III	132, 138, 247.
IV	120. (Appendix I.) 286.
VI	(Appendix I.) 281.
VII	(Appendix I.) 285.
XXI	136.
XXII	243. (Appendix I.) 281.

APPENDIX II

PROVERBS (*contd.*)	PAGES OF THIS VOLUME
CHAP. XXIV	30, 41, 243.
XXVIII	243.
XXX	122.
XXXI	(Appendix I.) 281.

ECCLESIASTES

I	(Appendix I.) 283.
III	94.
V	55.
VII	(Appendix I.) 285.
IX	241. (Appendix I.) 280.

SONG OF SOLOMON

II	41. (Appendix I.) 285.
IV	39.
V	180.
VI	(Appendix I.) 286.
VII	236.
VIII	236.

ISAIAH

I	204.
II	180. (Appendix I.) 284.
V	191, 247.
VI	90, 146.
VII	148.
IX	6.
XI	80, 203, 267.
XIV	139.
XXIII	(Appendix I.) 280.
XXV	74.
XXXII	118, 137, 184.
XXXIII	(Appendix I.) 280.
XXXV	103, 113.
XL	103, 156.
XLII	35, 103, 104.
XLIV	(Appendix I.) 283.

ISAIAH (contd.)   PAGES OF THIS VOLUME

CHAP.	
XLVII	245.
LII	181.
LIII	(Appendix I.) 281.
LIV	73. (Appendix I.) 281, 283.
LV	56, 128.
LVII	(Appendix I.) 285.
LVIII	183.
LIX	191.
LX	47, 231. (Appendix I.) 280.
LXI	(Appendix I.) 284.
LXII	(Appendix I.) 283.
LXIII	142.
LXV	167.
LXVI	208.

JEREMIAH

I	(Appendix I.) 280, 282.
V	164.
VI	179.
VIII	73, 179.
XVII	74.
XVIII	60, 74.
XXIII	22, 122. (Appendix I.) 282.
XXXI	164. (Appendix. I.) 283.

LAMENTATIONS

II	223.

EZEKIEL

I	51, 81. (Appendix I.) 280, 281.
XI	83.
XVI	246.
XXXI	89.
XXXVII	187.
XL	104.
XLVII	240.

APPENDIX II

DANIEL   PAGES OF THIS VOLUME

CHAP.
- III | 202.
- IV | 168.
- VI | 116.

HOSEA
- IV | (Appendix I.) 282.
- X | 185. (Appendix I.) 284, 286.
- XI | 130.

JOEL
- II | 191.
- III | 195.

AMOS
- VI | (Appendix I.) 285.
- IX | 259, 260.

JONAH
- IV | 91.

MICAH
- VI | 189. (Appendix I.) 284

ZECHARIAH
- VI | 20
- VII | 248.
- IX | 75.

MALACHI
- I | 221.
- III | 187, 188, 192.
- IV | 71, 94, 128. (Appendix I.) 283.

S. MATTHEW
- II | 33, 36. (Appendix I.) 279.
- III | (Appendix I.) 284.

APPENDIX II

S. MATTHEW (*contd.*)   **PAGES OF THIS VOLUME**

CHAP.	
IV	114, 148, 231, 237, 238.
V	27, 86, 87, 114, 158, 167, 193, 212, 245, 246. (Appendix I.) 281, 286.
VI	55, 79, 86, 93, 100, 103, 119, 131, 139, 147, 150, 217, 228, 230, 248. (Appendix I.) 281, 282, 285.
VII	(Appendix I.) 286.
VIII	147. (Appendix I.) 281.
IX	271, 272.
X	36, 37, 156, 158, 171. (Appendix I.) 281, 284.
XI	66, 81, 99, 178, 201, 231.
XII	103, 104, 116, 196, 232. (Appendix I.) 285.
XIII	43, 190, 196.
XIV	154, 155.
XVI	17, 136, 142. (Appendix I.) 280.
XVII	71, 114, 163, 237, 238, 239.
XVIII	31, 80, 131. (Appendix I.) 280.
XIX	105, 189, 198.
XX	91, 122, 152. (Appendix I.) 280.
XXI	21, 75, 140, 200, 236.
XXII	4, 55, 68, 75, 230.
XXIV	4, 51, 125, 142, 198, 226, 230, 240, 268. (Appendix I.) 282, 286.
XXV	28, 39, 158, 177, 178, 188, 190, 212, 273. (Appendix I.) 287.
XXVI	114, 174, 200. (Appendix I.) 286.
XXVII	(Appendix I.) 285.

S. MARK

I	65.
II	91. (Appendix I.) 285.
III	172. (Appendix I.) 279.
IV	4, 44, 190, 192. (Appendix I.) 284.
V	(Appendix I.) 283.
VI	102, 155, 159.
VIII	17, 201.
IX	208, 214, 237. (Appendix I.) 281.
X	17, 39, 189, 230.

APPENDIX II

S. MARK (contd.)   PAGES OF THIS VOLUME

CHAP.	
XII	236.
XIII	58, 125, 240, 241.
XIV	180. (Appendix I.) 279, 284.

S. LUKE

I	99, 122, 156, 158, 258, 259. (Appendix I.) 284.
II	32, 99, 176. (Appendix I.) 282.
IV	148.
V	119.
VI	226. (Appendix I.) 279.
VII	38, 87, 180. (Appendix I.) 286.
VIII	44, 78, 120, 190.
IX	41, 114, 161, 237, 238, 239. (Appendix I.) 282.
X	4, 7, 27, 73, 81, 97, 99, 200. (Appendix I.) 284.
XI	29, 86.
XII	56, 69, 93, 102, 142, 143, 156, 168.
XIII	212.
XIV	9, 272. (Appendix I.) 280, 281.
XV	165, 185, 189, 190.
XVI	15, 26, 55, 176, 189, 205.
XVII	230.
XVIII	105, 189, 230.
XIX	157, 177, 197, 202, 272, 273.
XXI	125
XXII	114, 174.
XXIII	182, 185. (Appendix I.) 286.
XXIV	34.

S. JOHN

I	63, 94, 134, 249. (Appendix I.) 283.
II	141. (Appendix I.) 284.
III	228.
IV	28, 84, 92, 154, 220. (Appendix I.) 280.
VI	20, 28, 29. (Appendix I.) 282.
VII	44.
VIII	3, 38, 94.
IX	44, 94.
X	20.

S. JOHN (*contd.*)   PAGES OF THIS VOLUME

CHAP.	
XII	75, 92, 180, 183.
XIV	6, 36, 201. (Appendix I.) 281, 286.
XV	(Appendix I.) 285.
XVII	244.
XX	34, 40, 142, 214.
XXI	29, 34, 37, 38, 100.

ACTS

I	22, 51.
II	21, 202. (Appendix I.) 280.
IV	172, 258. (Appendix I.) 279.
VII	(Appendix I.) 280.
XIII	258.
XIV	(Appendix I.) 280.
XV	258.
XVII	154, 194. (Appendix I.) 286.
XX	31.
XXIV	53.

ROMANS

I	68, 152, 207.
II	41.
III	80.
V	118.
VIII	14.
XI	(Appendix I.) 282.
XII	168. (Appendix I.) 279, 281.
XIII	5.
XIV	230.

1 CORINTHIANS

I	35, 69. (Appendix I.) 286.
II	206, 207.
III	125, 228. (Appendix I.) 281, 287.
VI	125, 194.
VIII	(Appendix I.) 286.
X	69. (Appendix I.) 280, 284.

APPENDIX II

1 CORINTHIANS *(contd.)*   PAGES OF THIS VOLUME
CHAP. XIII | 128, 159.
    XV | 22, 23, 91, **125, 232, 261.** (Appendix I.) **281.**

2 CORINTHIANS
    III | 144. (Appendix I.) 281.
    IV | 233.
    XIII | **13, 75,** 101.

GALATIANS
    II | 36, 77.
    III | 152.
    V | 67.

EPHESIANS
    II | 16, 129, 172. (Appendix I.) 280.
    IV | 125. (Appendix I.) 279.
    V | 16, 76, **122,** 125.
    VI | **17, 170.** (Appendix I.) **279.**

PHILIPPIANS
    IV | 68, 159.

COLOSSIANS
    I | 112.
    II | 125.
    III | 16, **67,** 122, **210.** (Appendix I.) 279.

1 THESSALONIANS
    IV | (Appendix I.) 286.

2 THESSALONIANS
    II | 125.

1 TIMOTHY
    I | (Appendix I.) 287.
    II | 229.

1 TIMOTHY (*contd.*)   PAGES OF THIS VOLUME

CHAP. III | 25. (Appendix I.) 279.
       IV | 173.
        V | 173.
       VI | 52, 55.

2 TIMOTHY

       III | 55.
        IV | 173.

TITUS

         I | 25.

HEBREWS

         I | (Appendix I.) 284.
       III | 125.
        IV | 236.
        IX | (Appendix I.) 284.
         X | 152.
       XII | 101, 124. (Appendix I.) 284.
      XIII | 52, 99.

JAMES

         I | 12.
        II | 32.
       III | 96, 188, 219, 252.
        IV | 194.
         V | 54. (Appendix I.) 282.

1 PETER

         I | 166.
        II | 173.
       III | 44.
         V | 25, 173.

2 PETER

         I | (Appendix I.) 281.
       III | 52, 156, 252.

APPENDIX II

1 JOHN		PAGES OF THIS VOLUME
CHAP.	II	(Appendix I.) 284.
	III	54. (Appendix I.) 284.
	IV	127, 196. (Appendix I.) 284.

JUDE

	I	215. (Appendix I.) 285.

REVELATION

	I	4, 51, 173, 212, 252.
	II	211, 212, 213, 214, 232.
	III	149, 186, 212, 214, 215.
	IV	46, 76, 112, 146, 201, 206, 211. (Appendix I.) 280, 285.
	V	77.
	VII	3.
	XI	199.
	XIV	(Appendix I.) 280, 282.
	XVII	166.
	XVIII	204.
	XIX	250. (Appendix I.) 287.
	XX	66, 173, 234. (Appendix I.) 280.
	XXI	4, 24, 52, 184, 195, 201, 211, 215, 228. (Appendix I.) 280.
	XXII	89, 90, 137, 143, 149, 193, 195, 211, 214. (Appendix I.) 280, 281, 287.

www.ingramcontent.com/pod-product-compliance
Lightning Source LLC
Chambersburg PA
CBHW030813230426
43667CB00008B/1190